# Better
## THAN SEX

# Better
## THAN SEX

MY AUTOBIOGRAPHY

Mick Fitzgerald
with Donn McClean

*To*

*Martin*

*Happy Christmas*

**RACING POST**

# DEDICATION

## *To my family*

Published in 2008 by Racing Post
Compton, Newbury, Berkshire RG20 6NL

Copyright © Mick Fitzgerald and Donn McClean 2008

The right of Mick Fitzgerald and Donn McClean to be identified as the authors of this work has been asserted by them in accordance with the Copyright, Designs and Patents Act 1988.

A catalogue record for this book is available from the British Library.

ISBN 978-1-905156-56-6

Cover designed by Tracey Scarlett
Interiors designed by Fiona Pike

Printed in the UK by CPI William Clowes Beccles NR34 7TL

# CONTENTS

# ACKNOWLEDGMENTS

I would like to thank Donn McClean for his hard work, dedication to the cause and humour whilst helping me write this book. Brough Scott for his persuasive powers resulting in this book. Julian Brown and James de Wesselow at Highdown for their hard work and energy.

I would also like to thank all the people who have made my career a success, of which a special mention must go to Nicky Henderson.

Finally to my parents for believing in me, my gorgeous wife Chloe, for putting up with me, and my two sons Zac and Oscar for being my inspiration.

# CHAPTER 1

## HANGING BY A THREAD

L'Ami felt good underneath me as we broke into a canter. April 5, 2008, Grand National day. You know when a horse is well and when he is not, and this fellow was very well, ears pricked, taking everything in.

I always loved the build-up to the Grand National. I suppose the fact that I won it before made me feel like I was a part of it all, a tiny part of its history. That day in 1996, 12 years before, that was a special day. Rough Quest was brilliant. It was one of those races in which everything just went right. Unfortunately, a lot of it passed me by. I was so young, dazzled by the attention, high on the moment, that I forgot to take it all in, to appreciate everything that was happening around me. I was a mere passenger on a wave of adrenaline. So I was desperate to win the great race again. Next time, I would make sure that I savoured every delicious instant.

I was riding L'Ami because AP McCoy had rejected him, but I was delighted that he had, and I had told AP as much. All week, AP had deliberated: Butler's Cabin, L'Ami or King Johns Castle, all three owned by his boss JP McManus, all three with a real chance of winning. All week I had told him that I thought L'Ami was the most likely of the three. AP is one of my best mates and I wanted to steer him right, even though I was in line for the ride on L'Ami if he rejected him. He did. Actually, as it turned out, L'Ami would have been his third choice. He chose to ride Butler's Cabin, and I thought, big mistake.

I looked back up at the stands as we made our way to the start and thought, take all this in. It's a fantastic feeling, the people, the occasion, the hum, the history, the greatest horserace in the world under the gaze of millions, and you are a part of it. Appreciate it, lap it all up, take the time to savour it.

I wasn't really nervous as we circled at the start. You know that there are 30 massive fences in front of you, and that more than half the field will not complete the course, but even so I rarely got nervous before the National. I had a game plan, and I was happy with that. Be handy enough, steer a middle to outside course where the fences are slightly smaller and therefore easier to jump, and don't track any suicide bombers. There are lads who love to go down the inside, the brave man's route, because they are brave, because they are men. I never went in for any of that shite. Why would you go down the inside, why would you jump Becher's Brook tight to the inside rail and increase your chances of ending up on the deck? Because it looks good on television? That stuff was never for me.

I found my mates from the weigh room as we circled and wished them luck, AP, Ruby Walsh, Dominic Elsworth, David Casey, and I meant it. You want everyone to come back in one piece. It's a strange thing that, as a jockey, your colleagues are also your rivals. The people you hang out with, the people you go to work with, you get out on to the racecourse and you just want to beat them. You go down to the last with someone else, you're both flat out, and all you're hoping is that you'll wing the fence and he'll end up on the floor. Afterwards you want them to get up and walk away, but at the time you're just drilling down to the last and you're thinking, fall you bastard.

The Grand National is different, though. You want everyone to be safe; you want everyone to do well. The sense of camaraderie overrides the feeling of competition. I saw the starter heading for his rostrum and I turned L'Ami around to face him. I was sure that, with all the talk about the delayed start the previous year, he would let us go first time, and he did.

I got a nice start. L'Ami jumped off well and we travelled nicely down to the Melling Road. He was taking a bit of a tug, but no more than you would expect and I was happy. Once we crossed the Melling Road, I wanted to get him back underneath me before we got to the first fence. The last thing you want is to have your horse overtaking himself going down to the first fence in the National. If that happens, there is usually no way back.

We met the first on a good stride. I noticed Timmy Murphy on Comply Or Die jink a little bit in front of me, but my fellow retained his concentration. He ran a little bit at it, but he was fine, hup, he jumped over it nicely and landed running.

It's always a little bit of a relief when you get over the first fence in the National. These fences are different to anything that L'Ami would have seen since his run in the race the previous year, and the first fence could have taken him by surprise, but it didn't, he jumped it well, and I was happy.

He was perfect in my hands going down to the second, just settling into a nice rhythm, not too keen, just travelling away nicely in mid-division, a little towards the outside, exactly where I wanted to be. I wouldn't have changed a thing at that point. We approached the second fence, meeting on a perfect stride, one, two, up. Only he didn't come up. He did nothing actually. It was almost as if he didn't see the fence until it was too late. It was the last thing that I expected from him; he hadn't fallen since 2004. He took an extra stride that took us in far too close to the fence, and suddenly, from being as happy as I could have been, travelling well, we were at the point of no return, too tight in to the fence for him to be able to pick his legs up and jump out over it. Nadia Comaneci wouldn't have got over the fence from there.

I remember hearing the crack of the timber, the horse's front legs hitting the bottom of the fence, and thinking, this is going to hurt. You try to brace yourself, like in an airplane that is going to crash land, adopt the brace position. This plane is going to crash and there's nothing you can do about it. You almost try to curl yourself into a ball while you are still in the air, because you know that you're not coming back, you know you're going to hit the ground hard and you know that you're going to feel pain. You don't hope that you won't fall, because you know that you will, so all you can hope is that it won't hurt too much.

I'm not sure which part of my body hit the ground first, but it must have been my head, because I just blanked out after that. I don't remember being speared into the ground. It all happened so quickly that I didn't have time to brace myself properly. I was just catapulted downwards, head first.

The next thing I remember is that I'm lying on the flat of my back on the grass, and all I can see is sky. I don't know how long I'm out for, it can't be for more than a couple of seconds, but the whole scene has changed. The thunder of hooves, the shouts of jockeys, the crash of timber has been traded for a hush that is broken only by the commentator's voice over the PA system. I look down and I can see a body, but it's not my body. It's wearing the same green and gold silks that I put on half an hour earlier, and it's wearing my breeches and my boots, but it's not mine. It can't be mine. I can't feel it. It's as if my head has become separated from the rest of me. There's my head, and then there's green grass between my neck and the rest of the body that's lying on the ground.

I tried to move my fingers, but nothing happened. I tried to move my legs, again no. My brain was sending the signals, I knew what I had to do, but nothing was moving. Then I panicked. The only thing I could think of was my family, my girlfriend at the time, now my wife, Chloe, my two little boys, Zac and Oscar. I was looking in disbelief at this lump, this green and gold thing that wouldn't do what I was telling it to do and thinking no, please no, this can't be happening to me, I want to be able to play with my boys as they are growing up, I want to be around for them, I want to be a dad for them.

All the while I was desperately trying to get something to move, desperately trying to establish some contact between my brain and my limbs. I could see that my body was jumping up and down involuntarily, jolting off the ground sporadically, but I had no control over it. Panic had almost turned to despair when I thought I felt my finger, then my arm, and an unbelievable sense of relief rushed through my head. My right arm was now my arm, belonging to me, attached to my brain, not some other arm that was lying on the ground attached to some body that had nothing to do with me. Then I could feel my left arm. I didn't do anything with my arms, I didn't move them, I could just feel them, and that was enough.

Then the paramedics arrived. I just heard the footsteps on the ground coming over to me, and one of them asked me if I was ok. They always ask you if you are ok.

'No I'm not,' I told him. 'It's spinal and it's serious.'

'How do you know?' he asked.

'Trust me, I know,' I said. 'I've broken my neck before and I've done something very similar this time. Just get the spinal board.'

The spinal board was crucial. If they had tried to move me without the spinal board, given the way the discs were embedded in my spinal cord, then that would have been it for me. Not could have, would have. I would have been paralysed. Lying on a spinal board is like being strapped to a marble floor with somebody standing on your head. You can't move a thing. It was essential for me.

All the while I was moving my fingers and my toes. I had established contact with them, and I wasn't going to give it up easily. I just thought that if I kept moving them, I wouldn't lose contact with them again. Of course it doesn't make any difference if you move them or not, but I was desperate that the feeling would remain.

As they were strapping me to the spinal board, the field was coming around again on the second circuit. Paddy Brennan, who had fallen off Fundamentalist at the third fence, was going mad saying that they couldn't jump the second fence, that I was still on the ground on the landing side. The marshals began putting up markers at the part of the fence where I was, and were set to divert the field towards the other part of the fence. But you never know where loose horses are going to go, and there were plenty of those around. It was fortunate then that they managed to get me on to the spinal board and off the course just before the horses came back around.

It's strange the way your mind works. Even as they were looking after me at the side of the track, and even as I was concerned that they were doing everything right, my mobility literally hanging by a thread, the rest of my life in their hands, I still had one ear cocked to the racecourse commentary to hear who would win the race. Comply Or Die and Timmy Murphy.

I didn't think any more about it as they put me into the ambulance. I didn't think about the contrast in our respective situations, Timmy on top of the world, as I had been 12 years previously, me on the flat of my back, unsure if I would ever walk again. I was just thankful for now that I had the feeling back in my body. Then they closed the doors, and the ambulance took off.

# CHAPTER 2

## BULLY FOR ME

If there is an affinity for horses in your genes, they say that it will come through. Horses are not apparent in my immediate family, but if you were to look at my page in a bloodstock sales catalogue, you would see the horses there all right.

My father, Frank, is from a place called The Harrow in Boolavogue in County Wexford, the place forever remembered in Patrick McCall's ballad, 'Boolavogue', which commemorates the Irish Rebellion of 1798 and Father Murphy's brave but ultimately failed stance on Vinegar Hill.

Frank's father, my grandfather, worked in the county council, and my dad went to school locally in Boolavogue, then went to the vocational school in Enniscorthy, about five miles away, before joining the army apprentice school in Naas and training to be a mechanic.

My mother, Alice, grew up in Killorglin in County Kerry, the place that is famous for its Puck Fair, where they used to capture a wild goat from the mountains, the Macgillycuddy Reeks. They'd keep it in a cage during the festivities, crown it King Puck, deny it food and water, and then slaughter it at the end. I suppose that was a bit barbaric, so they don't do that any more. They still capture a wild mountain goat, and he still presides over proceedings from on high, but they take him down every night to give him food and water, and they release him back to the wild when the festival is over. We never missed a Puck Fair when we were kids.

My mother was waitressing in a restaurant in Naas when she met my father, who was in the army apprentice school. Dad was then transferred to Cork, and they got married in October 1968. My brother John was born the following year, and I was born on May 10, 1970, Michael Anthony Fitzgerald. Shortly after my birth, dad was posted to Cyprus with the United Nations for six months. When he came home he bought himself out of the army and we moved to Killarney. My sister, Elizabeth, was born in 1972.

I went to school in the convent in Killarney for three years before I was moved to the monastery. I don't remember too much about the convent except that the nuns made me sit on my left hand and use my right hand. Left-handers were demonic or something like that, apparently, so the nuns made everybody use their right hand. The Irish for a left-hander is *citeog*, which also means awkward, so maybe there is something in that.

When I was nine we moved to Camolin, Wexford, for my dad. My grandfather was on his own, and my father decided that he should move back to look after him. I wasn't too impressed. It's tough for a kid having to leave his friends and the surroundings with which he is familiar and start again. A couple of days after moving, I suggested to my mother that it might be a good idea if we moved back to Killarney, but we didn't. Four months later, my grandfather died, but my parents decided that we would stay in Camolin.

Just before our first Christmas in Camolin, a tinker was going down the road trying to sell a pony, I suppose trying to get a few quid together for Christmas. My father's family had always been involved in horses in some way. His father used to train workponies and workhorses, and his uncle was a blacksmith, and dad had always had an idea in the back of his head that he would like to have horses around. So after a bit of haggling, he bought the pony from the tinker and he put him out on the small bit of land, no more than a large garden really, that we had behind the house.

That was how it all began for me. I was ecstatic: our own pony, my own pony. Nobody really taught me how to ride, I didn't get lessons or anything, I just hopped up and did what came naturally with some help from dad. John, Elizabeth and I used to ride the pony until we got another, and then another, so we had a pony each. There was a lot of work with them, but we didn't mind. We loved riding them, Elizabeth and I probably more than John.

It's hard to believe now, looking at the Ireland of today, but back then Ireland was like a Third World country. In rural Ireland, rural Wexford in the 1980s, nobody had any money. My father didn't have a pot to piss in. He used to sell cars out of the back of the house and the most expensive car he would have would be worth about £1,000, the same amount as you get for scrapping your car these days. If you could buy one of them, you were minted.

The ponies that he bought were absolute dirt, really useless things that he used to buy from the tinkers because they were all he could afford. Then we would ride them and get them going, and if any of them showed any ability at all, we used to have to sell them because we just couldn't afford not to.

My parents used to drive us to shows every weekend, to Arklow, the far side of Wexford, Carlow, Waterford, wherever there was a gymkhana, we would go. We would just head off early in the morning in a truck that they had bought for a pittance from my aunt, mam, dad, John, Elizabeth and me, the five of us and our ponies, and we wouldn't be home until late in the evening. Every time you went to a show, you got points if you jumped a clear, more points if you jumped a double clear, and all the points that a pony accumulated added to his value. I loved that, I loved the competitiveness of it, and I learned a lot, not only about jumping, about seeing a stride, about the behaviour of horses, but also about competition, about people watching and the pressures that brings.

We hunted a little with the local hunt, the Island Foxhounds. I was never a big fan of hunting. There was too much standing around, waiting around on other people for me. I just wanted to get on and do it, so I didn't go hunting that often. We never went pony racing. My father didn't think that we would learn anything about horses by going pony racing, believing that it was just a case of sit and point, go as fast as you can for as long as you can. With gymkhanas and shows, you were all the while learning about horses, about looking for a stride, about balance, figuring out what made horses tick, whereas with pony racing, it was only about speed.

I had a really good pony, Ballybanogue Bracken, that my father had bought from the tinkers for £150. He was a difficult pony, who used to refuse a lot when we first got him, until one day, my old man got a piece of electric wire and tied it to the end of a stick. When the pony refused at a fence, he got the wire on the back of his legs, just above his hocks, and skinned him. After that, he never refused again. My father used to wave the stick with the wire on it above his head, it would make a swooshing noise, and it was as if the pony knew.

He was a great pony after that. I won a lot of prizes on him in open competition, and my sister Elizabeth rode him after I had left home. She was more of a nervous rider, but there was no issue with Bracken. You just had to sit on him and point him in the right direction, then switch on autopilot and he would do the rest. He would jump anything, and he was quick when it came to a jump-off against the clock.

We had another really good one, a purebred Connemara pony that my father bought as a two-year-old, but we got him the year that I left to join a racing stable, and dad couldn't afford to keep him. He couldn't have had other kids coming in to ride him or look after him. The risks would have been too great and the cost of insurance too high, so we sold him. At the time, both dad and I thought that he could have been the best that we ever had and, regrettably, we were right. He turned out to be a top-class pony, and was sold at the age of 11 for £25,000, a huge price for a pony at the time.

School was tough for me in the beginning after we moved back to Wexford. The lessons were fine and I never had a problem keeping up in class. I always found that side of it fairly easy, but it's hard for a new kid to fit into new surroundings, in with new kids, and it was harder for me than it should have been because I was bullied. When you are older, you want to stand out from the crowd, you want to be different, but when you are a kid, all you want is to fit in, to be the same as everybody else.

I don't know why this fellow picked on me. Maybe it was just because I was new, maybe because I was small, and because he could. It was really terrible. Nobody can fully appreciate the effect that a bully can have unless they are on the receiving end. It dominated my life. I would wake up in the morning and it would be the first thing I would think of. I didn't want to go to school; I didn't want to be out in the playground; I dreaded the journey home from school.

People knew that it was going on. I know my dad knew, but I think he thought that it was something that I needed to sort out myself. He's old school. Stand on your own two feet. Nobody is going to be there to fight your battles for you when you are older, so stand up and fight them yourself. It's a tough one for parents anyway. If you get involved you risk making the situation worse. My brother John knew, but didn't do anything about it either. At the time I hated that he didn't, but it was tough for him too. He was a year older than me, but he was new as well and trying to fit in himself, so it was hard for him as well.

Although it was only one guy, the worst of it was that other kids stood around and watched, didn't do anything about it, so I guess I figured that they were on his side as well. You can't stand back from it and see that they probably just didn't want to get involved for fear of being bullied themselves. You just think they're on the bully's side because they don't do anything to stop it. All I wanted was to fit in, be inconspicuous, but with this bullying I was the most conspicuous of all, I felt like an outcast. The beatings were probably easier to take than the mental bullying. At least a hiding is over and you go home and that's it, you're sore all right but at least it doesn't linger. The mental abuse is different, it stays with you, it lingers, and there's nothing you can do.

I dealt with it as well as I could. I loved sports; I played hurling. They hardly know what hurling is in Kerry, all the kids play Gaelic football, so I didn't see a hurl until we moved to Wexford, but I loved the game. I wasn't outstanding but I was always on the team. I was small for hurling, but when you have a hurl in your hand everyone is the same height. I also immersed myself in the horses. When I was with my pony the bullying didn't matter, nothing else really mattered. When I was competing, it didn't matter if I was liked or disliked by others, or if I fitted in or not, all that mattered was the next turn, the next fence.

The bullying went on for more than a year. Then one day we were playing football out in the field. I was in goal, as I often was, and this guy, the bully, came towards me with the ball. Something just snapped in me. I felt a surge of rage, like a year's worth of torment boiling up inside me and exploding out through every pore in my body. Sense or reason didn't come into it. I hadn't thought it through, it wasn't a plan that had been hatching for days or weeks, or a decision that I had made the night before or even a couple of minutes before. I just snapped. I didn't even see the ball. I just saw this guy coming towards me, and I let him have it. I gave it everything I had and I flattened him, absolutely poleaxed him.

He could have got up and boxed me, but he didn't. I'm not sure whether he was more sore than shocked or vice versa, but I didn't care. I had no idea what the consequences or repercussions of what I had done would be. Like I say, I hadn't thought it through. It just seemed like the right thing to do at the time. Turns out, it was.

The bullying stopped. Things just moved on to normal for me. There are things that happen to you in your life that shape your future, that contribute to the person that you are, and this was a major one for me. It could easily have gone the wrong way, and I was lucky that it didn't. I'm not saying that I'm a great fellow, and that I took matters into my own hands and dealt with them, because I was desperate for somebody like my dad or my brother to intervene. I was just lucky that it stopped the way it did, because it was a nightmare while it was going on.

I don't know what the fellow is doing now, I couldn't really care and I'm sure I wouldn't recognise him if he walked past me in the street, but it's remarkable the impact that the actions of one individual can have on you. I think that the whole episode made me stronger as a person, but it's one of the things that gets me now. I'm a pretty even-tempered fellow, I think, but when my temper goes, it really does go, and there is nothing else that makes me as angry now as a kid being bullied. Even when I think about it I get irate. I'm not sure what I would do if my boys Zac or Oscar were ever bullied, but even thinking about the prospect makes my blood boil. Hopefully the situation won't ever arise.

# CHAPTER 3

## PUB CRAWL

It's difficult to remove the rest of my childhood from the bullying, because it was there all the time, always on my mind, but my home life was happy. School was grand after the bullying stopped, I didn't mind school at all, and I was well able to keep up with the minimum of effort. I got a job in a petrol station in the evenings, just so that I could earn some pocket money. That was the way in our house, if you wanted something, you went and worked for it. That was my father's way, it's how I was brought up, and it was good. It made you appreciate things.

I wasn't that good a manual worker. I definitely wasn't as hard as my brother John, who was probably more like my father than I was. I definitely wouldn't have cut it in the army like my dad or John did, that's for sure. I didn't really like manual work. One of the families that my mam used to babysit for when we first moved to Camolin had a farm, and the father of the family asked if John and I would go up one Saturday to pick stones in the field, that he'd give us a few quid for ourselves, so we did. The following evening, when mam went up to babysit, she asked the farmer how we had got on. The message came back that John was a great worker, but that I had spent most of the time in the kitchen with Mary, the mother, putting the cups in the dishwasher and chatting.

'He wasn't a bit interested in picking the stones.'

If I didn't want to do something, I mainly just didn't do it, and said so. I figured even as a kid that there was no point in pretending that you didn't mind doing something and just putting up with it if your heart wasn't in it. John would have been more inclined to just get on with it, even under duress. John had a job down in the local supermarket in Camolin. One morning he was sick, and he suggested that it would be a good idea if I went down and did his job for the day, earn a few quid for

19

myself, so I said I would. I was sweeping the yard in the morning when the manager came out to me and said, look, that's not the right way to hold the brush. So I just handed him the brush and told him that the best thing would be if he held the brush and I headed off home again.

My dad was tough, I'd say he was fairly hard in his day, and he was hard on us kids. It was simple, if you screwed up you got a hiding. It was black and white so at least you knew where you stood. But he was fair. He's a good lad, my dad, and I'm very close to him now. We are good mates now more than father and son, and I speak to my mother and father three or four times a week these days.

Dad was an alcoholic. He wasn't a messy alcoholic or a brutal alcoholic, and at the time we didn't know that he was, I'm sure he didn't realise it himself, but he would go down the pub every night without fail, have his couple of pints, come home and go to bed. It was like you would brush your teeth before going to bed, he would have his couple of pints.

He's just a typical Paddy. He's five foot one and a half, bald head, big red smiley face, and he loved his pints. He wasn't a binge drinker. He'd never go down the pub and come home at four or five in the morning, or he wouldn't disappear on Thursday night and come home on Sunday, he'd never do that, and we never saw drink as a bad thing for him when we were kids. I don't think I ever saw him drunk as a child. He just loved his pints.

My parents always wanted to have their own pub. It was a dream of theirs that they would own and run a pub in a small village or town, so when John, Elizabeth and I were all raised and had left home, they figured that they would give it a go. They travelled the length and breadth of the country looking for the pub; they reckon they went to see pubs in nearly every county in Ireland. Every Friday evening my mother would come home from work – she worked as a cleaner at the time – with the evening paper to check out the racing for the weekend, and one Friday there was an ad for a pub for sale in Kilfinnane, just outside Kilmallock in County Limerick.

My parents had hardly even heard of Kilfinnane, but my dad went to see it the following day, and they both went back the following evening. It was dark that evening, and it was lashing rain, so they didn't really check out their surroundings. It was only after they had bought the pub that they realised there were three pubs almost next door to each other, with the one they had bought in the middle, and that there were 12 or 13 pubs in or around Kilfinnane. But the price was good, it was a premises, and it was a home as they could live above the pub, so they figured they'd give it a go.

It wasn't easy. My father got a job in a garage in Charleville, so he would work his normal nine-to-five job there, then come home in the evening and look after the pub with my mam. He was effectively working two jobs, and for what? The pub would be dead during the week, one or two stragglers sitting over a couple of pints all evening, it would hardly pay for the heat and the light. It was a little more lively during the weekends, but my dad would sit up drinking with whoever was left until the small hours of the morning. He would often be up till four or five, and then up again at half seven the following morning to start the day again. It just wasn't sustainable.

In 2002 I went home for his 50th birthday party, which they held in the pub. It was a great night. I suppose it was a bit of a novelty for the locals that I was there, in behind the bar pulling pints. Mam was laughing afterwards. My idea of working behind the bar, apparently, was pulling a pint for someone and spending 20 minutes chatting to them. Meanwhile they'd be packed deep waiting to be served. I suppose it wasn't a very efficient way to be going on.

Three weeks later, mam rang to say that dad had been taken into hospital. I asked her what was wrong, she said she didn't know, she just wanted to let me know that he had been taken in. I had three rides at Stratford that day and I asked her if she thought I should give them up and come home, but she wouldn't hear of it. She told me not to be worrying, that he had just been taken in, and that she would talk to me again that evening.

I called my sister Elizabeth to ask her what she thought, and she said that she thought I should come home, so I phoned my agent Dave Roberts, told him I couldn't go to Stratford, and drove straight to

21

Birmingham airport, but I couldn't get a flight from there, so I turned around and went to Heathrow. I got to Limerick Hospital that evening and went straight up to the ward where dad was. I walked down through the ward looking for him, and walked straight past his bed. I didn't recognise him, this greyish, yellowing skeleton of a thing, it couldn't have been my father, but it was. I got an awful shock when I realised it was him. In three weeks he had faded away from this hearty and hale man, apparently in the prime of his health, laughing and joking with everyone, the life and soul of his own 50th birthday party, to this waif, this skeletal wreck, barely alive.

Sclerosis of the liver, it was, perhaps unsurprisingly. The drink had caught up with him. A couple of weeks later and it would have overtaken him and buried him, but the doctors got to him just in time. Nobody would tell him what was wrong with him. I suppose they were protecting him, but he knew that he was bad, and he was frustrated not knowing what was wrong, so he asked me to ask the doctors and to tell him. I figured he should know.

I wasn't surprised that he asked me to find out. My brother John and my sister Elizabeth were there before me, but they both have more of a father/son/daughter relationship with my dad than I have. As I said, my dad and I are more like good pals than father and son, so we could talk straight with each other. John is a mechanic, like dad, and he would ring my dad looking for advice about a car or something, just as my dad would ring John to ask him for his opinion on something. Elizabeth is the only girl, so of course she is the daughter. She's a good bird, my sister.

So I asked the doctor what the story was.

'Look, it's like this,' he said. 'His liver is in a bad way, he's got sclerosis, it's nearly gone. If he doesn't completely give up drinking, I'd give him two years, maximum three. And I'm not talking about cutting back, about having just a couple of pints at the weekend, I'm talking about total abstinence. His liver isn't able to handle any more. If he touches another drop, he won't live to be 55.'

'Right,' I said. 'So what happens if he doesn't drink at all?'

'If he doesn't drink another drop,' the doctor said, 'his liver will replenish itself. Within two to three years it should be ok and he can go on to live a normal healthy life. But I have to tell you, four out of five people who come in here in the state that he's in don't make it. I tell them the story, just as I have told you, I tell them the certainty of it, they know the implications, but they just can't help themselves, they go back and drink and they are dead within five years.'

It was all very sobering. I told my dad. He had two choices, carry on drinking as he had been and he'd be dead within a year or two; give it up, not a drop, and he'd live a healthy life. It seems like a no-brainer, but the statistics don't lie, four out of five people can't do it. You can understand how hard it is, and how difficult it was on my dad to hear the ultimatum, maybe all the more difficult because it was coming from me, his son. It would be like if you were to tell somebody that if they ate breakfast again they would die, or that they couldn't drive a car again. Something that was ingrained into your life, something that you did every single day, almost without fail, you couldn't do it again or you wouldn't live to see your next birthday.

Dad broke down. I had never seen my old man come even close to showing emotion before, and here he was, sobbing away in his hospital bed. I'm not sure if it was the fact that he couldn't drink again that got him, or the realisation of how close he had come, or of what had gone before and of all he had drunk. It may have been a combination of everything, and it was too much for him. I just put my arms around him. Take as long as you like dad.

Of course they had to sell the pub. That was a bit tricky, but they managed to get rid of it in the end, one of the neighbouring pub owners bought it. They were sad leaving it. They missed the activity and the people coming in, but they were happy to walk away when they did. Besides my father's health, they just couldn't make it pay. There were good nights, and I always enjoyed going back and doing my stint behind the bar, there was always a bit of craic there, but there were just too many pubs and not enough people around the area, and it was always a struggle.

My parents moved down the road to Kilmallock, my dad got a job in the NCT in Charleville and my mam began looking after kids. They're very happy now. Elizabeth and her three kids live nearby. Dad is almost six years on the dry now, and I couldn't be more proud of him. It's exactly as the doctor said, he's living a normal healthy life, working away, and he's back to his normal self, back smiling again, fair play to him. I'm not sure if I could do what he has done.

# CHAPTER 4

## SHOVELLING SHIT

If you look back on anyone's life, you can invariably spot several pivotal points, several things that happened that have had a profound influence on that person's life. There are things that occur that send a life down a particular path. Without the occurrence, that path may never have been trodden.

My life is full of such turning points, or at least events that had a profound influence. One such event happened one afternoon, not long after my 13th birthday, when I was out exercising a new pony that my father had just bought from the tinkers. This was a terrible pony. He wouldn't do anything, he wouldn't trot, he wouldn't canter, he wouldn't jump, it was all I could do to get him to walk in a straight line – a really horrible character.

At the same time there was a fellow in with my dad getting his car serviced, Sean Doyle, who worked at Richard Lister's racing yard over in Coolgreaney. Call it fate if you want, or happenstance, call it what will, but I suppose he saw me on the pony and, whatever I was doing to it or however I was handling it, Sean was obviously impressed. He asked dad if I would be interested in going up to Richard's on Saturdays or on school holidays.

At the time, I hadn't even considered racing. I didn't really know much about it, and I certainly hadn't entertained the idea of becoming a jockey, but the idea of going and riding a real horse in a real yard excited the hell out of me. So the following Saturday my dad drove me the 13 miles up to Richard's. They put me up on this filly and whoosh! I couldn't believe it. I didn't realise how fast a horse could run. I'll never forget it, it was such a buzz, such an adrenaline rush, and that was it, that was me sorted. All I wanted to do was ride thoroughbreds, ride racehorses. I suppose not many 13-year-olds know what they want to do with their lives, and I definitely didn't have a clue until that morning, but I was certain after that. Money, fame, notoriety, recognition – nothing else came into it. I just wanted to ride racehorses, and that was what I was going to do.

Richard was a really nice fellow, just a really good genuine guy. His mother was a lovely woman and his father, Basil Lister, was Master of the Wicklow Foxhounds for a time, a real gentleman. I loved going up there. Even though I was only a young fellow, I got on well with the lads. There were good lads there, Martin O'Reilly and Paul McMahon. David Parnell was Richard's stable jockey at the time. I started going up just on Saturdays and at weekends and during the holidays, but then I started going up just about every spare moment I had. My dad used to drive me there in the beginning. I'd say that's part of the reason why we are so close even today. He used to drive me up in the morning, 13 miles, leave me off, then come home, do his own day's work and go to collect me again in the evening. After a while, he used to drive me to Sean Doyle's house in Gorey and then I'd go in with him. Sean was a really good lad as well. He taught me a lot.

Richard had a great year in 1984. His flag-bearer was Anita's Prince, whom Sean used to ride out all the time, and who finished second in the King's Stand Stakes at Royal Ascot. That was fantastic and heartbreaking at the same time. I watched the race with all the lads in the yard, and we were sure that he had won. He took it up under Lester Piggott inside the final furlong, and Willie Carson came late on the odds-on favourite Habibti and just did him. He was called out first in the photo-finish as well. Mick Meade was leading the horse up on the day and, when they were coming back in, Mick was afraid to go into the winner's enclosure in case they hadn't won it, but Piggott wasn't so reticent.

'Michael,' said Lester, in his own inimitable way, 'go into the number one, we've won.'

I couldn't believe it when the result was announced. I don't think many people could, not even Carson. It was a real heart-sink job. All the lads had backed him, I had even had a few quid on myself, but I was more gutted for Richard and for the yard than I was for my money.

I was getting more and more into racing and more into jockeys. Where most lads my age would have had posters of footballers on their bedroom walls, Johnny Giles or Liam Brady or Steve Heighway or Johan Cruyff, I had pictures of jockeys. John Francome, Lester Piggott and Steve Cauthen were my heroes. I didn't discriminate between Flat and National Hunt. Francome was just great to watch over a fence, and I thought Piggott was all brawn, he never admitted defeat on anything. I remember watching him winning the Guineas on Shadeed in 1985, Willie Carson came at him on Bairn and looked like he was going to go by, but Piggott just sat down and drove Shadeed on, rat-tat-tat, he just wasn't going to allow the horse to get beaten.

Cauthen brought a whole new dimension to race-riding when he came over from America. He was Kid Cauthen, the Kentucky Kid, who had won the American Triple Crown – the Kentucky Derby, the Preakness Stakes and the Belmont Stakes – on Affirmed in 1977. Amazingly, Affirmed remains the last horse to have completed the Triple Crown. Cauthen was a real artist in the saddle. I remember him riding for Barry Hills and Robert Sangster, and riding all those good Henry Cecil horses, Reference Point and Oh So Sharp and Old Vic and Indian Skimmer, and winning the Derby on Slip Anchor, leading the whole way. He was so far clear around Tattenham Corner that the race was over before he levelled up for home. They said that he had a clock in his head, that he knew exactly how fast he was travelling at any stage of a race. He was sheer class.

Fortunately I was never really one for betting. I was probably turned off betting for life when another horse of Richard's, Miami Count, got beaten in a 2,000 Guineas trial at Salisbury. He had won the Birdcatcher at Naas the previous year, and Richard fancied him strongly going to Salisbury. It was probably because he was from an unfashionable yard in the arse end of Ireland, but they put him in as an unconsidered 33-1 shot for the race, and we all lumped on. I remember I had just got paid that Saturday morning, so I had my wages on as well as all the spare cash that I could muster. I had £55 on the horse, that was a massive amount of money in those days for anybody, and he got beaten half a length by a horse called Lidhame, a Hamdan Al Maktoum horse who was no good afterwards. I think that did it for me. I could never have been a punter after that.

Miami Count was second in the Jersey Stakes that year as well, and Richard's star was in the ascendancy. His string suddenly jumped from 25 to 50, and he was flying. I was dying to leave school and go full time riding, to take out an apprenticeship with Richard. I got on ok in my Inter Cert – it's now called the Junior Cert, the exam that you do after your third or fourth year in secondary school – but during that summer I knew that I wasn't going back to school. Richard was happy to take me on as an apprentice. I told my parents, and they were fine about it.

Mam and dad went up to the school that September to tell the headmaster, Mr McCormack, that I wasn't coming back. He wasn't as chilled about it as my parents were. I suppose he was looking at it from an academic's point of view. He thought that it would be a huge waste if I were to be allowed to leave school and go to work in a racing yard; he thought that I could be an accountant or an engineer or a doctor or a lawyer or anything I wanted to be. The trouble was that I wanted to be a jockey, nothing else. He couldn't see it.

I suppose he had a point. The number of people who make it as a jockey compared to the number who leave school and go into a racing yard at the age of 14 or 15 is very small. The percentages probably weren't that encouraging. I didn't care. I didn't even think about it. All I wanted to do was ride horses. Mr McCormack had a bit of a go at my parents.

'If you want him to be shovelling shit for the rest of his life,' he said to them, 'then let him go. If you want him to make something of himself, then make him go back to school and do his Leaving Cert.'

Mam was quite upset by this. It wasn't as if they were uncaring parents who were just letting me do whatever I wanted to do. They knew how much I wanted this, how much I wanted to ride horses, how nothing else mattered. Who knew that I wouldn't make it as a jockey? And even if I didn't, I still wanted to work with horses. They figured that I wanted it so badly, they weren't going to stand in my way.

The day I won the Grand National on Rough Quest in 1996, one of the many phone calls that mam received at home in the pub was from Mr McCormack to congratulate her and us. In fairness to him, he admitted that he was out of order saying what he had said to her all those years ago. She appreciated the call, but she never forgot the comment. Hindsight is a wonderful thing.

I'll never forget my first ride on the racecourse. April 16, 1986 at Gowran Park on a horse called Being Bold, in the Thomastown Colts and Geldings Maiden. I still remember the name of the race. I don't know why Richard decided to put me up, maybe he just thought that he'd better give me a ride in order to keep me happy. I couldn't believe it when he told me the day before the race. Dreamland. I hardly slept that night. I remember going into the weighing room at Gowran Park and being completely overwhelmed. I saw Mick Kinane's peg there, and all his gear on it, Stephen Craine was there, Squibs Curran, all the lads I idolised, and here I was, in the same room as them, sharing a changing room. Kevin Manning and Charlie Swan were the two up-and-coming young apprentices at the time. I couldn't imagine that I would ever be as much in demand as they were. The jumps boys were there as well. Conor O'Dwyer was there. He was just getting going then. This was rabbit in the headlights stuff.

I tried to look like I wasn't star-struck, but I'm sure I failed miserably. I tried to make it look like I knew what I was doing, but the little things gave me away. First day at school, first day in a new job. I wasn't sure if I was sitting in the right place, I wasn't sure about weighing out, about when Richard would come to get the saddle and what I had to do then, about attaching my cap to my helmet, and then there were the tights. I took them out and tried to put them on, but I had never put on a pair of tights before – it's not something you feel that you need to practice in your bedroom – and I made a complete mess of it. Schoolboy error. Then we were called and I went out to the parade ring. I saw Richard there and I just went over to him and stood there in my silks and my breeches and my boots, a real jockey.

It all happened so quickly after that. Leg up, canter down to the start, behind the stalls, into the stalls, gates crash open and suddenly we're off, I'm off, me, Mick Fitzgerald, not yet 16 years old, apprentice jockey riding in a real horserace. I wasn't really sure if I was doing everything right, or even if I was doing anything right, or if I was in the right place, or if I was allowing my horse to do too much, or if we were too close to the front, or not close enough. Suddenly we were into the final furlong and I rode him out as best I could. We finished fifth. He ran a cracker, and I was probably a passenger for most if not all of the race, but I was buzzing, exhilarated. Riding out at home was one thing, it was great, but it was only riding out. This was a race. This was a different planet.

I didn't know it at the time, but my parents had come to watch me. That was a big deal for me. I didn't see them until after the race, and I was delighted to see them there. I think they were proud of me. I hope they were.

I had a good few more rides for Richard, about 20 in total, but I never even came close to a winner. The fickleness of this business never ceases to amaze me. Richard had a quiet year the following year, the two-year-olds who we thought might be all right just never came through, and his team dwindled. I didn't know it at the time, but Richard was a semi-professional poker player as well as a racehorse trainer, and he used to go to Dublin to play cards in order to win money so that he could pay the staff wages. It was a strange scenario. I can imagine him behind a card table, though, he looked a bit like John Denver, holding pocket aces and maintaining a poker face.

Richard's string fell sharply from 50 to about 15 in a year, and the opportunities for a young apprentice who had very little experience were limited to non-existent. I realised very quickly that I would have to leave if I was going to progress, if I didn't want to end up shovelling shit for the rest of my life. I used to go through the *Irish Field* every week looking for job vacancies. John Hayden had an ad in there looking for staff one week, which I answered, and he took me on. The only difficulty was that John Hayden was on The Curragh in Kildare, about 60 miles from Camolin. I didn't care. If that was where I needed to be in order to get on as a rider, or increase my chances of making it as a jockey, that was where I would be.

I was 16 when I left home. It didn't faze me, not even a little bit. I didn't really think about the fact that I was leaving home, and that I wouldn't live there with my mam and dad ever again. If I had thought about it, I might have been a little sad, but I didn't, I was just going to be a jockey. You could say that I was focused, but I wouldn't be that scientific about it. When you focus on something, it implies that you have to concentrate, you have to willingly and knowingly block out other things that might distract you. For me, there was no effort, there was nothing else, I just wanted to be a jockey, there was nothing to think about. I needed to go to John Hayden's to take the next step on that path, so that was where I was going.

I had a motorbike at the time, a Yamaha 100, which was just about one step up from a bicycle, and I drove that up to The Curragh. My parents followed on in the car with my stuff. John had no permanent accommodation for me, but he did have a caravan, which was mine if I wanted it, which I did. It was a roof and that was all I needed.

You might not think it, but there is a big difference climatically between Wexford and Kildare. I didn't appreciate the sunny south-east until I had to trade it for the vast expanses of The Curragh, but in that 60 miles, the climate changed from warm to not so warm. I had a gas heater in the caravan, so I'd be all nice and cosy in the evening, it would be lovely and warm going to bed, but then you'd wake up in the morning, freezing. I'm not joking, the curtains on the inside of the caravan would be frozen to the window in the morning. So I'd get up and get on my bike and drive to John's to ride out.

After a little while I moved into John's house. We had great craic there, the Haydens were such lovely people. John's wife Bernadette was great, there was a physically handicapped kid there, Simon, and John and Bernadette's own son, Stephen, who had Down's syndrome, and John John, who was my age. We all lived in the house together. The Haydens' daughter, Alice Mary, was away at college.

There was another guy there, Elliot Siquibi, a black kid from Zambia who had been kicked out of Newbridge College, so the Haydens took him in and set him to work. I think his father was some big cheese in Zambia, a fellow called Bronco Siquibi, who owned a bus company, Bronco Roadways. Anyway, I had never seen a black person before in real life, so

Elliot was a novelty to me, and he was great craic. He called himself Angel Cordero – he thought the Puerto Rican jockey Angel Cordero was black, or at least he claimed that he did.

Elliot was my age, but he was a big guy. We taught him how to ride, but he wasn't really a jockey. It was so funny to see him on a horse. He was so big, he almost looked too big for the horses he was riding. He was a sprinter, a really fast runner, and he was built like one. He was lazy as well. We used to send him down the yard to sweep up or muck out, and we'd go down later and find him combing his hair.

One day, we were out exercising the horses, out in one of the big fields. Elliot was riding College Boy, a small horse who he probably shouldn't have been on. The boss asked him to do a canter, left-handed first, then right-handed, just a nice swinging canter so that he could stretch his legs, nothing too strenuous, and then come up the middle the last time, just come up by us and stop. So Elliot says right, he sets off, left-handed canter, no problem, stops, right-handed canter, no problem. But when he turned to come up the middle past us, he gets his whip out and he starts flaking into this horse. It was one of the funniest things I have ever seen. This big dude who wouldn't look out of place in the 100 metres final trying to ride out this little horse, not much bigger than some of the bigger ponies that we used to have at home, trying to be a jockey on him, and the boss beside us going berserk.

'Stop, stop, fuck, stop!'

I think he just did it for the craic. He knew that he shouldn't have been doing it, and I don't think he ever fancied himself as a jockey. I think he just did it to piss the boss off and to give us lads a bit of a laugh. He fully succeeded on both counts.

Johnny Murtagh started on The Curragh around the same time as me, and I got to know him well. Johnny's a good lad. He had been with John Oxx while he was at RACE, the apprentice riders' school on The Curragh, and he joined Oxx then as an apprentice after he finished at RACE. He was riding in all the apprentice races for Oxx, and riding plenty of winners for an apprentice, with the result that he started getting plenty of outside rides, and all of a sudden Johnny was the man.

I was thin and small and light at the time, able to ride at 7st 2lb. Even when I was 17 I was still able to do 7st 11lb or 7st 12lb. Mam says that I didn't grow an inch from my confirmation until I was 17. But that summer, my weight just shot up. On the first day of the Flat season 1988, I was 17, almost 18, I was booked to ride a horse who was set to carry 8st 5lb. As an apprentice who had never ridden a winner, I was able to claim off him. However, while I was able to do the 8st 5lb all right, I wasn't able to claim, I'd got that heavy. You might not think that 8st-odd is heavy for an 18-year-old lad, of course it isn't, but it is for an 18-year-old lad who is trying to make it as a Flat jockey. I lost the ride. That was a real eye-opener.

It wasn't as if I was eating or drinking too much. Quite the contrary. I was starving myself and doing everything that I could to keep my weight down, but it wasn't working. Nature was beating me. I went to see a food guru about helping me lose more weight, and he told me that if I tried to lose any more weight I would kill myself. Do yourself a favour, so I did. I took his advice. I stopped trying to kill myself. Jump jockeys can be a lot heavier than Flat jockeys. The minimum weight that a horse could carry at the time in a National Hunt race in Ireland was 9st 7lb, compared to just over 7st 10lb for Flat horses, so if you weighed less than 9st 7lb, you were not precluded from riding anything over jumps because of your weight. That seemed to me to be the way to go.

I started drinking that summer. I hadn't touched a drop until I was 18, I was so intent on keeping my weight down and making it as a Flat jockey that I wasn't going to do anything that was going to jeopardise that, but once I had decided that my future lay over jumps, and that it was okay if I put on a little weight, I figured that it would be ok if I had a drink. I got a bit of a taste for it that summer, and I had a blast.

I went away that summer, the summer of 1988, with a few of my mates to the Canaries, myself, Peg Cullen and Brian Lynch. It was my first time on a holiday with my mates, and I had just started drinking, so it was a fairly lethal cocktail. I was very quickly realising that there was another world out there outside of horses and racing. I had only just begun to go to nightclubs, I hadn't really bothered before, I wasn't really that into it, I was so worried about keeping my weight down. I was getting the hang of it now though and enjoying it lots.

Our first night in the Canaries, I overdid it a bit, I treated it like it was our last. I was absolutely upside down before the evening had really started, puked everywhere, so the boys had to bring me home and put me to bed before heading out again themselves. Our apartment was a two-bed affair with a pull-out bed, so we were all going to take it in turns sleeping in the pull-out bed. Peg was in it the first night. I got up in the morning, feeling great, I had got everything out of my system, went into the sitting room and saw Peg, a pool of sick beside his bed and his false teeth in it. So that was it, poor Peg was stuck in the pull-out bed for the entire holiday. We had great craic, though, eating and drinking plenty and going a little bit mad, trying to get up on women, everything. We didn't have a care in the world.

During the period when I'd been trying to keep my weight down, I'd been going regularly to the sauna in Newbridge that a lot of the jockeys used at the time, and one day I got chatting to Stanley Moore. Stanley was working for Toby Balding in the UK, and he told me that there were lots more opportunities in England than in Ireland. There wasn't nearly as much racing in Ireland as there was in England, and England wasn't as much of a closed shop as Ireland, where all the top jockeys had the top yards and the top horses sewn up.

Stanley got me a job at John Jenkins' yard in Royston, in Hertfordshire in the south of England, and I decided that I would go. It was a no-brainer really. There were very few opportunities for a claiming National Hunt jockey in Ireland. The only place where you would really get an opportunity was at Francis Flood's in Grangecon, but you really had to be able to ride at 9st in order to get the opportunities there, as you had to be able to claim off 9st 7lb. I couldn't do 9st, I would have struggled to do 9st 7lb at that stage.

I'm not sure that my parents were too happy about the prospect of me moving to England. It was one thing moving to The Curragh, up to Kildare to be in the heart of racing country, it was quite another going to England on my own. They thought I was too young, and they were probably right, but I was going, I had my mind made up. It made all the sense in the world to me.

Ryanair had just started at the time, and I got one of the first Ryanair flights from Dublin to Luton. My dad brought me to the airport. It was a bit sad heading off, but I knew that it was the right thing. I think he did too, but he was a bit nervous for me. That's only natural. I just said good luck and I was off.

# CHAPTER 5

## HOOF OIL AND MARMALADE

The first thing that struck me about England was the accent. I wasn't quite sure what to expect, but we all look alike, we all speak the same language, so I wasn't expecting the accent to be so strange.

'Y'all right mate?'

After a little while, though, I realised that half of Ireland was in England. You'd go to Newmarket for a night out and you'd meet most of the lads that you were with on The Curragh a couple of months previously.

Royston was all right, but we were Paddies and the English didn't really like us a lot of the time. Bassingbourn Barracks was just three miles from Royston, and the army lads used to come in to the town at night-time and at weekends. They weren't too friendly to us, and I'm sure we weren't very friendly to them. This was in the late 1980s, the Troubles were still going on in Northern Ireland, and I suppose they had colleagues or friends posted over there. Whenever they heard the Irish accents, they would prick their ears, and there were a few nights when we had to do a runner fairly sharpish or even fight our way out of pubs.

Maurice Ahern, a good friend of mine, was at Jenkins's yard as well, he was doing fairly well for himself there, getting on well, and we used to go out for a few pints together. Maurice would be fairly fiery when he would get a few pints in him, and I wasn't exactly a shrinking violet myself. We wouldn't go looking for trouble, but we wouldn't allow ourselves to be walked on either, so I suppose if the army lads were looking for a scrap, they could press our buttons fairly easily.

'Fucking Paddies,' they'd say when they'd hear our accents.

'Ah go fuck yourself.' Maurice wouldn't be able to let it go.

'What did you say Paddy?'

'I said go fuck yourself.'

And that would be it, all in, a proper fight, a proper boxing match. We weren't big, but we could handle ourselves fairly well, and we never came off too badly, although it wasn't pretty.

Later on, when I was working with Jackie Retter in Exeter, I used to come up to Lambourn a little and go out there with another friend, Christy O'Connor. Christy and I had been together on The Curragh, he was with Michael Grassick when I was with John Hayden, so we got to know each other well then. He was with David Murray Smith in Lambourn. This night, out on the beer in Lambourn, with plenty of drink on board, we were at a party in the Catholic Club, quite a big party spot in Lambourn, when lo and behold a row broke out between Christy and his girlfriend. It was just a little tiff at first, then it grew to more than that, and a guy came over and told Christy to back off. Christy saw red, another guy telling him to back off his own girlfriend. He went to hit him, and the next thing there were three of them on top of him. I had no option, I had to get involved to protect Christy, so I did, and all hell broke loose. I have to admit I was a bit of a scrapper when I was younger.

Anyway, we got it sorted, we got out of there, and everything was all right. We heard later on that a couple of the lads who were involved in the fight were looking for us, but I didn't really care that much, I was back off down to Exeter and I wasn't likely to be in Lambourn for a while.

Turns out, I was wrong. Six months later I was back, when I came up to Nicky Henderson's place to talk about taking on the role as his stable jockey. I went in to see Nicky in the office, all fine, had a good chat, sorted out the details, grand, then as we were walking out Nicky introduces me to his head lad, Albert Browne, Corky. I just shook his hand and said how're'ye, thought nothing of it, look forward to working with you. When Nicky's phone rang, though, Corky looked me in the eye.

'You owe me a new shirt,' he said.

'You what?'

'You owe me a new shirt.'

I looked at him, and suddenly the realisation dawned as he continued to speak.

'Catholic Club, about six months ago, I'm the fellow you pinned to the wall. You're a lucky boy.'

That was my first encounter with Corky. He's a good lad, we're the best of mates now, but he didn't forget that night, he never forgets.

It was all a bit of a culture shock for me, but the craic was good and the Irish lads looked out for each other. The English girls were great as well, very different to Irish girls, a lot more forward, and we were all fairly successful on that front, which was grand, but it wasn't helping my career.

I liked John, even though he hardly gave me any chances. I had one ride in a bumper for him on a horse called Blue Finch at Huntingdon in October 1988, and he was useless. Absolutely useless. We finished seventh in a desperate race. He didn't even come close to winning a race afterwards.

I have ridden winners for John since, but he wasn't inclined to put me up then, when I was trying to get going. John wasn't as big when I joined him as he had been through the early 1980s, but he still had some good horses, Grey Salute, who won the Lanzarote Hurdle and the Tote Gold Trophy, and he had a horse called Another Rhythm, a sprinter whom I used to ride all the time at home who was owned by Patsy Byrne, one half of the Byrne Brothers Plc from Duagh in County Kerry who sponsor the Cleeve Hurdle and a host of other races, and who has owned some really good horses in the past including Maelkar, Tolpuddle and Cristoforo.

If you were in the yard on a Saturday afternoon and you heard John coming down, you knew that you were in trouble, that you were going to get roped into something that wouldn't be in your interest. I remember one Saturday, by the time I heard him coming it was too late to disappear. Ah no, what's he going to get me to do now?

'C'mere,' he said to me. 'Give me a hand with something here will you?'

'No I can't,' I said. 'It's Saturday evening, I'm going out in a minute.'

'Just come on,' he said. 'It won't take a minute. Just give me a help out, will you?'

So I said right, I would. It was hard to say no to John. He brought me into the school where he had this horse tacked up and ready to go.

'I need you to ride this thing out for a bit,' he said. 'I've got the owner coming down to see him tomorrow and he hasn't been out for a while. I just want to knock the freshness out of him, I don't want him being too free tomorrow when the owner comes to see him.'

'Ah, you're joking me.'

So I got up on this thing anyway. Well it wasn't that he was a bit fresh – he was an absolute lunatic. He buried me three times that evening, got rid of me and left me on the flat of my back on the ground, and each time I got back up on him like an eejit. John didn't say that much, but he was a lot happier than I was.

The next morning I got up on this thing again and he was as quiet as a lamb. A different horse. Turns out that the owner coming to see him that morning was Patsy Byrne. When Patsy asked me what he was like, I just mumbled something like, not too bad. I didn't tell him that he nearly killed me the previous evening.

That was John all over, he was a bit of a character, but likeable with it. There was a horse in the yard, Ricmar, who Maurice and I thought had more ability than his handicap mark suggested. We backed him at Windsor when he got beaten, and then we backed him again at Southwell in a really awful handicap hurdle, but he got beaten again. Next time he was running at Taunton with Simon Sherwood booked to ride. We figured, ah look, forget him, he's probably no good, so we went hunting and didn't back him. He won at 13-2. I met John that evening.

'That Ricmar,' I said. 'I've backed it on its last two runs and then it goes and wins today.'

'I knew you backed it the last two times,' he said with a smirk. 'They weren't his days. Today was his day. That'll teach you.'

I realised fairly quickly that I wasn't going to make the breakthrough at John's. Johnny Francome and Steve Smith Eccles and Richard Dunwoody and Simon Sherwood used to come in to ride the good horses, and there were other younger fellows around John's, like Maurice, who were always going to be ahead of me in the pecking order. I was constantly checking the *Sporting Life* for job opportunities. I saw this job advertised with a small trainer down in Devon, Richard Tucker. I didn't even know where Devon was, but I didn't care. I'd have gone to Outer Mongolia if I was going to get to ride in races. I was completely mobile, suitcase packed, gone. I got the train down to Devon to meet Richard and have a look. He was basically a farmer who had a couple of horses. I didn't mind at all, in fact I quite liked the idea of being with a small trainer. A young jockey can get a bit lost in some of the more fashionable yards, as I found out at Jenkins'. It's often better to be a big fish, or the only fish, in a small pond than a tiny fish in an ocean.

I liked Devon as well. It was very like Ireland, rural and quiet, totally different to Royston, and the people were really nice, real salt of the earth. I got digs with this lovely older lady, Freda Samson, a real motherly-type figure who looked after me well.

My first ride over hurdles for Richard was on a horse called Lover's Secret in a conditional jockeys' selling hurdle at Ludlow, just before Christmas 1988. The standard of races doesn't get much lower than a conditional jockeys' selling hurdle at Ludlow just before Christmas, but I didn't care, it was a ride and I wasn't used to getting many of them. Lover's Secret wasn't much good, but he had run ok at Exeter on his only previous outing that season, and he liked good ground which, unusually for December, it was at Ludlow that day.

Richard didn't give me many instructions, he just told me to have him handy and finish as close as I could, so I kicked him on and tracked the leader, the favourite Sharp Order. Going to the second-last, I moved up on the outside and had just about taken it up jumping the flight when the favourite came down. I would be lying if I said that I was disappointed to see him go down, but I think I was travelling better anyway. I just put my head down then and rode down to the last, scrambled over it as best we could and rode for all I was worth up the run-in.

It was a strange feeling winning, riding my first winner. Every time before that when I had finished a race – and I had had about 80 rides up to that point without getting close to a winner – there were other horses in front of me. You'd finish third or fourth and think, not so bad, but there were always other horses in front of you, you were always behind something else. That day at Ludlow, there were no other horses in front of me, nothing there except green grass, just me and wide-open space. I was first, I had won. It was a bit surreal, but it was a great feeling.

My next ride was two days later at Hereford, three days before Christmas Day, on a filly called Lurex Girl in another conditional jockeys' selling hurdle. She ran a cracker for me. We took it up at the third-last and I kicked for home but, no sooner had I done that than another horse, Below Zero, came up on my outside, and went past. Even so, my filly kept on well to finish second.

My third ride over jumps for Richard was four days after Christmas in a conditional jockeys' handicap hurdle on a horse called Corston Springs. There was a little bit of controversy surrounding Corston Springs's previous run on Boxing Day at Newton Abbot, when he was pulled up under Peter Scudamore. It was unusual, perhaps, for Scu to be at Newton Abbot on that day, one of the busiest racing days on the calendar, when the showcase events, including the King George, were at Kempton. But Scu's trainer Martin Pipe didn't have anything in the King George, and he was sending a strong team to Newton Abbot on the day, including an exciting novice chaser Sabin Du Loir, who duly obliged at 1-2. Richard took the opportunity to book Scu for Corston Springs in the handicap hurdle but he was pulled up. Richard wasn't happy with the ride that Scu had given him. He was a funny old horse though, who had his own way of doing things. I rode him five days later at Hereford and he won.

I was delighted with the ride that I gave Corston Springs that day. I dropped him in nearly last, went right around the inside, just kept him interested, crept and crept, and didn't produce him until we had jumped the last. When we did, I asked him to quicken, which he did, impressively, and we won going away.

I was flying. I had had three rides in eight days, two winners and a second, and I thought, I've got this sorted now. This jumping game is the way to go. I had got the taste for riding winners and I just wanted to continue doing so. Life felt great.

If you had told me then that it would be 18 months before I would ride my next winner, I would have told you that you were mad, but it was. The same thing happened to Richard Tucker as had happened to Richard Lister. Horses dwindled, a couple went wrong or started regressing and they just weren't being replaced. I was on the phone a lot to a couple of the smaller trainers and permit-holders around. Any time I saw a conditional jockeys' race in the paper, I was straight on the phone to the trainers with entries asking if I could ride their horses. I got quite a few outside rides like this, but none of them was any good, none of them won.

I was getting disillusioned. You get a bit of a break, you ride a couple of winners, you're on the crest of a wave, buzzing, it's happening for you now, you're the next big thing, or you hope you are anyway, you're just waiting for the next winner, but it doesn't come, you wait longer, it'll come, just be patient, you work harder, ring more trainers, burst your balls, but still no winner, not even close. Gradually the wind goes out of your sails, the momentum slows until you feel that you are stopped or even going backwards. Time is moving on and you're not progressing.

There just weren't the opportunities for me any more at Richard's, he just didn't have the horses, so I moved to Ron Hodges. It didn't bother me that I was moving around a bit, there was always a reason for a move, each move, I felt, was increasing the prospect of me getting going, getting a couple of winners, getting a little momentum behind me, a bit of recognition.

I liked it at Ron's, we got on well together. I lived in the house with Ron and his wife Mandy. Chris Maude lived there as well, he was just getting going himself. I thought that it was a good move for me. Ron had given his conditional riders good opportunities in the past. Simon Earle had made it there, Wally Irvine was doing well there, Maudey was in the process of getting on well there, so I figured that it would be a good move for me. He had a couple of nice horses as well, Smartie Express, Highway Express, who won at Cheltenham's January meeting, and Hard To Figure, owned by James Mursell, who won the Ayr Gold Cup a few years later.

But it didn't happen for me at Ron's either. I don't know what it was, I got on really well with him, and we'd all have great craic together in the house in the evenings, but he didn't give me many rides, in fact he rarely gave me a decent opportunity. Maybe we were just too close, maybe I was so friendly with him that he just regarded me as part of the furniture and figured I'd stick around anyway even if I didn't get any rides. Maybe he thought that I wasn't good enough, and maybe I wasn't. Who knows? And it wasn't as if you could go up and ask him why you weren't getting on any, it just wasn't the done thing. It would be like a football player asking the manager why he was sitting on the bench all the time and wasn't getting a chance in the team.

My disillusionment grew deeper. It's like anything, if you put the effort in and you get rewarded, you will continue to put the effort in because you can see that your efforts are worthwhile. But if you put the effort in and you don't get rewarded, in any walk of life, you might continue to make the effort for a while, but you can't continue indefinitely. You can't continually bang your head against the wall if you can't see any progress being made. I was in danger of getting into a rut. I was comfortable at Ron's, I had a grand comfortable lifestyle, nice family to live with, a few pints at night-time or at the weekends, working with horses, and just about enough money to live on, but I wasn't getting to race-ride, I wasn't getting on in my career, and I'm sure I never would have if I had stayed there.

Like I say, the craic was good. The local hunt used to meet at Ron's once a year, just before Christmas, before heading off for their day's sport. We used to have to get up early, start early in the morning and be done with the horses before the people would start arriving at about 11 o'clock in the morning. Maudey and Wally and I were the ones who were given the responsibility of serving the drinks as the people arrived, port and brandy and the like, to keep them warm for the day I guess. So we went around with a tray of drinks each, we walked around the yard, from one end to the other with this tray, how're'ye, how's it goin, and the hunting people were taking a glass of port or brandy from the tray. When we met back up at the top of the yard, we still had a couple of full glasses each left on our trays. I looked at Maudey and figured, why not, so we drank whatever we had left, then re-loaded and headed off around the yard again.

The three of us met back up at the top of the yard a second time and we had even more full glasses left over, so we lowered them as well. These were glasses of port and brandy, and Ron didn't skimp on the measures, so we were getting nicely warm and jolly. We did the round once more, maybe twice more, until the hunt pulled out and everyone was gone from the yard. At this stage we were nicely pissed and happy. We had to be back in the yard for three o'clock to ride out final lot, so we figured we'd go to the pub for a couple of hours. So the three of us piled into an old Nissan that I had just bought from Maudey and we headed off down the track at the back of the yard, across the field to the pub. After a couple of pints there we could hardly stand up. We came out of the pub fully intent on riding out at three o'clock, but we couldn't walk in a straight line never mind get up on a horse.

I drove back across the field and crashed into the fence at the back of the yard. Wally was scared shitless that we'd be caught, so he tried to get out of the car before it had stopped. Sure, when I saw him trying to escape I just drove off. I can still see Wally hanging off the door, trying to get out of the car as the car accelerates across the field.

We met the head girl, Jane Parker, on our way back in. We were crawling up the old path to the yard. We couldn't walk, we were laughing so much. She wasn't a bit impressed. Of course we couldn't ride out, so she just sent us to the house to go to bed. In my wisdom, I went into the tack room and fell asleep. When I woke up later that evening, my shoes were gone and there was hoof oil and marmalade in my hair. The other lads weren't impressed with us either, they had to do our horses while we were incapacitated, so they had obviously decided to have a little bit of fun with me while I slept. I suppose it could have been a lot worse.

I walked up to the house through the rain, no shoes, feet soaking wet, and got into the kitchen to see Maudey sitting there, looking terrible. However he looked, I'm sure I must have looked much worse. I didn't know until later about the foreign substances in my hair.

Ron heard about the incident later. He didn't say anything, but it definitely didn't do me any good in terms of getting rides for him. I was well into my time with Ron then anyway, and had already figured that I wasn't going to get on there. I don't think I would have done something like that or allowed something like that to happen if I was getting on. I think I would have made sure that I kept my bib clean.

I wasn't sure where my next winner, my next ride, was going to come from. Things looked a little bleak.

# CHAPTER 6

## TRESPASSERS WILL BE SHOT

It's difficult sometimes to extricate yourself from your comfort zone. You can go about your business from day to day, you can be fairly happy with what you do from the time you get up in the morning to the time you go to bed at night, but when you stand back from it and look at your life, what you are doing, where you are headed, if you are not happy with what you see, then you need to do something about it. People do it. They go about their day-to-day lives, in jobs they don't really like, with people they could live without, and then, by the time they realise they really aren't that happy, they figure that it's too late to do anything about it.

I could have trundled on along at Ron's indefinitely. I was riding horses, which was all I wanted to do, I had enough money to live on, I had good mates, a decent boss, and a good place to live, but I wasn't going anywhere. My career was static. At least I realised that it was, and that was half the battle. I decided in the spring of 1990 that I wasn't going to stay at Ron's. I had got to know New Zealander Andrew Nicholson. Andrew is a top-class horseman, a three-day-eventer, who rode for New Zealand in the Olympic Games six times. Although he won a gold medal at the 1990 World Equestrian Games in Stockholm, he is probably, regrettably and unfairly, best known for his performance at the 1992 Olympics in Barcelona when, as last man to go for his team and country, he could have had eight fences down and New Zealand would still have won the gold medal. As it happened, he had nine poles down, which resulted in New Zealand dropping to the silver medal position and Australia winning the gold. My plan was to go out to Andrew's brother John in New Zealand to ride out there.

Andrew said that there were good opportunities for young riders in New Zealand. I had no idea what I was really going to be doing out there with him, and it would have possibly meant moving out of racing, but I was disillusioned with the way my career was going in England, or not going, and the thought of New Zealand quite excited me. I was young and free-spirited, I had no ties, no mortgage, no wife, no long-term girlfriend (just lots of short-term ones), no kids, just me and a suitcase, so I figured, why not?

I was coming up to another one of those crossroads. If I had gone to New Zealand, who knows what type of life I would have led or what I would be doing now? I could be sitting at the end of a bar in Auckland, beer stains on my vest, telling anyone who would care to listen to me for a few minutes, anyone who hadn't been forewarned by the barman, that I used to be a jockey in England.

'You? A jockey?'

'I was, yeah. I rode two winners.'

'No way mate. Of real races, real horseraces?'

'Yeah, one at Ludlow and one at Hereford. Look, I have a couple of photos here in my pocket.'

'Wow, you've put on a lot of weight since then, mate.'

I was just really passing the time with Ron until it was time for me to leave. About six weeks before I was due to go, I started riding a little for Ray Callow. Ray was another small trainer who lived down the road from Ron and used his gallops. He saw me riding out for Ron and asked me if I would ride a horse for him, Sunset Sam, in a selling handicap hurdle at Newton Abbot. We finished eighth.

Sunset Sam was entered again in a selling hurdle at Hereford a month later, on Easter Monday, and Ray asked me if I would ride him again. This time we won. The horse appreciated the faster ground and he picked up well on the run-in. It may have been only a selling hurdle at Hereford, but it was a huge deal for me, just my third winner and my first in a year and a half. Something clicked with me then, the buzz I got out of winning reignited something in me and I thought that it would be a real shame to give this up. If I left and went to New Zealand, who knew what I would end up doing? It was difficult to think that whatever I ended up doing could possibly give me a greater kick than the kick I got out of riding the winner of a seller at Hereford.

This was the spark that I needed, the kick on the arse to make me go and try to make it work for myself. I was still going to leave my cosy life at Ron's, but I was going to stay and try to make a go of it in England. Ray Callow knew Gerald Ham, a bigger trainer with more horses than Ray, and he said that he would put in a word for me with him. Ray had only about ten horses, whereas Gerald was having about 25 or 30 winners a season at the time, so hooking up with Gerald was a great move for me. Gerald was at Rooks Bridge in Somerset, just about 20 miles from Ray's place at Somerton. It meant that I could base myself between the two yards and ride for both, while at the same time pestering other trainers for rides. It was the first time that I felt that I was making real progress.

I rode a few winners for Gerald, and my confidence began to grow. I became re-energised, phoning other trainers looking for rides, and my efforts were being rewarded, while I continued to ride for Ray. Sunset Sam was a great servant to me. I finished fifth on him in a decent enough handicap hurdle at Chepstow a couple of weeks after we had won at Hereford, and then we finished second in a good race at Stratford in June 1990.

Duncan Idaho came along again a couple of months later. I had ridden him in his first three races for Ray about a year previously, but he was useless. Then I got back on him in a conditional jockeys' handicap hurdle at Taunton in December 1990, and we won, totally unexpectedly, at 20-1. I won on him twice more at Stratford and Leicester in the following two months, and things really got going for me.

I owe those two horses and those two trainers an awful lot. Were it not for Sunset Sam and Duncan Idaho, and the opportunities that Ray Callow and Gerald Ham gave me, I have no doubt that I would not be in the position that I am now in, looking back with immense satisfaction on a career of which I am very proud. They provided the momentum that fanned the flames and the vehicle through which to promote myself.

The second week in March 1991 was a huge week for me, nothing to do with Cheltenham, but all to do with the two meetings, Sandown and Uttoxeter, that book-ended Cheltenham week. In going through the entries for the Saturday before the Cheltenham Festival, I noticed that there was a horse in the bumper at Sandown, trained by Jackie Retter, who didn't have a jockey. In those days, only conditional riders and amateurs could ride in bumpers in the UK. Bumpers, or National Hunt Flat races, are actually an Irish invention, so called because of their confinement to amateur riders who may not be as adept at steering their mounts as professionals. They are still the sole preserve of amateurs in Ireland, but in the UK professionals can ride in them these days. Back then, they represented big opportunities for me.

I went up to Jackie one day at the races and asked her if I could ride Rafiki for her at Sandown. It was a measure of how far I had come in terms of confidence. Just one year previously there was no way I would have walked up to a trainer at the races and asked them if I could ride a horse for them. I may have gone home and rung them, or I may not have even asked for the ride at all. If you don't ask, you can't be refused. I think Jackie was quite taken aback, a young lad so brazen. She said she'd think about it and get back to me. I'm sure that if I had phoned her she would have said no thanks. It's a lot more difficult to say no when you are face to face.

Jackie knew Gerald Ham quite well, so she rang him and asked him what I was like. Luckily Gerald put in a good word for me, so I got the ride. That was a huge deal for me. Ok, it was only the bumper, and Rafiki was a 16-1 shot, but it was Sandown, it was Imperial Cup day, and it didn't get any bigger for me.

Rafiki was brilliant. He may have been having his first run since his racecourse debut almost two years previously, but Jackie had him as straight as an arrow. We moved up going around the home turn, took it up early in the straight, I gave him a kick in the belly and he was off. I didn't look beside me or behind me, it is a steep hill at Sandown and you don't want to give them any excuse not to go up it. I just kept kicking and pushing until we reached the winning line, 15 lengths clear of our closest pursuer.

The following Saturday, Midlands Grand National day at Uttoxeter, I rode Duncan Idaho for Ray in a handicap hurdle. This was a little different to Sandown. While Rafiki had little chance and was well under the radar, Duncan Idaho had won three of his last five races and was joint-favourite. And while at Sandown I was riding against fellow conditional riders, at Uttoxeter I was riding against the big boys, Peter Scudamore, Richard Dunwoody, Lorcan Wyer, Ronnie Beggan, Jamie Osborne. It didn't faze me. I jumped Duncan Idaho out the back, made my ground steadily down the back straight, took it up at the last and won well.

I was on top of the world. A winner at Sandown, one of the top tracks in the country, on Imperial Cup day, one of its biggest National Hunt days, and then a winner on Midlands National day at Uttoxeter. Ok, so everyone is a little punch-drunk after Cheltenham, but Midlands National day is the biggest day at Uttoxeter, and the race was shown live on Channel 4. Winning a seller at Hereford or Ludlow was brilliant, but this was a different league.

It's remarkable. If Rafiki had finished in mid-division I may not have had another ride for Jackie Retter. Success is a potent tonic. I rode a few for her then over the next few weeks and we had three winners. At the end of the season, she asked me to come down and base myself with her and ride all her horses. You're not really riding that many for Gerald anyway, she figured, so why don't you come down to me? So I went down to her place in Whitestone, just outside Exeter, had a look around, liked the place, and figured, why not?

Jackie and I hit it off straight away. I liked the way that she went about things. She was a trainer who really trained her horses, she knew them inside out, every one an individual, each with different requirements, and she trained them as such. She loved her horses, she lived for them. They were fit, like hard fit – she really made her horses work in a different way to the other trainers I had been with before. They worked hard every time they went out, whatever they did, even when they went walking on the roads they'd come back dripping in sweat. They were made to walk properly with their heads in the right place, their body moving in the right way. All her horses were ridden on the roads in exercise and dressage saddles so they were made to work and use their muscles properly. She was very, very hot on things like that.

She got inside horses' heads, tried to find out what made them tick. It showed me a whole new way of looking at horses, and I learned an awful lot with Jackie, but she brought it to an extreme, and ultimately it was probably her downfall. She spent too much time on horses who were no good, trying to get them to develop. At the end of the day, they were just no good – it wouldn't have mattered if you had stitched four more legs on to them. She couldn't have it, she just wouldn't accept that a horse was no good, she'd try to find out why it wasn't running faster. She was stubborn like that.

But Jackie was just a very good trainer, brilliant with horses. It was the people that she couldn't deal that well with. She had a sign up on her land saying 'Trespassers will be shot', a sign that Richard Dunwoody happened upon in later years when he got lost during one of his orienteering treks. Fortunately Woody escaped with a cup of tea and a mild bollocking.

If training racehorses was only about training, Jackie would have been one of the most successful trainers in the country, no question. But there is so much more to being a successful trainer than just training horses. It's as much about dealing with people as it is about dealing with horses, and Jackie just wasn't great on the people front, which is probably why she didn't enjoy long-term success as a trainer.

A couple of years later, just after Nicky Henderson offered me the job at Seven Barrows, I was playing golf with Jim Old and Tim Thomson Jones, and they were saying to me, wait until you get to Cheltenham, wait until you're riding a fancied horse for Nicky in the Cathcart, you think he's all nice and happy now, wait till you see him at Cheltenham, then you'll know what pressure is. I just told them that, whatever pressure I would feel at Nicky's, it wouldn't have been a patch on what I felt at Jackie's. Every race for her was a Gold Cup, even a £1,000 race at Exeter, because so much was put into every horse, she put everything into preparing a horse for a race, and if you messed it up from the saddle, you got a bollocking, simple as that. I've seen her reduce men to tears. We would sometimes go days without speaking to each other, which was difficult given that we worked together, all because of a disagreement over a ride that I gave to one of her horses. But she was great, Jackie, and on the whole we got on great.

I was her assistant trainer effectively. We planned everything together, I worked very much in tandem with her, I rode all the work and I planned all the entries with her, so it was very much a team effort. We had two great years and my career took off on the back of my association with her. To put it into context, I had ridden two winners during the 1988-89 season, just one in 1989-90, and 11 in 1990-91, all of them between Easter Monday and the end of the season, so there was definite progress being made. But in 1991-92, my first season with Jackie, I had 38 winners and finished second to Adrian Maguire in the conditional riders' championship. Quantum leap.

I had a fairly bad fall at the end of the 1991-92 season off a horse of Simon Christian's called Ryton Guard. It was at Wincanton at one of their evening meetings in May 1992. I'd given him a lovely ride as well, crept around out the back, moved up early in the home straight, took it up at the second-last and we only had to jump the last to win. He got it all wrong and he came down, firing me into the turf. I was out cold for about five minutes and it took me a long time to regain my senses. I'd say it was about ten days before I began to feel right again, until the feeling that I was in a dream left me.

When you are concussed for five minutes, you take a mandatory 21 days off. So that was the end of the season for me. It was a real pity in one sense, because I only had three winners to go before I lost my claim. I would have loved to have ridden out my claim that season, and I had a great chance of doing it. However, the silver lining was that I was still able to claim 3lb at the beginning of the following season, which meant that I was able to ride as a conditional rider for the entire season. I resolved that I would try to go one better in the conditional jockeys' championship.

I made another massive leap forward in the 1992-93 season, mainly courtesy of Dave Roberts. Jockeys' agents weren't a big thing at the time, particularly in National Hunt racing. A jockey was generally attached to a yard and booked his own rides outside of that yard. But Dave was beginning to make his name as an agent. He was the only one doing it at the time really. He already had Dean Gallagher and Richard Guest on his books, as well as the latest riding sensation to come out of Ireland, Adrian Maguire, and he was making a success of it. I'd come in after first lot at Jackie's and there'd be a message on the office answering machine.

'Hello, this is Dave Roberts. I've got Adrian Maguire and Richard Guest available for Southwell on Monday.'

I could see the attractiveness of it from a jockey's point of view. You didn't have to worry about getting on the right horses or off the wrong ones, you didn't have to spend hours on the phone, or waiting for trainers to phone you back, and you didn't have to ring begging for rides. You had somebody else to do all that for you, and you paid him ten per cent of your cut of the prize-money. The better you did, the better the agent did, so it was in his interest to get you on the right horses. I asked Dave if he would take me on, add me to his books, and he agreed that he would.

Dave is a great agent. He has refined it now to an art, and he is brilliant at what he does. He knows the form book inside out, and he knows the type of rider that each trainer looks for, which jockeys suit which trainers. As soon as the entries came out, he would be on the phone trying to book rides for all his jockeys. He figured that the better the riders that he had on his books, the easier it would be to get through to the trainers. That's what he figured, and he was tireless, absolutely monotonous. He built up his 'stable' of jockeys until he got to the stage that he is at now, where he is the first port of call for trainers when they are looking for a jockey. The one regret Dave has, I would say, is that he never made Adrian Maguire champion jockey. He got damn close, and he nearly killed the two of them trying during the 1993-94 season, when Adrian finished the season on 194 winners, enough to win the championship hands down in a normal year, but that wasn't a normal year. Dunwoody rode 197.

I got on great with Adrian, Muttley. We used to go racing together a lot, we'd share the driving if we were both riding at Kelso or Hexham or somewhere miles away. Sabrina, his girlfriend at the time, his wife now, was great as well, she was there with him from day one, and they have two great kids. Adrian is doing well for himself now as a trainer down in Mallow in County Cork. He's the man who discovered Denman, and he has trained a couple of good horses already in his short time as a trainer, including Celestial Wave, who won the Christmas Hurdle at Leopardstown in 2006. Look out for the white bridle.

People used to say to me that if it wasn't for Adrian I would be making all the headlines, I would have won the conditional jockeys' championship, I would be getting a lot of the rides that Adrian was getting. I remember the commentator and Channel 4 pundit Simon Holt, who used to write for *The Sporting Life*, asking me about it one day after I had ridden a couple of winners, but I didn't look at it like that. I was delighted that Adrian was doing so well, really I was, and I rooted for him. He put so much into it, he deserved to do as well as he did. I'm not a begrudger; I don't have that mentality. If somebody has the talent and puts the effort in, they deserve to do well, and good luck to them. Good luck to Adrian. My time would come.

It's very different if someone has talent and they couldn't be bothered putting the effort in. There are few things that annoy me more than seeing somebody who feels that the world owes them a living, that racing owes them a living, and they expect to just go in and pick it up without working for it. We are the privileged few, we are the ones who are in a position to make a living doing what we love doing, working in a sport that we love.

I remember one morning in 1997 I was riding out at Henrietta Knight's. Jason Titley and I were riding a few for Henrietta. We were there one morning at 7.30. When you are pulling out at 7.30 at Henrietta's, you pull out at 7.30, not 7.32, or 7.30 just let me finish this cigarette and I'll be with you. It's 7.30 on the dot. This morning, another jockey who was due to ride out wasn't there. At 7.30 the phone rings, Terry Biddlecombe (Henrietta's husband, multiple champion jockey of the last generation) answers, it's the missing jockey. He said he couldn't come in, he had a puncture and his spare wheel was flat, so he was really sorry but he couldn't come in.

Of course, the truth was that he had been out on the piss the night before, had woken up, didn't feel like coming in, and decided that he'd make up this story. As stories go, it wasn't that good. He must have still been pissed when he dreamed that one up. So Terry says, don't worry, we want you to ride out anyway, we'll come and get you, and he sends a lad up to get him. The jockey panics and lets the air out of one of his tyres and the spare, just in case the lad checked the spare. Of course the lads told us all what really happened afterwards anyway, so his efforts at deception failed miserably.

The great thing about Dave was that he favoured none of his riders.

'I have Gallagher, Fitzgerald and Maguire, who do you want?'

As he got better and more established, the more trainers would call him.

'This has a chance in the handicap chase at Sandown on Saturday, but I don't have a rider for him yet. Who have you got?'

Of course, they would mainly want Adrian if he was available, but as I got more established, demand for me increased. Chicken and egg. The more successful you are, the more in demand you are. The more in demand you are, the more rides you get, the better rides you get, and the more successful you are. So how do you begin? That's the difficult part. Where does the circle begin?

I was busier than ever after I joined Dave, and it was great, although my petrol bill rocketed. Hexham, Sedgefield, Kelso, Newton Abbot, Dave was merciless, he didn't care, he'd send me anywhere to get me a ride, to try to get me a winner. I wasn't complaining. All I wanted to do was ride, and I would have gone to Timbuktu for one. You might go to a meeting for five rides and you'd think you were in the big league now, five rides at one meeting. You were like the top jockeys. Four of them might have no chance, one of them might have a small chance, but I didn't care. I was getting rides and I was getting my name about. Worst-case scenario, you get to meet trainers, you get to ride for trainers, you begin to develop a relationship with them so that they will think of you when they have a runner with a decent chance. And it was an income – £68 per ride, if you were going to Hexham anyway you might as well have five rides as one, even if four of them have no real chance of winning. When you were young you didn't care. You were living the dream and getting paid to do so.

I got rides for lots of different trainers through Dave. I rode a fair bit for Howard Johnson, Tim Thomson Jones, Henrietta Knight, Nick Gaselee. It was all about getting in the shop window. Dave was like my PA. I'd ring him on my way to the races:

'Well, where am I going tomorrow?'

'You're at Hexham tomorrow, probably Kelso on Wednesday and Market Rasen on Thursday.'

I had the car packed up and ready to go wherever the rides were, and it all began to snowball. Suddenly from having a handful of rides a week, I was going racing five or six times a week with an average of three or four rides at every meeting, and it was mostly down to Dave Roberts. Jackie wasn't overly impressed, she was used to having me around the place at home. I used to ride almost all of the work. She wanted her horses worked in a certain way, and she knew I understood that, so she wanted me to come in to ride work or to school every morning, even the mornings when I was riding in the afternoon, so that was tough. I dealt with owners a lot of the time as well, she wasn't so good in that department, and it wasn't ideal for her that I was off to Hexham or Kelso when she wouldn't have any runners.

If she did have a runner, of course I had to go and ride that, wherever it was. That was the deal, I rode all her horses. There was never any question of getting off one of hers to ride something else in the same race or to go somewhere else to ride for someone else. No way. You wouldn't even ask. You wouldn't dare.

I bought a house in Exeter. I figured I'd better start thinking a little about the future. It cost £32,000. I couldn't believe that I was forking out that type of money, or that I was able to get a mortgage for it, but I had a great accountant, Di Wright, who got it all sorted for me.

The ride on Henry Mann came along pretty much out of the blue. He was trained by Simon Christian and owned by Lynn Wilson, who was tragically killed in a car crash in early 2008. He and his wife Judy were great supporters of the game and became great patrons of Nicky Henderson's after I teamed up with Nicky the following year. Lynn built up his business, Wilson Connolly, gradually and ended up selling it to Taylor Woodrow for £480 million in 2003, but he was always a gentleman and we became great friends. His untimely death was so sad, and it still dismays me that I wasn't able to ride a winner at the Cheltenham Festival for him. If I had been told that I could have ridden a Cheltenham winner for just one owner at Nicky's, and I could have chosen, I would have chosen Lynn.

He had two winners at the Festival, and I rode neither. Actually, I got off both of them. I got off Barna Boy in the 1997 County Hurdle to ride Cheryl's Lad. Nicky had two in the race and I thought that Cheryl's Lad had the better chance. That was a real killer, not just because I didn't ride the winner for Lynn, but because I had finished fourth on Barna Boy at the previous year's Festival. To make matters worse, Dunwoody got the ride! Neither of us had ridden a winner at that Festival up to that point either, and the County Hurdle is always the last race.

I got off Greenhope in the 2006 Grand Annual to ride Tysou. I had ridden Greenhope in a handicap hurdle at Newbury two weeks before Cheltenham. I thought he was a certainty that day, he was thrown in at the weights on his chase rating, and he ran like a hairy goat. Honestly, he hardly lifted a leg. So I thought, well there's no way this fellow will have improved enough in the space of two weeks to win a Grand Annual, so I rode Tysou instead. I was tailed off on Tysou, Greenhope won the race under Andrew Tinkler. That was doubly galling because it was the Johnny Henderson Grand Annual Chase, named after Nicky's late father, and it was a race that Nicky was desperate to win. I was delighted for Nicky and Lynn, but I was a little sorry for myself.

So Simon Christian called me one day out of the blue and asked me if I would ride Henry Mann in a handicap chase the following Saturday at Newbury. I was a bit surprised, but delighted. Here was a horse who had won the Golden Hurdle Final (the modern day Pertemps) at the Cheltenham Festival and who had finished second in the William Hill Chase the previous season on just his fourth run over fences. He had unseated Graham McCourt at Aintree and had run well to finish second at the Cheltenham April meeting, but I don't think that Simon or Lynn were too happy with the ride that Graham gave him that day, so they thought they'd go and ask me to ride him for the 1992-93 season. I was sorry for Graham. Graham is a great fellow and he was one of the strongest riders in a finish that I had ever seen, but you have to take the opportunities that you are given in this game.

Henry Mann ran like a drain at Newbury. He never travelled and finished seventh. I rode him two more times, the following January in the Timeform Hall of Fame Chase (later better known as the Pillar Chase) at Cheltenham and the following February at Leicester, no good either time. In fact, he never won another race, even after he was moved to Nicky's in 1994. I was actually asked to ride Sibton Abbey in that Cheltenham race by Ferdy Murphy. Adrian Maguire was committed to Toby Balding's horse, Cool Ground, on whom he had won the Cheltenham Gold Cup the previous season, so he asked me if I could ride, but of course I couldn't as I was already committed to Henry Mann. It just shows you. I went from having no ride in the race to having two in a couple of days. You know how this story ends – Sibton Abbey won the race with Steve Smith Eccles on him, I was fourth on Henry Mann.

I rode Smartie Express for Ron Hodges in the Mildmay of Flete at the Cheltenham Festival that year. Dunwoody had ridden him to win his previous two chases, but he got off him at Cheltenham to ride Belstone Fox for David Nicholson. I was gutted to finish second. We had landed upsides the winner over the last and I battered him going up the hill, as you do. I knew I was going to get suspended but I didn't care. I wasn't going to get this close to a Cheltenham winner and let it go for the want of a couple more smacks with the whip. Alas, it wasn't enough, the horse just couldn't go on any more. We finished second, and I did get suspended.

Top of my wish-list as a rider was a winner at the Cheltenham Festival, and I had got so close. The first four horses go into the winner's enclosure to unsaddle at Cheltenham, so I was led in there all right, which was an experience, but the cheers weren't for me, they were for Graham McCourt and Sacre D'Or. I was more gutted at not winning the race than I was delighted at finishing second.

The outside rides were great, but Jackie was my bread and butter and, while she was great for me, I have no doubt that I was good for her as well. The two seasons I had with her were her two best years. We complemented each other well, and we worked hard, dawn till dusk every day. She had some very decent horses from whom she managed to extract their best. Mottram's Gold was a flag-bearer for us, and so was the mare Kalogy, on whom I beat the Nicky Henderson-trained Billy Bathgate in a novice hurdle at Newbury in March 1992 (it wasn't the last I would see of Billy Bathgate). Broughton Manor was a great mare. I won seven races on her. We beat Smartie Express a couple of times in novice chases and handicap chases, and we beat a really decent mare of David Nicholson's, Deadly Charm, who had been third behind Bradbury Star in the Scilly Isles Chase at Sandown two runs previously, at Wincanton in March 1992.

Boscean Chieftain was a bit of a star. I rode him in seven races, all of them in a six-month spell between December 1992 and May 1993, winning four times, finishing second once and fourth twice. I finished second on him in the Daily Telegraph Hurdle at the good Ascot meeting in February. That was a strange race – there were only four runners and the other three were trained by Martin Pipe. So there was Jackie and me versus the might of Martin Pipe, and we were 25-1 outsider of the field. Even so, we nearly won it. When we took it up going around the home turn I thought we were going to go close, but Sweet Glow and Peter Scudamore came and collared us.

Still, we rounded off the season well by winning the Long Distance Hurdle at Haydock in May, again at 25-1, the outsider of seven. That was Swinton Hurdle day, the last big day of the National Hunt season, and the BBC cameras were there. Julian Wilson interviewed me live on BBC after that race, which did me no harm at all. It was grand, I was a little nervous, but not too much.

I rode 54 winners during the 1992-93 season, and won the conditional riders' title. I was really happy about that, but I was even more delighted at getting the Lester award for top conditional, because that was down to a vote. It usually goes to the leading conditional, but it was still a great honour, it was great to be accepted and honoured like that by my peers. I was well on my way.

# CHAPTER 7

## BIG LEAGUE

Ascot Sales, July 1993, I'm standing there with Jackie, we have come down to see if we can pick up one or two horses for not too much money. It's not easy. You would think that, at a relatively low-profile sale like this, one or two horses might fall through the cracks, but everyone is here, most of the top trainers and agents, so there aren't many cracks. I'm just standing there, leaning over the rail with Jackie, minding my own business, when I get a tap on the arm.

'Can I have a word?'

I had never met Nicky Henderson before. He had been one of the top trainers in the country for a few years now. I didn't know anything about him when he spent four years as assistant trainer to the great Fred Winter in the early 1970s, nor when he started training in his own right in 1978. I wasn't really aware of the good horses that he had during his early years as a trainer, Zongalero, The Tsarevich, Classified and their ilk. I was more a Flat-racing fan at the time as a kid, but I did follow John Francome, and I noticed the Henderson name when Francome rode for him.

I was very aware of See You Then, however, whom Nicky trained to win three Champion Hurdles in a row from 1985 to 1987, the first horse to do so since Persian War, and I knew about Travado and Remittance Man. The whole world knew about Remittance Man, it seemed, winner of the Arkle and the Champion Chase and on the brink of world domination. And I knew that Nicky was looking for a jockey.

There was a bit of a jockey-go-round going on at the time. Peter Scudamore had just announced his retirement, and Richard Dunwoody consequently had just been taken on as first jockey to Martin Pipe. Woody had been in an enviable position up to then, effectively having the pick of the horses from David Nicholson's and Nicky's yards, and it must have been a huge wrench for him to give that up, given the quality of horses that he had at his disposal, but he wanted to be champion jockey, he wanted to ride more winners than anybody else, and he figured that the best way of maximising his chances of so doing was to join Pipe.

As a result the Nicholson and Henderson jobs were vacant. Adrian Maguire was a shoo-in for the Nicholson job, so that really wasn't an issue, but there was much conjecture on who would take on the Henderson role. Irish champion Charlie Swan was mentioned, as was Norman Williamson. Indeed, Norman was offered the job, but he decided not to take it, probably because Woody was going to keep the ride on Remittance Man and a couple of other horses in the yard. Norman figured that it was all or nothing. He was offered the Kim Bailey job at the same time, and he decided to take that instead, which wasn't a bad decision, as it turned out, as two years later he rode Master Oats to win the Gold Cup and Alderbrook to win the Champion Hurdle for Bailey.

I was being mentioned as a possible contender for the Henderson job. I liked that I was, but I didn't think about it too much. It was a measure of how far I had come that I was being thought of even as a possible for one of the top jobs in the country, but I was just getting on with my business with Jackie. So when Nicky came up to me at Ascot, I was surprised, but not to the point where I was picking myself up off the floor. He asked me to come up and see him the following day, and we'd have a chat.

That evening as I drove back from Ascot, I thought, this could be it, this could be my big break, my big step into the big league. Nicky was a top-class trainer (still is) and a big Cheltenham man. For me, it was all about Cheltenham. Even when I was first getting into National Hunt racing, it was the Gold Cup that was the pinnacle, not the Grand National, it was Dawn Run who made the hairs stand up on the back of my neck, not West Tip.

I tried not to allow my thoughts to run away with me. I phoned Jackie to tell her that I was going to see Nicky the following day. She wasn't very pleased. Jackie didn't hide her emotions very well.

'Give me a ring after you've seen him and let me know how it went.'

The interview the following day went well. It was more of a chat than an interview, just sorting out the details. He was always offering me the job and I was always accepting it, although there were a few caveats. Dunwoody would keep the ride on Remittance Man, that was set in stone. He would also ride some of the Michael Buckley horses, Tinryland and Thumbs Up, horses like that. Jamie Osborne would continue to ride Travado, and I would ride the young horses. I said fine, perfect.

'One thing I do want, though,' I said to Nicky. 'I want the riding decisions to be made early. I don't want to be sitting around until the last minute waiting for Dunwoody to decide what he's going to ride, where he's going to go, because all the rides at the other meeting would be gone. I want to know early where I'm going to be. Dave Roberts is a very good agent, but he needs to know in good time where I'm riding. As long as I know, then that will be grand, and if Dunwoody turns around at the last minute and lets you down, I'm not going to be able to change my plans.'

We shook hands. I could hardly believe it, me, Mick Fitzgerald, stable jockey to Nicky Henderson. Amazing. On one level it was a bit surreal, on another it was a natural progression. It was all I could do not to explode with excitement. I have no idea why he picked me. He didn't know me from Adam. He had seen me ride all right, and he must have thought I was ok, but he didn't know anything about me, and I think he asked a lot of people for their opinions which, fortunately, must have been positive. But I thought that I deserved the job, or at least a shot at it. Scu was gone, Dunwoody was with Pipe now, Maguire was with Nicholson, Osborne was with Oliver Sherwood and Charlie Egerton and Henrietta Knight, so he wasn't an option. After those, I was the obvious choice surely, the up-and-coming youngster, the leading conditional rider.

I was never lacking confidence in my own ability. Some people may mistake that for arrogance, but I don't think I'm an arrogant person. I just genuinely believed in my ability as a rider, I really believed that I was good, and I hope that didn't or doesn't come across as arrogance.

Corky could have scuppered the whole deal when we met him outside, but if he told Nicky about the small altercation that we had had in the Catholic Club, and I would be amazed if he didn't, Nicky didn't allow it to influence his decision.

I left Seven Barrows and drove to Ridgeway Hospital in Swindon, where I was going to get my collarbones operated on. When I got there I rang Jackie.

'So how did it go?' she asked.

'It went well,' I told her. 'We had a good chat, he seems like a good guy.'

'And what do you think? Will you take the job?'

'Ah, I'd be mad to turn it down, Jackie,' I said, a bit sheepishly. 'It's too good an opportunity.'

'Well I'm very disappointed.'

That was it. She hung up. We didn't exchange another word. I was in hospital then for a few days getting my collarbones sorted, so I didn't get to see her until about a month after that when I called down to the yard. She was getting organised and was in the process of trying to find herself a new jockey.

'Nicky is very good,' I told her. 'I'm sure I will have lots of opportunities to ride for you still.'

'But that's not going to work, is it?' she said. 'He's not going to let you off to ride my horses when he needs you himself.'

'Look, he just said play it by ear, we'll see how it goes,' I reasoned.

Jackie shook her head.

'No,' she said slowly. 'It's just not going to work.'

End of.

It was sad that we couldn't continue our association, but it was reality. To turn down the job with Nicky so that I could continue to ride for Jackie just wasn't an option, it wasn't realistic, and she knew it. Nothing lasts forever. If you are going to progress, you have to take the opportunities with which you are presented, at least put yourself in a position to exploit them. I learned an awful lot during my time with Jackie, but it was time to move on.

Other doors began to open for me. I started riding out for Jenny Pitman, Henrietta Knight and Nick Gaselee, three top trainers at the time. Jenny famously became the first woman to train the winner of the Grand National when Corbiere won the race in 1983. She also won two Gold Cups with Burrough Hill Lad and Garrison Savannah, who almost became the first horse since Golden Miller to win the Gold Cup and the Grand National in the same season when he just got caught on the run-in by Seagram in 1991. She was succeeded when she retired by her son Mark, a top trainer himself, who had ridden Garrison Savannah to his Gold Cup win and his Grand National heartache. Nick Gaselee trained Party Politics to win the National in 1992, while Henrietta Knight, of course, was the mastermind behind Best Mate entering the history books as the first horse since Arkle to win three Gold Cups.

My first morning down at Jenny's, Dean Gallagher and Graham Bradley were there as well. Jenny always liked to have a lot of jockeys riding for her, and I was schooling a nice young horse. First fence, I see a nice stride, up, jumps it well. Second fence, this horse is eyeing it up, he wants to have a cut at it, I see a stride, let him go, up, flies it. Down to the last, the horse's blood is up, his confidence is high, he wants to have a go, I see a stride again, give him his head, and zing, he absolutely wings it. I pull up, come back around to Jenny, big smile on my face.

'You see if you ever do that to one of my young horses again,' she screams at me, 'I'll pull you down off the fucker.'

I'm flabbergasted.

'If he did that at Cheltenham,' she continues, 'he'd end up in a big black hole at the back of one of those ditches.'

'Right,' I say, 'well what do you want me to do?'

'Hold him in underneath your hands,' she says. 'Let him pop over them.'

We go to the top of the school again, and this horse is dying to have another go. He's by Strong Gale, a lovely horse, a natural jumper, but I'm hanging on to him going to the first fence. He's looking at the fence thinking, 'Let me go, let me go', but I keep a hold of his head, he gets right into the roots of the fence, almost kicks it out of his way, does well to stand up. Down to the second, same thing, I keep a hold of his head and he makes a complete mess of the fence. Jenny is standing at the second fence looking on. So we're down to the third fence, this horse is frothing at the mouth now wanting to get on with it, so I see a stride, let him go, and he wings it, brilliant jump.

'There you go,' says Jenny when I turn back up. 'The only reason he jumped the last one so well was because you did what I told you at the first two.'

I school a couple more young horses, Brad and I school two together and when we pull up, Jenny is screaming at us again.

'You fucking amateurs!'

We're scratching our heads. I don't have a whole lot of time for too much messing. I have to get home and have a sweat before I go racing.

'Mark, get your helmet,' she says, 'show these lads how to school a horse.'

Mark, Jenny's son, looks on a little uncomfortably.

'I haven't got my helmet Mom.'

'What do you mean you haven't got your helmet?' berates Jenny. 'Didn't I tell you to bring your helmet in case you had to show these lads how to school a horse?'

Brad looks at me.

'Bah,' he says in his best Yorkshire drawl, 'she's some fucker!'

I liked riding for Jenny though. She had a tough streak, but she was fair. I rode for her quite a bit after I got going, and was on Artadoin Lad for her when he finished second behind Barton in the 1999 Royal & SunAlliance Novices' Hurdle. Jenny called a spade a spade, there was no beating around the bush, she told you what she thought, but she was always fair. She had her own ideas about how her horses should be ridden and once you did it her way, you were all right.

Brad actually cost me a Champion Hurdle winner. In the mid-1990s, Jamie Osborne was riding most of Wally Sturt's horses, most of whom were in training with Jim Old, and I was more or less riding the Sturt horses that Jamie couldn't ride when my commitments to Nicky allowed. Brad was riding a few for him as well. Osborne rode Collier Bay for Wally and Jim to win the AIG Europe Champion Hurdle at Leopardstown in January 1996, and I was sure that he would ride him in the Champion Hurdle at Cheltenham, but Jamie chose to ride Mysilv for Charlie Egerton instead. Jim called me the week before the race.

'Look,' he said, 'Wally wants Brad to ride Collier Bay if he's available, but if he rides Alderbrook, which it looks like he will, then you ride Collier Bay.'

I was made up. I had been down to school Collier Bay that week and he went very well for me. He was a better horse on soft ground than he was on good ground, but if there was even a little bit of cut in the ground at Cheltenham, I thought he would have a right chance.

Alas, fate conspired against me. The week before Cheltenham, Dean Gallagher had his 30th birthday party. All the jockeys were there, most of them a little the worse for wear, but Brad was worse than most, absolutely upside down drunk he was. He was supposed to go up to Kim Bailey's to school Alderbrook the following morning, he set his alarm, but there was a power cut that evening and his alarm didn't work. He might not have made it anyway, but with no alarm he had no chance. He missed his appointment at Bailey's to school the horse and lost the ride on the Champion Hurdle favourite. Bailey got Dunwoody to ride Alderbrook, so Brad switched to Collier Bay, which left me riding Land Afar for Paul Webber.

Going down the hill in the race to the second-last, I was under pressure going nowhere and Brad goes past on Collier Bay pulling a train. I wasn't happy at the time, but it's swings and roundabouts. I would get on plenty of big winners in the future that could have been another jockey's ride.

I was good friends with Jamie Osborne and he put me in for a lot of good rides. He's a good fellow Jamie, he was a good lad when he was riding and he's doing well now training on the Flat. He always gave the impression that he was Jack the Lad, but he was really professional. He studied form and past races in at least as much detail as I did and he was one of the first jockeys to get an equiciser – a mechanical horse for all the world – into his house.

Jamie was riding a good bit for Henrietta Knight, but he was also riding for Oliver Sherwood and Charlie Egerton, so he wasn't available all of the time, so Henrietta asked me if I would be happy if she had second call on me when I wasn't riding for Nicky. This was unbelievable. From being out in the wilderness, a mere conditional who was intent on riding out his claim, here I was with a job with one of the most powerful National Hunt yards in the country, a second option with another really strong yard, and in demand with lots of other top yards.

The first time that I was up at Henrietta's, we rode out in the morning and then all went in for breakfast, Henrietta and me and Jimmy Duggan, who used to ride Aonoch, and the late John Durkan, who used to ride for Henrietta as well, and a couple of others. Henrietta is all very prim and proper, speaks with a nice posh English accent, very correctly and carefully. Her mother was lady-in-waiting for the Queen Mother, so it's hardly surprising that she is so correct. And here was I, a bog man from Ireland, in having breakfast with this person for the first time, so I was very careful about my manners and my language.

'Jimmy was down in London yesterday,' said Henrietta directly to me, 'and he very kindly brought me back a present.'

'That's nice,' I said, a little bemused, as she dug into the pile of newspapers and magazines on the table. She picked out a magazine and put it down in front of me.

'What do you think of that?'

I looked at the page. There's this bird, stark naked, bending over, about to get rammed up the arse by this guy, also starkers. I almost fell off my chair. Henrietta Knight, prim and proper Henrietta Knight, former schoolteacher, one step removed from royalty, showing me this picture of a bird and a guy about to get it on. They were all sitting there around the table waiting to see my reaction, trying not to burst out laughing. Jimmy Duggan was sniggering away. I was quite stunned, and I'm sure it showed. It was one of the only times in my life that I've been at a loss for something to say, but I had to say something, they were all waiting for my response. I was thinking, 'lucky bird' or 'lucky guy'. What I really wanted to say was, 'Henrietta, I'm shocked!'

'Well somebody is about to be very happy,' I bumbled, barely audibly, as the laughter exploded.

More coffee anyone?

# CHAPTER 8

## WOODY WOES

I was bowled over by Nicky's place, Seven Barrows. It was at Seven Barrows that Peter Walwyn used to train, and from where he sent out Grundy to beat Bustino in the 1975 King George, the one that is generally regarded as the greatest race ever staged on British soil, and Humble Duty to win the Guineas and Polygamy to win the Oaks. Nicky had trained from Windsor House Stables, also in Lambourn, before that, but he and Peter swapped stables a couple of years earlier as Peter was scaling down and Nicky was cranking up. Meanwhile I rented out the house I'd bought in Exeter and moved to Faringdon, just beside Lambourn.

My first ride for Nicky was on a horse called Palm Reader in a handicap chase at Worcester in September 1993. He was a horrible horse. I hated him. He was as free as the wind, you couldn't hold one side of him. He'd just gallop headlong into fences without thinking what he was doing, and he wouldn't listen to you. You'd try to shorten him up going into a fence, but he wouldn't do it, he'd just gallop away into it and then go, uh oh, I need to jump this now.

I wanted to do well, I wanted to give this a good ride and win if possible. Dunwoody had just ridden a winner for Nicky at Bangor, typical, so that added to the pressure, at least in my head. I gave Palm Reader his head a little bit in this race at Worcester, and we were about ten lengths clear down the back straight. At the second-last fence in the back straight, he galloped straight into it, clouted the fence in the middle and turned a somersault, sending me flying. Inauspicious start.

Thankfully I didn't have to wait too long for my first winner. It wasn't like I was under pressure, or that Nicky was making it difficult for me, but I was fairly anxious to get my first winner for Nicky on the board. It's like when a striker joins a new club, you know he can score, you've seen him score for other teams, but if he goes a couple of games without scoring for his new team, the media start talking, the fans start getting anxious and the pressure grows. The more the pressure grows, the more difficult it is. So I just wanted to hit the back of the onion bag for my new team nice and early, no fuss, no pressure.

Billy Bathgate was a nice young chaser, who was owned by Michael Buckley, a good friend of mine now. He had been a good novice hurdler, and he hadn't been that far off the top novice chasers the previous season, but he had desperate wind problems, and they held him back. He used to choke badly in his races, and you had to give him enough time to catch his breath. If you asked him to do too much too early it would be like someone stuffed a cork into his windpipe and he just couldn't breathe. But he had loads of gears, so you had to ride him with a lot of confidence. That suited me. I loved riding out the back, riding for a turn of foot.

I thought I gave him a nice ride that day at Kempton in October 1993. I always loved riding at Kempton, Nicky always liked having runners there. He has been leading trainer at Kempton and I have been leading rider for a good few years now. People think I'm mad when I say that Kempton is very like Cheltenham, but in many ways it is. On the face of it, they couldn't be more different. Kempton is right-handed, Cheltenham is left-handed, Kempton is as flat as a pancake, Cheltenham has more hills and valleys than a Welsh shepherd, but actually, the attributes that you need in a horse for success at Cheltenham are the exact same as the attributes you need for success at Kempton. If you are not travelling at Cheltenham, you have no chance of getting home, and it's the same at Kempton. If you don't jump at speed, if you don't get the distance, if you don't fully get home, you'll win nothing at either track.

You often hear it said, especially in the context of the King George, if he's going to get three miles anywhere, he's going to get it at Kempton, but you really need to get the distance. You see it often, horses in a bunch turning for home but spread out like washing by the time they reach the winning line. It isn't a coincidence that horses who win or run well at the Racing Post Chase meeting at Kempton in February invariably do well at the Cheltenham Festival. Contrast that with other tracks, like Ascot or

Newbury. Albertas Run in 2008 was the first horse in about 60 years to win the Reynoldstown Chase at Ascot and go on to win the Royal & SunAlliance Chase at Cheltenham, even though you would think that it would be the ideal prep race.

I just hunted Billy Bathgate around out the back in the early stages, made ground around the home turn, took it up at the second-last and sent him clear. I got off the horse and thought, yes. Everything had gone well, the horse had done it well and I was off the mark. That was a nice feeling. Nicky was very pleased. 'I hope it's the first of many.'

It was. Nicky had good horses and it was a pleasure to ride so many of them. I won a novice chase on Amtrak Express at Newbury the following week. I just kicked him out of the gate and we never saw another rival. He was a lovely horse, but he was tiny. Sitting on him was like sitting on a razor blade. He was much better than his size should have allowed him to be.

I broke my nose off him the following month at Fontwell. He was well fancied, an even money favourite, we were in front going to the fourth fence, the one down the hill, when he met it wrong and came down. Then, as he was getting up, he just flicked his head back and caught me a sucker punch right on the nose, smashed it to bits. There was an old doctor at the track and he started pulling and dragging it, trying to get it back into place. 'Oh, it looks like you've broken your nose there all right, here just hold still and I'll click it back into place.' I nearly passed out with the pain. Facial injuries are the worst. I'm not sure why. Maybe it's because your face is closer to your brain than your arm or your leg, but a broken nose is bloody sore.

The doctor couldn't get it back into place so they sent me off to hospital, where they told me that I had broken it in ten or 12 places, so they had to reset the whole thing. I went back into Nicky's the following day with my face all blue and yellow and all different colours, and he said, 'Where are you going? You're not riding out with your nose like that.' He was right, it was ridiculous, but I was just champing at the bit, dying to get back, dying to get going. Dunwoody was there like a thorn in my side, always present even when he wasn't, always a factor. He was there like a nagging dull pain that just won't go away no matter what you do. I wanted to be as good as him, I almost wanted to be him, but I wasn't, I couldn't be him, there was only one Dunwoody and I felt that I was in his shadow for the first two or three years at Nicky's.

The day I came back after breaking my nose, I was riding this thing at Towcester for Kim Bailey. The first thing he did, you wouldn't have believed it, was fire his head back and hit me on the nose. Whack! Nose gone again, splattered all over my face again, blood everywhere, bastard of a horse. My nose is in bits now, it's been broken so many times. Ruined my prospects as a male model.

Dunwoody or no Dunwoody, I got on well with Nicky from the start, but it was very much a boss/employee relationship in the beginning. Our relationship evolved from that though to a point now where I number him among my very best friends. I was thinking about this recently and trying to put my finger on when we moved from superior/subordinate to just good mates, but I couldn't. There was huge respect there from the start, I totally respected him as a racehorse trainer, and it was a gradual evolution from there. We used to travel to the races together a lot in the early days. He didn't have a driver then and he'd call me in the morning and ask me how I was getting to the races or if I was going with anybody. Usually I would be travelling on my own, so he'd offer me a lift. He'd drive there and I'd drive home, so we got to know each other very well.

We'd often stop off for a drink on the way home, or when we'd get to his place, where my car would be parked, he'd ask me in and we'd have a drink together. It didn't matter if we had had a successful day or not. I was always honest with him, I would always tell him what I thought about a horse after riding him in a race or even after schooling him, and he knew that. If I thought a horse was useless I'd tell him.

As time went on we got closer, to the point where, when I broke up with my first wife, Jane, in 2001, I told my parents, I told my best friend, Shane Donohoe, I told AP McCoy, and the next person I told was Nicky. That's how close we were even then. When my divorce was going through, I told him that I hoped he never had to go through what I was going through. Ironically and regrettably, some years later when Nicky and Diana were separating, I met him in Scotland, just after it had all been finalised, and I asked him how he was.

'Ah not too bad,' he said through misty eyes, 'all things considered. But you know, I never forgot what you said to me all those years ago, and you were dead right.'

There would be just the two of us in the car on the way home from the races, so we shared everything, the good days and the bad days, although sometimes after a particularly bad day you'd wish you were driving home on your own.

One such day was February 19, 1994, the day that I got Current Express beaten at Nottingham. It was about a two-hour drive to Nottingham, so it was a fair way to go for just one ride, but I thought Current Express would win. He had finished fifth behind Flown, who was also trained by Nicky, in the Supreme Novices' Hurdle at the Cheltenham Festival two years previously, then he had a year off with leg trouble, and I had won on him at Kempton on his only previous run over fences the previous month. He was a very talented horse and Nicky thought an awful lot of him.

I was a very busy rider in those days. I'd gun them at every fence. I'd see a stride and I'd fire them at the fence, you're coming up for me, no arguments. There was no mistake, this horse might not come up, it was my way or the highway. It wasn't the best way to be. You have to ride a horse as you find it, you might see a stride, but it might not be for the horse, he might not have the energy nor the inclination to make it, so you have to treat every situation differently.

So I was gunning Current Express down over his fences and we had gone clear. He was a super jumper, he had so much scope over a fence, he had jumped great at Kempton and he had come up for me every time at Nottingham, until we got to the second-last. I saw a stride, it was a long one but it was a stride so I kicked him into it, come on, you're coming with me. But he had a look and didn't fancy it. 'Are you sure?' He put down on me and belted the fence, which knocked him sideways, halted his momentum and knocked the stuffing out of him. He did well to stand up. He made another mistake at the last and finished a very tired third.

I was disgusted. All I could think was that he should have come up for me. I couldn't believe that he hadn't. I could tell by Nicky's face when we came back in that he didn't agree. That was a long drive home. I had had just one ride, Nicky had had just one runner, and I had got him beat in Nicky's eyes. I still wasn't so sure about that myself, but I didn't want to argue until I had seen the race again. I was dying to get home to watch the race again. Nicky didn't say much on the way home in the car. That was his way, the silent treatment, he'd never bawl you out of it, but you didn't want to be on the receiving end of the Henderson silent treatment. He usually forgot about it very quickly afterwards though. That was the great thing about Nicky, he'd put these things behind him very quickly. No sense in dwelling on them. Move on.

I got home that night and turned on the video. That was my way of dealing with these things. I got SIS into my house in Faringdon for that very reason. Although it wasn't cheap, it was worth it to me. I must have watched that race about 40 times. I'd analyse my ride, figure out if and where I had made a mistake, and try to put it right for the next time. I did it so that I could learn from it, not so that I could torment myself, although it had that effect as well. With Current Express, Nicky was absolutely right, it was completely my fault. I didn't need to gun him down to the second-last like I had. I hadn't realised that we were as far clear as we were, and the horse had so much speed anyway that he would have won doing handsprings if I had just let him go in tight and pop the fence.

I should have won and I lost. That killed me, that always killed me. I was disappointed for the horse, disappointed for Nicky, disappointed for the owners and I was gutted that I had made the mistake. I had been doing a little bit of work with Yogi Breisner before that. If there is something that Yogi doesn't know about jumping horses or riding a horse over a fence, it is not worth knowing. He was a top event rider himself, and he managed the Great Britain team that won the silver medal in the Sydney and Athens Olympics, but it is for his mastery with National Hunt horses and riders that he is known in racing circles. Nicky used him a lot for horses who needed to learn more about jumping than they knew, and for jockeys.

After Current Express, Nicky wanted me to step up my work with

Yogi. I'm sure the timing wasn't coincidental. He was keen for me to get it right. Once I had it right, it would benefit him and it would take the pressure off him. I spent hours with Yogi. His objective was to get me to sit more still over a fence. I was like a boy in a classroom who just couldn't stop fidgeting, a bit like AP McCoy is now, although he is getting better as well. In his younger days, AP wouldn't be able to let a horse just walk around at the start without slapping it or kicking it until you'd just want to shout at him: 'Would you ever give over!'

I was still quite raw when I got to Nicky's, no question. I had never really had any training or schooling on how to ride. I had gone down to Caroline Beasley a little bit when I was a kid but, beyond that nobody had ever given me any tuition, no more than most of the other lads riding around then. It's different now, most young lads rising up through the ranks now have had formal training. Most lads at that time didn't. You just took what you could from different riders, watched the riders you liked, Woody and Osborne and Francome, and tried to imitate their best attributes.

The big thing that I learned from Yogi was that it was ok to do nothing over a fence. I was very busy with my hands. I was too eager to get a horse to jump and I was getting ahead of him, with the result that I would be putting all my weight on the front of the horse and he'd have no power from behind to actually jump. The jumping action has to come from behind.

It was a psychological thing. You always felt that you needed to do something, you needed to help the horse in some way, teach it how to jump. The most difficult thing to do over a fence was nothing. The horse can jump itself. At the end of the day, it's the horse who has to jump the fence, not the jockey. You can't do it for him. How many horses fall at fences when they are running loose with no jockey on their backs to interfere with them? Very few. This was something that I needed to get my head around, and it took me a while.

Even though I was stable jockey in name at Nicky's, first jockey, the fact that I wasn't riding any of the established stable stars meant that I felt very much like the second jockey. Woody was always around. Golden

Balls. He could do no wrong in Nicky's eyes. I knew Woody very well, I was good friends with him, I quite liked him, but it didn't matter, I used to look at him and think, you bloody smoothie. He'd be all smiles with Nicky, but he'd shaft you on the racecourse or on the schooling grounds if it would further his cause. They said he'd ride over his grandmother for a winner, and I didn't doubt it.

Woody would often come in to school at Nicky's. I used to school a lot with him, two horses upsides, over the four schooling fences. At Nicky's you'd come in from the left and turn left, then the one on the inside would wait for the one on the outside to catch up before you'd jump off, or that was the way it was supposed to happen. But Woody would always make sure that he was on the inside coming in, always, it was unbelievable, then when he straightened up he wouldn't wait for me to get upsides, he'd just kick off, steal a half a length, which would be impossible to make up over four schooling fences when you weren't supposed to be racing anyway. That's how competitive he was, even when he was schooling he'd have to win. Everything was a race. He'd pull up at the end of the school, and look back at me, typical Mona Lisa smile on his face that said, what happened to you there? Could you not keep up?

The odd time you'd catch him on the hop, the very odd time you'd get the jump on him and you'd be off and he wouldn't be able to catch up. He'd get down to the end and he'd look at you and kind of shake his head, as if to say, 'you're so immature, imagine trying to win a school'.

'That didn't jump very well, Woody, did it?' you'd say.

'What do you mean?' he'd respond, all defensive. 'He jumped fine.'

Then Nicky would ask him how the horse jumped, and he'd say, fine. Just fine. That's all you ever got out of Woody. Not, 'oh, this is a lovely jumper' or 'he's got a bit to learn' or 'he shortened up well at the second'. Just fine, that was all.

I remember Woody and Jamie Osborne coming in to school together the same day, Woody was schooling Remittance Man and Jamie was schooling Travado. They turned in at the bottom of the school, and they both took off, each of them trying to out-do the other. Johnny Kavanagh and myself were taking a couple of young hurdlers over the schooling hurdles beside them, but we stopped when we saw Woody and Oz take off, full pelt.

Before they even got to the first fence, Nicky started screaming from the top of the school. Nicky would never have a go at Woody, but he was going bananas this morning. Here he was, getting these two top jockeys, two of the best jockeys in Britain at the time, in to school his two best horses, possibly the two best two-mile chasers in the country, and they were acting like school kids. Each one was trying to do the other, make him make a mistake, get the upper hand. These two horses, hugely valuable commodities, fragile beasts, going 40 miles an hour over these fences, schooling fences for sure, but they were proper fences, proper racecourse size. Fortunately for everyone, there were no mishaps. The two horses were brilliant. The two lads pulled up with big ear-to-ear smiles on their faces, what's all the fuss about? Nicky's coronary averted.

It was good fun for them, but it was stupid and I could understand why the guvnor was going mad. Ok, so it was only a one-off, and Oz and Woody were top class at schooling young horses, but schooling is exactly that, it's about teaching, it's not about seeing what a horse can do or going as fast as you can and having a bit of fun. I was forever telling the young lads at Nicky's, it's not about putting on a show, it's about teaching and learning. You're trying to teach the horse to jump a fence the way you want him to jump it, and you're learning about how he does it.

Some trainers don't believe in schooling too much. To my mind, that's a mistake. Nicky always schooled his horses well. You do your work at home on the schooling ground so that horse and rider both know what to expect when you get to the racecourse. As a rider you get to learn what each horse will do in any given situation, how far it will stand off, how tight it will go, if it jumps left or right, and that gives you an edge. You are all the while looking for an edge.

John Francome is a great man to school a horse. He comes to Nicky's once or twice a year, not for Channel 4 or anything, he just comes in to school because he loves it. And he is still brilliant. He's 55 years of age and he is still a top-class rider, poetry over a fence. I try to get the young lads to watch him, and I try to teach them myself. I never had anyone to teach me when I was younger. I would have loved to have had someone take me aside and tell me what I was doing wrong, or give me some pointers on how I could improve, so I try to give the young lads pointers when I can, but you might as well be banging your head against the wall sometimes. Sometimes I just can't seem to get through to them. I'd say I'm quite an aggressive teacher. But it's frustrating. You tell a lad something once, you're doing them a favour, you would think they'd take it on board, but not a bit of it sometimes. Then you see them doing the wrong thing again, without any apparent effort to take on board what you took the time to tell them or show them.

Take Andrew Tinkler, for example, nice lad, nice rider. He was riding in a bumper one day at Ludlow. He comes around the top bend at Ludlow, quite a sharp right-hand turn, with his stick in his right hand, wielding this thing like Zorro, gives it a smack and the horse runs away to his left. He ends up getting beaten half a length after giving away about six lengths by running wide off the bend. Andrew comes in and says, 'Aw, it ran all over the track.' Funny that. You hit a horse with your right hand coming off a sharp right-hand turn and he runs away to his left?

'Right,' I said to him afterwards. 'Do you not think that on a right-handed track you should carry your whip in your left hand?'

'Yeah.'

'You can't use your stick in your left hand, can you?'

'Not as well as in my right.'

'Right, well I'll tell you what,' I said. 'Every day you're riding out at Nicky's, carry your stick in your left hand. Riding, schooling, working, always carry it in your left hand. Every time I see you at Nicky's, I want to see the whip in your left hand. And if you are riding a horse and it's moderate, and you think it needs a smack to get it going, give it a smack with your left. Gradually your left hand will get better and you will be able to use both hands. Ok?'

'Ok.'

Three or four days later, he was riding at Hereford, another right-handed track, same thing, comes around the home turn and gives the horse a smack with his right hand, horse veers out to his left. This time, however, the horse wins. So Andrew is back in the weigh room and all the lads are saying well done, and he's smiling and delighted with himself for riding a winner.

'Well done Andrew,' I said to him.

'Thanks.'

'But did you not hear me when I told you to carry your whip in your left hand on a right-handed track?'

He looked at me, startled.

'Well, he needed a smack, and I wanted to give him a good smack, so I decided I'd use my right hand.'

'But the horse ran across the track,' I said. 'If you had got beaten, that would have been the reason again. He didn't need a smack at that point. He just needed to be balanced.'

'Right.'

The next day, the very next day, you wouldn't believe it, I was down schooling at Nicky's and I saw Andrew, laughing and joking with one of the other lads, stick in his right hand.

'Look Andrew,' I said to him. 'Put your stick in your left hand. It needs to become second nature.'

This all happened when Andrew was 16 or 17. He's about 23 now, and I still don't think he's as effective as he could be with the stick in his left hand. It's disappointing. Some lads just won't take things on board. Andrew is a nice rider, he still rides for Nicky, but he just hasn't progressed the way that I thought he would, the way that I hoped he would. He's not a bad lad though, and he's young still, so he could still be good.

As a young jockey, I had nothing but respect for Richard Dunwoody. He was brilliant, the best there has ever been I'd say. When I was a kid I looked at Francome and Jonjo and thought they were the best, and they were at the time, but Woody was better. Everyone wanted to be like Woody. He just oozed class in the saddle. On the one hand I enjoyed seeing him close up, seeing him school, present a horse to a fence, seeing his balance, his communication with the horse, and I'd try to learn. On the other hand I used to think, what chance have I got? This is my competition. I'll never be that good.

Adrian Maguire said something to me coming out of Ludlow one day. I was travelling with him this day, he lived in Faringdon as well and we used to often go racing together. I had just ridden a treble, one for Nicky and two for outside yards, and I was feeling pretty good about myself.

'Why are you trying to be like Dunwoody?' Adrian asked.

'You what?'

'You're trying to be like Dunwoody on everything you ride for Henderson,' he said. 'You're putting yourself under too much pressure, you're trying too hard, you're panicking. When you are riding for other trainers, you just ride your own race, you're much more relaxed, and it's better. It's like chalk and cheese. You don't have to be like Dunwoody, find your own way, play to your own strengths. You're not Dunwoody. You don't have to be Dunwoody.'

He was right. I was putting myself under more pressure when I was riding for Nicky. I was always trying to ride the perfect race, trying too hard, trying to get horses to do things that they just weren't able to do, asking them to make jumps that they just weren't able to make. I was just so desperate for it to work, I was desperate to succeed for Nicky, to make the job a success. I wasn't trying to ride like Dunwoody, I wasn't trying to copy his style, I was just trying to be as good as him.

But after Adrian said that to me I began to realise, I didn't have to be someone else, I didn't have to be another jockey, I just needed to be my own jockey and be as good as I could be. Sometimes when you want something so badly you try too hard to make it happen. So I began to relax more when I was riding for Nicky, just ride my own race, every ride doesn't have to be the perfect ride, every winner doesn't have to be a copybook race. You can win ugly too.

I was desperate for analysing rides. That was my way. I'd go home at night-time after a day's racing, stick on the video and watch all the races in which I'd been involved that day. The winners were fine, I didn't focus too much on those, but I used to replay the losers over and over again to try to figure out where I had gone wrong. The shorter the margin of defeat, the more I analysed it. How could I have made up the length by which I was beaten, the neck, the short head? What if I had done this,

80

what if I had asked him for a long one there, or sat tight there? What if I had held on to him for longer, or kicked for home earlier? You could always find at least a length.

I would study the videos for a long time, not just to beat myself up over a defeat, but to learn for the future, to learn about individual horses and about my own riding. Maybe a horse idled when he hit the front, so next time I would resolve to hold on to him for longer. Maybe he jumped a little to his right over the last two fences, maybe he didn't quicken as readily as he felt like he would. All of these pieces of information went into my mental database for use in the future. I learned about other horses as well, what they did well and what they didn't do well, and how I could beat them the next time I met them.

I probably studied videos and form more than most jockeys, but I thought that it was only right that I should do it. It's a competitive world out there, and you had to equip yourself with every possible piece of armoury if you were to succeed. I didn't feel that I was so talented, that I had so much in hand of any other rider, that I was able to allow myself the luxury of not being as well prepared as I could be.

By studying the form book and the videos I was able to pinpoint the strengths and weaknesses of the horses who I would ride and the horses who I wouldn't ride, and that was extremely useful information. Before I would go out to ride a race, I would know what might lead, what might be held up, who the good and bad jumpers were, who the main dangers were, who would definitely stay the distance, who would benefit from a slow early gallop, and I was able to work out from there how I would ride my horse.

I became quite good friends with Woody, we used to socialise quite a bit together, him and his wife Carol. But he was a difficult guy to get to know intimately. One year, after he had split up with Carol, we went on holidays together, just the two of us, to Portugal, and we had a ball. We just had great craic there, we got on great, out drinking and messing and pulling birds, just the pair of us for about five days. A week later I saw him at Cheltenham, not the Festival but the January meeting, and he blanked me. Completely blanked me. Not a 'How're 'ye' or 'Have you recovered from Portugal?' Nothing. It was as if he didn't know me. But that was just his way. He didn't do it out of malice, he was just so focused on riding that nothing else mattered, he was just on a different wavelength, he didn't seem to care about anything else.

Woody's focus got the better of him one day at Ascot in February 1999. He was just coming towards the end of his career, his right arm was giving him hell. He had ridden Marlborough in the opening race of the day, the novice chase. He had gone to the last fence upsides Jamie Osborne on Lord Of The River, tried to use his stick in his right hand, didn't have the strength to hit him, and put his right hand back on the reins just before the final fence. The horse got the fence wrong and came down.

In the second race, I was riding Bluedonix for David Nicholson, Chocolate Thornton having chosen to ride Castle Owen instead. Woody was riding Sadler's Realm for Philip Hobbs. Down around Swinley Bottom, about a mile from home, he went for a gap on my inside that wasn't really there. It was quite a strange manoeuvre, it wasn't as if we were going to the second-last fence, or that it was make or break for him in terms of securing a position, it was as if he just did it for the hell of it. I finished third, he finished well down the field, but when we got back to the weigh room, I asked him what he thought he was doing. He just mumbled something indecipherable and went on about his business.

The next race was the big race of the day, the Mitsubishi Shogun Chase. I was riding Super Coin for Richard Lee, Woody was riding Direct Route for Howard Johnson. Again around Swinley Bottom, Woody went for a gap that wasn't there. It really was bizarre. He was going between me and Carl Llewellyn on Chief's Song, who was on the rail. There was half a gap there, but definitely not enough room for a horse, and he had no right to go there. I leaned into him to block his path. Timmy Murphy, riding Challenger Du Luc, who was on my outside, saw what was happening and he leaned in towards the rail as well. But instead of taking a tug, Woody kept pressing. The net result was that we all leaned in towards the rail and Carl on Chief's Song had nowhere to go and almost came to a standstill. The horse did well to stay on his feet and Carl did well to stay in the saddle.

It was crazy what Woody had done. It was probably difficult to tell what happened if you had been watching from the stands or on television, it just looked like it had all got a bit tight and Carl had come off worst, because he was on the rail, but riding in the race, there was no question that it was Woody's fault. He had no right to go where he was trying to go. It just wasn't the done thing among jockeys. There is a certain etiquette, there has to be. You have two ambulances following you when you work, you have to play by the rules and you have to be sure not to do anything that is going to place any of the lads in danger. It was as if Woody knew that the end of his career was in sight and he just thought, to hell with it. It was as if he was trying to prove to himself and to everyone else that he still had it, that he still had no fear and was able to ride better than anyone and go wherever he liked. More likely he didn't think, he was just so caught up in himself and the inexorable move towards the end of his career. It was sad to see it. He didn't need to do it. He was such an exceptional rider, so talented, that it was sad to see him reduced to this.

The favourite Teeton Mill and Norman Williamson won the race, I finished fourth, but that was almost irrelevant. I got back to the weigh room, I saw Woody in front of me on the way in and I saw red.

'What the fuck do you think you were doing out there?' I called after him.

'Fuck off,' he retorted. 'What did you think you were doing, leaning in on me like that?'

'You had no right to go where you were going.'

'Go fuck yourself, just because you're riding a few winners now.'

He grabbed my goggles from my neck, and that was it. We started laying into each other. We fell on the floor, kicking and punching each other. The lads and the valets eventually managed to break us up. Woody says in his book that the fight was my fault, that I was on a good run, and that I was always a little louder when I was riding plenty of winners. That's not the case. I was livid with him, he shouldn't have done what he did, and I would have confronted him even if I hadn't ridden a winner all season.

The lads were all brought into the stewards' room to try to explain the incident down at Swinley Bottom. I wasn't called in as they weren't attaching any blame to me for the incident, but I had no doubt that the entire incident was caused by Woody. Unbelievably, it was Timmy who was blamed for the whole thing, for coming in from the outside and tightening everybody up. He was suspended for ten days while Woody got off scot-free.

I didn't mind too much that I was effectively still behind Woody in the pecking order at Nicky's. I was happy to bide my time. I learned very quickly in this game that there is nothing to be gained from throwing your toys out of the pram. If you burn a bridge, the only effect it has is that you can't cross that bridge again. Where's the benefit in that? Maybe you get some slight personal satisfaction from venting your spleen, but the likelihood is that you just get yourself more riled, and you blow a good relationship. It's a long road that doesn't turn, and I take pride in the fact that I rode winners for nearly every one of the trainers for whom I rode after I left them – Jackie Retter, Gerald Ham, Ron Hodges, John Jenkins, every one of them.

About two months into my time with Nicky, in November 1993, he had runners at Kempton and Hereford. Woody was down to ride at Hereford, and I asked Nicky if he wanted me to go to Kempton, but he didn't, so Dave got on and booked seven rides for me at Hereford. It was only a Wednesday meeting, but it was a decent card. Seven races and I had seven rides, including a good one for Kim Bailey, Richville, who was probably going to be favourite in the handicap chase.

I was at Nicky's on the Tuesday morning riding out, and he said to me that he wanted me to go to Kempton to ride one in the novice hurdle. Now I knew the novice hurdler and he was useless, one of those home-breds that wouldn't run out of its own way.

'What do you mean you want me to go to Kempton?' I asked.

'Well, I've got this novice hurdler,' said Nicky, 'that I want to run at Kempton tomorrow and I want you to ride it.'

'But I'm not going to Kempton,' I said. 'I'm going to Hereford.'

'Well I want you to go to Kempton.'

'I'm going to Hereford, simple.'

Nicky got all flustered, as he does.

'You know, this horse,' he stuttered, 'he's got to run at Kempton tomorrow, and I want you to go and ride it.'

Perhaps I am too stubborn for my own good sometimes, but this was a point on which I wasn't going to budge. It was one of the main things that I wanted sorted before we started. I was fine with Dunwoody riding Remittance Man and some of the other high-profile horses in the yard, I was grand with Osborne riding Travado, I was happy to play second fiddle for now behind those two. They were established names, big-game boys, and I was only a freshman.

More importantly, that was part of the deal. I knew that that was the way it was going to be when I agreed to take on the role. Everything was set out in front of me, that was the deal, take it or leave it, and I took both of his hands off. But the other part of the deal was that I would know where Dunwoody was going early so that I knew where I was going, so that Dave could get on and book my rides. We were two months in and already Nicky was trying to do an about-turn on that one. I have no doubt that, had I given in and gone to Kempton, that would have set a precedent, and that would have been a nightmare for me and for Dave, and I would have ended up pissing off all the other trainers for whom I was riding and with whom I had struck up relationships.

Maybe my mother was right about me. Back to the brush in the yard at the supermarket where my brother used to work. If I didn't want to do something, I just said that I didn't want to do it, and I didn't do it. Much better that than agree to do it and end up doing it begrudgingly. Life is too short for that kind of carry on.

'It's simple,' I said to Nicky again. 'I'm going to Hereford.'

I didn't expand. I didn't remind him of our agreement, that I would know early where I was going, or that I had seven rides booked at Hereford, or that I didn't want to be upsetting the other trainers. I didn't need to. He knew. I just walked out the door.

He could have told me where to go right there and then. I could have lost the job before I had got a run at it. But I didn't. Nicky's a bigger man than that. I didn't turn to see his face, but I imagine he was a little taken aback. Maybe I got my just deserts at Hereford the following day. I didn't ride a winner. Worse than that, I fell off Richville at the first fence in the handicap chase, just a three-horse race for which he was sent off the 10-11 favourite. To rub salt into the wounds, Woody won the race on one of Nicky's, Freeline Finishing. Woody rode two other winners there that day as well, including another for Nicky, Tudor Fable in the novice chase, in which I finished second on James The First for Paul Nicholls. And I was second on Kelling, another odds-on shot for Nicholls, in the novice hurdle. Maybe it was karma, maybe I got my comeuppance. Even so, I was glad I stuck to my guns.

Looking back on it now, on an amazing association that I had with Nicky, in 15 years as his stable jockey, it was one of only two times that we exchanged cross words. I didn't have to wait too long for the second time.

# CHAPTER 9

## OPPORTUNITY FLOPS

There are some horses who transcend racing, horses who are more important to a yard than the races they run in or the races they win, and Remittance Man was one of those. Nicky Henderson loved Remittance Man. When he spoke about him, he swelled with pride; when he watched him on the gallops in the mornings, he glowed. Remittance Man was the crown jewels. I have no doubt that he would have slept in Nicky's bedroom if he had fit – maybe not on the bed, but definitely on the floor between the bed and the door. Remittance Man and Richard Dunwoody – now there was a dream team.

Remittance Man's racing record was quite incredible. In 14 races over fences up to and including February 1994, he had been beaten just once. That was when he finished third in the 1992 King George over three miles, a distance that proved to be beyond him. Even that day, he had travelled like a winner down to the third-last under Jamie Osborne, but he hit that fence, which knocked the stuffing out of him, and he failed to get home, but was still beaten just three and a half lengths by the top-class French horse The Fellow. He had won the Arkle Chase at Cheltenham in 1991 and he had gone back to win the Queen Mother Champion Chase at the 1992 Festival. He had loads of gears, his jumping was fast and accurate, and he was pretty much unbeatable over two or two and a half miles.

He had trouble with his legs after he won the Peterborough Chase at Huntingdon in November 1992, so Nicky had given him time, but had brought him back to win the Emblem Chase at Kempton in February 1994 emphatically, reunited with Dunwoody, beating Deep Sensation and Wonder Man, two high-class two-milers. It was a hell of a training feat by Nicky to get him back to win such a competitive race, and the bookmakers made him favourite to land the Champion Chase again the following month on the back of it.

Remittance Man was Dunwoody's ride. He had ridden the horse in all but two of his chases, once in that King George, when he remained loyal to the racing institution that was Desert Orchid, and once in the 1992 Champion Chase, when he rode Waterloo Boy for the late David Nicholson instead, having committed to him in February when it wasn't certain if Remittance Man was going to run in the race or be good enough to beat the established two-mile chasers even if he did.

I was never in line to ride Remittance Man. I didn't mind. That was part of the deal from the outset. I was happy enough with how I was doing. Besides the established stars like Remittance Man and Travado, Nicky didn't have many really exciting young horses coming up through the ranks. Even so, I had ridden about 20 winners for him before February and almost the same number for outside yards, so I was well on track to beat my previous season's best-ever total of 54 winners.

The Cheltenham Festival is the pinnacle of the National Hunt racing year. The degree to which a jockey or a trainer's entire season has been successful will often be largely determined by how he or she does at the Cheltenham Festival in March. And if the magnitude of most trainers' efforts in gearing their horses towards Cheltenham was seven or eight out of ten, the magnitude of Nicky's would be 11. It is all about Cheltenham, no exceptions. When he is looking at a three-year-old store horse at the Derby Sale or the Land Rover Sale, he is thinking Gold Cup or Champion Chase. When he starts schooling the young horses, he is thinking Supreme Novices' Hurdle or Arkle. When the horses come back in towards the end of the summer, he is thinking about their possible Cheltenham targets. Most trainers will tell you that there are 361 days in the year, and then there is the Cheltenham Festival. Nicky will tell you that there are four days in the year, and 361 others.

The big race for Nicky at the 1994 Cheltenham Festival was the Queen Mother Champion Chase. It is often a race that is dominated by no more than a handful of top-class two-mile chasers, and Nicky had two of them at Seven Barrows, the peerless Remittance Man, and Travado, who had won the Arkle, the championship two-mile race for novice chasers, the previous season. Of course I wasn't in line to ride either, Remittance Man was Dunwoody's and Travado was Jamie Osborne's ride. Actually, I wasn't sure what I was going to be riding for Nicky at Cheltenham. Raymylette was a nice horse, an ex-Irish horse, who would probably go in the Cathcart, but Woody had ridden him when he had won well at Leicester, and I couldn't see him getting off him. Barna Boy was on track for the Supreme Novices' Hurdle. Woody had ridden him on his first two runs over hurdles, but I had ridden him at Kempton on his previous run when Woody was riding one for Pipe, so maybe Barna Boy. Billy Bathgate in the Grand Annual maybe.

Then something happened that dramatically altered my path to that year's Festival. It was just an ordinary card at Nottingham in early March, but Dunwoody and Adrian Maguire were both riding at the meeting, and they were in the middle of their championship struggle that would go to the last day of the season and see Dunwoody claim the title by 197 winners to 194, so the fact that they were both at Nottingham added a degree of interest to the meeting.

Adrian was riding the favourite in the selling hurdle, Mr Geneaology, Woody was riding the third favourite, Raggerty. Woody was leading on the approach to the second-last when Adrian tried to go up his inside. Woody was having none of it. He tugged on his left rein, closing the door on Adrian, with the result that Mr Geneaology ran out. He could have crashed out through the rail, it could have been very dangerous, and it didn't look good. There is an unwritten rule among jockeys that you don't try to go up the inside of a senior jockey, so there was an element of Adrian trying to get one over on Woody. That said, it looked bad on Woody's part. The stewards don't take any unwritten rules into account, written ones are all they are interested in. They disqualified Raggerty and suspended Woody for 14 days. The timing was disastrous for him, as it ruled him out of the Cheltenham Festival.

That left Remittance Man without a jockey in the Champion Chase. So the debate ensued as to who would ride him. There was talk of taking Jamie off Travado and putting him on Remittance Man. Jamie had ridden

Remittance Man to win the Champion Chase in 1992, but he had struck up such a successful partnership with Travado, he had won on him four times over fences, including in the previous year's Arkle, so it didn't make sense to take him off him. After that, I was the obvious choice. Ok, so I was young and relatively inexperienced, and this was the big time, it didn't really get much bigger, but I was going to have to take my place on the big stage at some point if I was going to be Nicky's stable jockey, and needs must, Dunwoody was out. I was desperate to be given the opportunity.

Nicky called me into his office about a week before Cheltenham and said, right, we've decided, we're going to leave Jamie on Travado and put you on Remittance Man. My heart did a little somersault. I remember as I was leaving his office that morning, I turned around to Nicky and just said: 'Thanks guvnor, I won't let you down.'

Four days before the first day of the Cheltenham Festival I went to school Remittance Man. This was a big deal. I had never sat on him before, I had never been allowed to. It was like a child going into a fun park every day, being allowed to go on the swings and the slides and the bumping cars and the swing chairs, but never being allowed to get on the roller coaster. Every day he looks longingly at the roller coaster, sees the other kids on it, hears their shrieks of horror and excitement, and wishes that he could have a go. Then, one day, his parents say he can get on the roller coaster. Ecstasy.

Ian Major always rode Remittance Man at Nicky's. The only time he didn't ride him was when Woody came in to school him. This morning, Ian rode the lead horse and I was given the leg-up on Remittance Man. He wasn't that big, I knew he wasn't, but he felt good beneath me, a compact ball of muscle and energy. We did a little piece of work up the gallop and pulled up at the end.

'Well, what did you think?' asked Ian.

'Fucking hell,' I said, 'this thing wouldn't win a seller!'

Ian was surprised. He thought he had worked well.

'He's always like that,' he said. 'That's just him, that's what he does.'

We got back down to Nicky and I told him what I thought.

'Right,' said Nicky, 'you're going to have to ride him over a couple of fences.'

Nicky had four fences on the schooling ground at Seven Barrows at the time. I got down to the bottom on Remittance Man, turned him around to face the fences, and whoosh! He just took off. I couldn't believe it. He was like a different horse, a different species. Over the fences he was dynamite. He would just eye each one up in turn, one-two-zing, one-two-zing, like an archer would eye up a target, bullseye every time.

I couldn't stop smiling when we pulled up. My face hurt, but the smile went from my left ear to my right ear involuntarily, and I'd say it stayed there until I went to sleep that night. I hadn't experienced anything like it before, or anything like the transformation in a horse just by putting a couple of obstacles in front of him. I knew then what all the fuss was about.

The first day of the Cheltenham Festival didn't go too well that year. In the opener, the Supreme Novices' Hurdle, I got knocked sideways at the first flight of hurdles on Barna Boy. You can get away with something like that in an ordinary race on an ordinary day, but at Cheltenham it's 100 miles an hour the whole way, and we didn't have time to recover. In the circumstances, the horse did well to finish sixth. I only had one other ride on the opening day, Everaldo in the Gold Card Final, also for Nicky, whom I had to pull up before the final flight because he had gone lame. Nicky's luck wasn't any better without me. Charlie Swan rode Thumbs Up in the Arkle, and he was travelling really well when he was brought down by Coonawara at the third-last. Windy Ways's fourth placing in the Kim Muir, the amateur riders' race, under Charlie Vigors, was the closest he got.

It was all about the second day for Nicky. For me though, it was all about the Champion Chase. Nicky had the first and second favourites in Remittance Man and Travado, but really it was all about Remittance Man for him as, obviously, it was for me. I didn't feel nervous going out to ride him, I didn't feel like I was under any pressure, although I was, riding the favourite in the Champion Chase with the weight of expectation that brings, heightened by the fact that I was a freshman, never having ridden a winner at the Festival before, and that I was standing in for Richard Dunwoody, probably the greatest National Hunt jockey of his generation.

I was very happy in the early stages of the race. Remittance Man was coasting underneath me, just behind Space Fair and Viking Flagship and Katabatic, jumping with the zest that I had seen on the schooling ground at Seven Barrows five days earlier. We jumped the ditch well at the top of the hill, the fourth-last, and then turned to come down the hill. The pace increases when you turn down the hill on the far side at Cheltenham. There are just three fences to jump then, the third-last and second-last are on that downhill stretch before you round the home turn, jump the last, and climb the final hill to the line.

As we turned to face the third-last I gave Remittance Man a little squeeze. The pace was increasing and the last thing I wanted was to get caught behind the front-runners who might have been coming back. Also, I wanted to give him a clear sight of these two fences.

We were going helter-skelter down to the third-last. These were the fastest steeplechasers in Britain, competing over National Hunt racing's sprint distance, and we were going pell-mell down the hill. Remittance Man didn't pick up as well as I had expected him to. I was travelling so well at the top of the hill, and I knew all about his talent, all about his gears, so I expected that, when I gave him a little squeeze, he would just go up another gear effortlessly. He didn't. Actually, he was struggling to hold his position with Viking Flagship and Travado on the approach to the third-last.

I saw a stride. It was a long one but it was a stride and it was one I was sure he could make. If we didn't go long, if we went in tight and popped the fence, we would lose a length, maybe two, the race could be over for us on the landing side of the third-last, the others could have had too much of a lead on us from that point. I didn't want to forsake any ground at that fence, I couldn't, not to horses of the calibre of Viking Flagship and Travado, especially when I was riding such a good jumper, the best jumper in England.

I went for my horse, gave him a kick, c'mon! I expected him to take off, to soar over the fence and land running. Nothing. In that instant, when he didn't come up for me on that long stride, I knew we were gone. He obviously thought he couldn't make it, he knew he couldn't, he didn't have the energy. He tried to put in a short stride and fiddle his way over the fence, but it was too late. We had got in too close to the fence, I had put him in too close and we were going too fast. He clouted the top of the fence and the pair of us came crashing down on the landing side.

I lay on the landing side of the fence winded, gutted. I lay there for a moment and heard the thunder of hooves and the shouts of jockeys fade off into the distance. I sat up. What have you done? You've put the best jumper in the country on the floor, that's what you've done. That's it. That's your job gone. There's no way Nicky Henderson is going to allow this one to pass. Remittance Man just doesn't fall, it's simple, he'd jump a Puissance wall for you and he'd land running. And look, if you're honest, the job wasn't going that well anyway. You were trying too hard and you were still playing second fiddle to everyone. Then you get your big chance and you blow it.

The Land Rover arrived to pick me up to bring me back to the weigh room. The race was still on and the commentary was on the radio in the car. Travado was in front, challenged by Viking Flagship. Suddenly, a ray of hope. If Travado won the race, if Nicky won the race anyway, Remittance Man's fall wouldn't seem so bad. Success can paper over many cracks. I started shouting at the radio. 'Go on Travado! Go on Jamie!'

'Viking Flagship on the far side, Travado on the near side,' the commentator was saying. 'There's nothing between them.'

'Go on Travado!' I was screaming. The driver of the Land Rover must have thought that I had flipped.

'Viking Flagship wins the Champion Chase,' said the commentator, 'from Travado in second, Deep Sensation is third . . .'

My heart hit my boots. That's it. Disaster. It seemed like a long, long way from there back around to the enclosures. You just want to get into the sanctuary of the weigh room, talk to nobody, see nobody, you just want to go and hide and hope that not too many people noticed.

Nicky came in shortly after I got there. He said nothing, just looked at me.

'I'm sorry,' I said.

He nodded and walked off.

I rode Lemon's Mill for Martin Pipe in the next, the Coral Cup. Nowhere. I rode Bibendum for Robert Waley-Cohen in the Mildmay of Flete. Nowhere. I rode Feels Like Gold for Martin Pipe in the last, the Bumper. Nowhere. That day was all about Charlie Swan, he had ridden a treble, including the Irish banker of the meeting, Danoli, in the opener, the Sun Alliance Hurdle. I just wanted to get out of the place and get home.

Once there, I sat down in front of the video. I watched the whole race again, I watched from the fourth-last over and over and I watched the third-last fence. Play, wince, rewind, play, wince, rewind. I'd say I watched the race about 50 times that evening trying to come to terms with what had happened. It was difficult to watch, torturous even, but in a way it was also therapeutic. I didn't do it to torture myself, I did it in order to see if there was something that I could learn from the incident, the disaster, something that I could pick up that would enable me to minimise the chance of the same thing happening again, and that was therapeutic. I just needed to salvage some good from a horrible situation.

I concluded that it was my fault. I shouldn't have asked him to make that jump. I wasn't going well enough. 'You weren't going well enough.' I said it over and over to myself, out loud. 'You weren't going well enough.' It's a tricky fence, the third-last on the Old course at Cheltenham. You come into it going downhill, so you often think that you are travelling better than you are, then the ground levels off just before the fence, you actually jump it on a bit of an incline, and jockeys often ask horses for a bigger jump than they can give.

On Remittance Man, however, I wasn't travelling that well and I knew it. I asked him to make the jump because I thought he had to in order to stay in the race, and because I thought he could. He was such a marvellous jumper and he had never fallen before in 14 chases and nine hurdle races. Of course it would have been better to allow him go in tight and pop the fence, better to have stayed on his feet and finished fourth than to have ended up on the deck. At least I wouldn't have gone down in history as the only man to have put the greatest jumper in the country on the floor the only time I rode him in a race. But hindsight is 20-20. At the time I was certain he would make the jump. Going in tight didn't even seem like an option.

I didn't sleep very well that night.

Above: *Me (on the right) with my brother John.*

Left: *Me with Father Christmas as Mum holds my brother John. Father Christmas looks a little startled. I must have asked him for a pony.*

Left: *John, my sister Elizabeth and me.*

Bottom left: *Looking very happy with myself.*

Bottom right: *Jumping a makeshift fence at home in Camolin on my pony Ballybanogue Bracken.*

*Giving it loads in my parents' pub with my Uncle Jimmy on guitar.*

*Having a pint with friends (Adrian Maguire in the striped shirt) in my parents' pub.*

*Me, Elizabeth, Mum, John and Dad at John's passing-out parade in The Curragh.*

*Sunset Sam and me at Hereford in April 1990. He and Duncan Idaho, trained by Ray Callow, were the two horses who got me going.*

*Jumping a hurdle on Duncan Idaho in the Christmas Pudding Conditional Jockeys' Handicap Hurdle at Taunton in December 1990.*

*Duncan Idaho carrying me to victory again in a handicap hurdle at Uttoxeter in March 1991.*

Above: *Jackie Retter.*

Above right: *Big Matt in full flight at Ascot in May 1995.*

*Raymylette, my favourite horse, and me in the Cathcart Chase at Cheltenham in March 1994.*

*A worm's-eye view of me jumping the last in the 1996 Grand National on Rough Quest with three lengths to make up on David Bridgwater and Encore Un Peu.*

**Above:** *Me and Woody at Kempton in February 1999, a month after our Ascot bust-up. Looks like we're not exchanging pleasantries again yet.*

**Left:** *Grand National winner.*

**Below:** *Jumping the final flight on Katarino in the Murphy's Juvenile Hurdle at Cheltenham in November 1998.*

*On the way to the most coveted winner's enclosure in racing after winning the Queen Mother Champion Chase on Call Equiname in 1999. (Looks like Paul Nicholls has acquired a new fan!)*

*Stormyfairweather was brilliant in the 1999 Cathcart Chase.*

*Unbridled joy after winning the 1999 Gold Cup on See More Business, with his owner Paul Barber.*

*Savouring the moment, being led in past the packed grandstand at Cheltenham after landing the Gold Cup.*

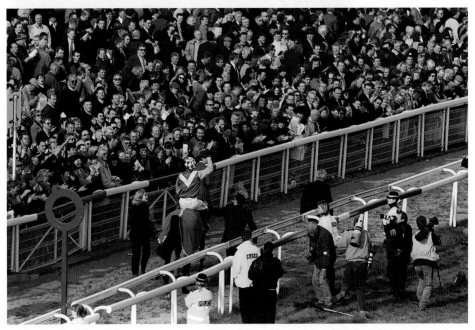

*Tiutchev and me out-jumping Cenkos and David Casey on the way to winning the 2000 Arkle.*

*Getting my riding instructions from the Queen Mother at Ascot, as Nicky fixes his hair.*

*Bacchanal winging a ditch in the Reynoldstown Chase at Ascot in February 2001.*

# CHAPTER 10

## SWEET SPOT

It was great to be riding at the Cheltenham Festival, it was great to be a part of it all, it was some change for me in a couple of years from watching it at home on television, looking on longingly, but it can be a lonely place when things are going against you. Remittance Man was still on my mind when I arrived there the following day, the Thursday, the last day of the Festival, Gold Cup day.

Things didn't get any better either. I fell at the second-last on Dayadan in the opener, the Triumph Hurdle, and I pulled Capability Brown up in the Gold Cup, which was won by the French horse The Fellow. Capability Brown was a 200-1 shot, the outsider of the four horses that Martin Pipe ran in the race and, while I was happy to have had a ride in the Gold Cup, it was frustrating riding something that had been pulled up on his only previous run that season against the best staying chasers in the business.

Things got even worse. I was riding Billy Bathgate in the Grand Annual, the third-last race of the Festival, for Nicky and owner Michael Buckley, and we thought that he had a chance. I had won a handicap chase on the horse at Ascot the previous December, beating two decent horses in Wonder Man, who had finished second to Travado in the previous year's Arkle, and Uncle Ernie, admittedly getting plenty of weight off them. Even so, Billy Bathgate was a difficult horse. His wind wasn't great and he always shit himself on the big days. I could tell as we came in to line up at the start that he was afraid of his life. It was a big occasion, there was lots of fanfare, lots of noise, lots of other horses about, so when the tape went up he didn't move, he just stood still for a couple of seconds and allowed the other horses to go before he consented to move off himself.

The nightmare continues. This was like one of those Laurel and Hardy movies where everything that could possibly go wrong was actually going wrong, only it wasn't comical. We were miles behind the leaders jumping the first fence and they were flying, as befits a 17-runner two-mile handicap chase at Cheltenham. There was no point in trying to make up the ground early, they were going so fast. If I had, I would have ended up bursting him and ruining his admittedly slim chance. So I figured that my only chance of salvaging anything from the situation was to sit tight, make sure he jumped and hope that they would go too fast in front so that I could pick them off coming home.

As it turned out, they did go off too fast in front, but just not fast enough. We started making a little ground going down the hill on the far side, and we flew home, but realistically we were never going to get near the leaders, and we were a fast-finishing fifth, about 20 lengths behind the winner.

Nicky wasn't happy.

'That was a waste of fucking time then, wasn't it?' he said to me when I came back in and dismounted.

'He just planted himself at the gate,' I protested. Nicky wasn't listening. My defence lacked confidence and conviction anyway.

'You might as well have pulled him up after the first fence, you were so far behind. You cannot win from that position at Cheltenham. It's not possible.'

I wasn't happy, I thought I was being blamed for being in the wrong, but I didn't say anything. What could I say? The horse planted himself at the start, there was nothing I could do about it, and actually I thought I made the best of a bad situation, but there was no point in getting into a slanging match with Nicky, not there, not in the unsaddling area at Cheltenham. What would Dunwoody have done? Dunno, probably something similar to what I had done. He wouldn't have got left at the start, though, that's what Dunwoody wouldn't have done. Golden Balls. It was difficult to be positive.

There were two races left at the meeting and I had a ride in each, Raymylette in the next, the Cathcart Chase, and Arabian Bold in the last, the County Hurdle, both for Nicky. I had never ridden Raymylette in a race, but I had ridden him at home, and he was tricky enough. He consistently hung to his right, which was no good at Cheltenham, where you are turning to your left all the time. He had won his only two chases for Nicky, both times ridden by Dunwoody, but he struggled to go left. His first win had been at Leicester, a right-handed track, his last win had been at Warwick, a left-handed track, when he had hung and jumped to his right the whole way. Nicky was fitting a special bit today that would help me steer him, that would hopefully prevent him going to his right, but I wasn't too optimistic, especially the way the Festival had been going.

'This horse is going to pull me all over the place and make me look like an eejit,' I thought.

If you had offered me a helicopter ride out of Cheltenham there and then, as I sat in the weigh room contemplating my ride on Raymylette, I would have thought long and hard about taking it. Go home, go to bed, avoid everyone, forget about it all for a while, that would have been a very attractive option.

Nicky came in to get the saddle. Here we go again. He was so upset about Billy Bathgate, he seemed to be so angry, there was no way he could have calmed down in 20 minutes. I braced myself for the continuation of the bollocking, or at least the progression to the silent treatment, I hardly looked him in the eye as I gave him the saddle. I didn't know what to say.

'Look, you know this horse,' he said to me. I looked up, a little startled.

'You've schooled him,' he continued. 'You've seen him race. Don't mess him about. If something else wants to give you a lead, fair enough, take it, but this fellow jumps well, so give him his head, don't be pulling him or dragging him, just let him run and jump.'

That instant, right there, summed Nicky Henderson up for me. I couldn't believe that he could wipe the slate clean, start again as if he hadn't been spitting fire 20 minutes earlier, as if Billy Bathgate hadn't happened. That's how professional he is. The past was gone, nothing could be done about it, it couldn't be retrieved, focus on the future.

His words made a hell of a difference to me, to my frame of mind. Something clicked. In an instant I was transformed from somebody who couldn't have really cared less if he was there or not, who would rather have curled up in a ball and hidden from the world, or retreated to the sanctuary of his home away from prying eyes, as go out and ride a fancied horse in the Cathcart Chase, into someone who was right up for the job. So I thought, ok, let's get this one right.

Nothing else wanted to go on, so I just gave Raymylette his head, let him stride on. Everything was going well, he was jumping really well and travelling well underneath me, until we came down the hill on the far side. There are two courses at Cheltenham, the Old course and the New course. When the Festival was a three-day affair, they used the Old course for the first two days and the New course for just the last day, Gold Cup day. So when we were going down the hill on the far side, we were on a different course to the one we were on for the Remittance Man debacle, but it still didn't stop the memory flooding back to me. There are two fences in the home straight on the new course, so the third-last is the last before the home straight.

Remittance Man flashed through my mind as we approached it. We were still in front and travelling well. I didn't feel under as much pressure to hold my position as I had on Remittance Man the previous day. I didn't feel like we had to wing the fence in order to hold our position. Five strides away and we were meeting it on the exact same stride as Remittance Man. I couldn't believe it. What to do? Everything flashed through my mind in an instant. Remittance Man, how he couldn't make the jump, the whirr of the video, watching it over and over, 'you weren't going well enough', crashing through the fence. Then I thought of Yogi Breisner. 'The most difficult thing to do over a fence is nothing.' Sit still. Yogi wasn't lying, it wasn't easy, but I decided to do it, to try to sit still. I left it completely up to Raymylette. If you want to go long, go for it, I'll go with you, but if you don't feel like you're up to it, if you think it's too long and you want to go short, I'm here for you too.

Raymylette went long. He jumped right out of my hands, barely brushed over the top of the fence and landed running. Nailed it. In that moment I learned more about jumping a fence than I had in the previous five years.

It was all there in the contrast between Remittance Man and Raymylette at almost the exact same point on the course. I was amazed at how no effort on my part could result in such a perfect jump. It's all very well being told to do nothing over a fence, but until you do it, until you can bring yourself to do it, you don't really get it. It's like being told how to drive a car. Release the clutch gradually and press gently on the accelerator at the same time. The first time you do it the car jumps forward and stalls. The next time you do it the car revs and smoke spews out of the exhaust. You try it a couple more times, each time without success, you just can't get it right, then one time it comes right. You just apply the correct amount of pressure to the accelerator and release the clutch simultaneously at the right speed, and the car moves forward smoothly. That's it, you think. I've got it. But you've only got it because you did it, you learned by doing, trial and error. So it was with jumping a fence. If there was a sweet spot to be hit in jumping a fence, Raymylette hit it right there at the third-last in the 1994 Cathcart.

It wasn't over yet. As we rounded the home turn I could sense something coming at me on the outside. We jumped the second-last well and I asked Raymylette for everything going down to the last. Our challenger was Buckboard Bounce, Charlie Swan wearing John Mulhern's red silks with a white question mark. How ironic. Raymylette zinged the last just as he had zinged the other 16 fences, and he gave his all up the hill. He did hang a little bit to his right on the run-in, but that was more than acceptable, he had given his all, and we clung on to get home by three-quarters of a length.

I couldn't believe it. A winner at the Cheltenham Festival. I had just ridden a winner at the Cheltenham Festival. Nothing else mattered. The mishap on Remittance Man was suddenly a distant memory. And Billy Bathgate. Billy who? This was my dream and I was living it. When I started riding, even when I was riding on the Flat, my dream was to ride a winner at Cheltenham. Jonjo punching the air on Dawn Run was the person I wanted to emulate, not Tommy Stack winning the Grand National on Red Rum, not Piggott or Cauthen winning the Derby, and here I was on Raymylette, walking down the path in front of the stands on my way back to the winner's enclosure at Cheltenham. All the hard work, all the heartache, it was all for this. At that moment, if you had told me that I wouldn't ride another winner, I wouldn't have cared.

The winner's enclosure at Cheltenham is like an amphitheatre of sound with people packed deep on the steps that surround the winner's circle. When I came in on Raymylette, the faces and the noise hit me like a wall. It was an unbelievable feeling, I almost burst with pride, relief, satisfaction, elation. I hoped my parents would be proud of me, I was sure they would be. All the time spent trucking around the country to gymkhanas and shows, all the heartache with leaving school, going up to The Curragh, coming over to England, all the uncertainty, it had all led to this point, the winner's enclosure at Cheltenham.

Andrew Lloyd Webber, the composer, who owned Raymylette, was there, beaming, with his wife Madeleine. Nicky was delighted obviously. It had been a long Festival for him. This was the second-last race of the meeting and he hadn't had a winner up to that point, which was tough on a yard that concentrates on and gears so much towards Cheltenham.

'You don't know what this means to me,' he said to me when I dismounted.

I think I did. What I didn't know, however, and still don't, was exactly what it meant for my relationship with Nicky. I didn't think about it too much at the time, but looking back now, maybe my job with Nicky wasn't hanging by a thread, but it certainly wasn't rock-solid.

Look at it objectively. Nicky hadn't had a great season by his standards, neither of the two stable stars was my ride, then when I did get my chance, I blew it. I had put Remittance Man on the deck and I had given Billy Bathgate a terrible ride in his eyes. In those circumstances, any normal employer would have to have a serious look at his new employee, probably still on probation, and he had to have been under pressure from owners. Like I say, success can make up for many failings, and I owe Raymylette an awful lot.

# CHAPTER 11

## SPRINGBOARD

If you look back on any successful jockey's career, you can usually pinpoint a horse who was the springboard, the catalyst to that success. Sure, you need to have the talent and you need to have put in the graft to put yourself in the position to get the ride on a decent horse in the first place, and you need to have the ability to exploit the opportunity fully when it does arise, but you do need that horse.

Racing is a fickle business, and there are lots of really talented riders who were just never fashionable because they never got the breaks, they never got on that top-class horse who carried them into the limelight. For Adrian Maguire, it was Omerta. For Timmy Murphy it was Beef Or Salmon. For Richard Dunwoody it was probably West Tip, and just about any horse he sat on in the mid-1980s. For me, it was Raymylette.

People often ask me who my favourite horse was. See More Business or Rough Quest or Trabolgan or Marlborough or Fondmort? It was Raymylette. He was the horse on whom I won my first big race, on whom I realised my childhood dream of riding a winner at the Cheltenham Festival. He was the one who catapulted me into the limelight, from young rider with potential, Mick Fitzgerald, to Cheltenham Festival-winning rider Mick Fitzgerald. He was the one on whom I learned to ride over a fence properly, on whom Yogi Breisner's advice about doing nothing became actuality. He had bags of talent, he was a super jumper and he was as honest as the day is long. He would have lain down on the ground and died for you.

Raymylette's first run the following season, the 1994-95 season, was always going to be in the First National Bank Chase at Ascot in November. It was the obvious race for him, a chase restricted to horses who were in their second season jumping fences, as he was. Remarkably, he was having just the third run of his life over fences when he won the Cathcart. He was still a really inexperienced steeplechaser and he was still improving.

I was beside myself wondering if I was going to keep the ride on him. On the one hand, I thought that Nicky wouldn't take me off him, surely? He couldn't take me off him, not after me winning the Cathcart on him and providing Nicky with his only winner at the 1994 Cheltenham Festival. On the other hand there was Dunwoody. There was always Dunwoody, standing there, peering over my shoulder, smiling. Woody the Ubiquitous.

Woody would probably be on the phone looking for the ride in the First National. That was his way. Neither mates nor camaraderie nor anything else came into it. He just saw a race, saw a horse who he wanted to ride, who he thought he should ride, and he or his agent was straight on the phone. He didn't think of the other guy, the Mick Fitzgeralds of the world who would be left without a mount, sitting on his arse when the horse that he should be riding was carrying Dunwoody up the run-in. It wasn't that he was selfish, he was just focused, he just saw it from his point of view, didn't think of the consequences for others. Then again, maybe that is selfishness, seeing the universe through your own eyes without stopping to think of how others might see it.

Exactly a year earlier, November 1993, First National Bank Chase day at Ascot, it was also and is always Becher Chase day at Aintree. The Becher Chase is usually an early-season sighter for the Grand National, given that it is run over the big National fences. Woody was going to Ascot to ride a couple for Nicky and for Pipe. I headed off to Aintree, primarily to ride Wont Be Gone Long in the Becher Chase for Nicky, a horse on whom Woody had won the John Hughes Chase over the big fences at the Grand National meeting three years previously, and I had got on a horse in the first race, a two-mile race run over the Grand National fences, for Jeff King, Little Tom. There was myself, Adrian Maguire and Johnny Kavanagh in the car. Johnny was riding for Nicky at the time as well, he's a good lad Johnny, but he was out with a broken leg, so he just came along with me and Adrian for the day.

As luck would have it, Ascot was called off. As soon as we heard the news, Johnny says, 'Ah here we go now, you know Woody will be on to Nicky looking to go to Aintree instead.'

'No way, he will not.'

I obviously didn't know Woody that well at the time. Sure enough, half an hour later my phone rings. Woody. Unbeknownst to me, he had been on to Nicky looking to go to Aintree, looking to jock me off Nicky's horse, and me halfway up the road to Liverpool. Nicky did a Pontius Pilate on it. 'You'd better give Mick a ring and sort it out among yourselves.'

The conversation went something like this:

'All right Fitz?'

'All right Woody.'

'Ascot's been called off.'

'Yeah, I heard.'

'I've just spoken to Nicky,' he said, 'and he said I should talk to you. You know, I'd like to ride Wont Be Gone Long in the Becher Chase. What do you think?'

'No,' I said simply. 'I'm riding him.'

'Eh, right,' he said. 'But I won the John Hughes on him, and I'd like to ride him today. I'm coming up to Aintree now anyway.'

'I don't care Woody,' I said. 'I'm riding him.'

That was the end of the story as far as I was concerned, and it was, except that the day didn't pan out as I had hoped. Little Tom buried me at the first fence in the opener. I was going well on Wont Be Gone Long in the Becher Chase when he clouted a fence and turned a somersault, like really turned a somersault. He broke a vertebra in his neck, the poor horse. He was ok, he didn't have to be put down, but it can't have been pleasant for him. It certainly wasn't for me; I hobbled away in bits.

It wasn't a good day for any of the incumbents of Adrian's car. Howe Street buried Adrian at the second-last in the first race, then he was probably going to win the Becher Chase on Ushers Island when the horse came down at the second-last and gave Adrian a desperate fall. Adrian had to give up his later rides and Dunwoody, who had hot-footed it up from Ascot, got on most of them. It was probably a good thing that he didn't manage to win on one of them.

So there we were in the car on the way home, Johnny still with his broken leg, the only one of us who hadn't deteriorated significantly since the journey up, Adrian so sore that he couldn't drive and me, who could barely move, lumbered with the job of driving us all the way back from Liverpool to Faringdon.

But that was the way Dunwoody was. There was one day, in May 1992, when he was riding at Hereford during the day and Johnny Kavanagh was down to ride Acre Hill for Nicky at Newton Abbot that evening. As it turned out, Acre Hill was the only horse declared for the handicap chase at Newton Abbot, so it was going to be a walkover, Johnny would just have to ride the horse down past the stands and back up again to collect the prize and notch a winner for himself. But Dunwoody figured that it was his ride. He got on to Nicky and said that he wanted to ride Acre Hill, that he was trying to catch Scu in the jockeys' championship and needed every winner that he could get. But he was about 40 behind Scu at the time, he had no chance of catching him. Anyway, Nicky says ok, if he could get down to Newton Abbot on time.

Dunwoody rode Tinryland to win at Hereford at five o'clock. He would have weighed in at about 5.15. Acre Hill's 'race' at Newton Abbot was at 7.40, so he had about two hours to get from Hereford to Newton Abbot, a distance of about 150 miles that should take more than two and a half hours. He got into his car, Hywel Davies went with him, and they took off. They were done for speeding on the way, but Dunwoody didn't care, he got there on time to weigh out and he got the ride on the horse. He jocked Johnny off. You couldn't make it up. He jocked Johnny off a walkover.

The winner's purse for the race was just over two grand, Dunwoody's cut would have been just over £200. It would hardly have paid for the petrol. When you add in the mileage, the speeding ticket, the time involved, the risk to your life going 100 miles an hour down the M5 and the ill-will that it generated, not just between Dunwoody and Johnny, but between Dunwoody and all the lads in the weigh room who would have been sympathetic to Johnny in that situation, and ask Dunwoody was it worth it, just for one more winner on the board. The answer would have been unequivocal. Yes.

I rang my agent Dave Roberts to make arrangements for the weekend, First National Bank Chase day in November 1994, exactly a year to the day after that eminently forgettable Becher Chase day. I told him that I thought that I would be riding Raymylette in the feature race at Ascot, that I wouldn't be going to Aintree, but that I couldn't guarantee it.

'Yeah, you ride Raymylette.'

'I do? Are you sure?'

'I am, the guv'nor was on.'

My heart did a little flip. Brilliant. I would have been desperately disappointed if I hadn't been riding him, but I was elated now that I was. It was a bit strange that it was Dave who told me that I was riding him and not Nicky, but Nicky just presumed all along that I would, he felt that he didn't need to say anything to me, so it wasn't an issue for him. That was another turning point in our relationship and in the cementing of my position as number one jockey. It was a huge vote of confidence in me, in my talent as a rider, in my ability to perform on the big stage in a big race, both from Nicky and from the owners, Andrew and Madeleine Lloyd Webber, and I was really looking forward to riding Raymylette again.

It was a really competitive race, as it always is. Jonjo O'Neill had a progressive young chaser in it, Beachy Head, Pipe was running Lord Relic, who would finish second in the Hennessy on his next start and whom Dunwoody was riding, Charlie Brooks ran Couldnt Be Better, who would win the Edward Hanmer and the Hennessy the following year, and Nicky also ran Thumbs Up, whom Jamie Osborne rode. We were carrying top weight of 11st 10lb, so even though we had won the Cathcart we were 10-1 shots. It didn't matter. Raymylette jumped out of the gate and I let him stride on. He was such a good jumper, he was so honest, he did hang a bit to his right, but that really was fine at Ascot, which is right-handed. Ascot is a lovely course to ride when you are on a good jumper. He was bang on at every fence, didn't even miss one, and we never saw a rival. Couldnt Be Better and Graham Bradley came at us on the run-in, but Raymylette dug deep and we fought him off.

That was another huge day for me. As well as winning a big race, another high-profile race that was live on BBC television, it was also a lucrative prize. You're not thinking, well if I win this race I'll win this much money, you're only thinking about riding the race, about winning it, the prestige of the race, the profile, but it's nice when you get back and realise that you've also won a lot of money as a result. The race was worth £26,000 to the winner, so I was looking at around two-and-a-half grand. That was a huge amount of money at the time, when you consider that I had bought my first house a year earlier for £39,000, and had a £30,000 mortgage. That was one-tenth of my mortgage in five minutes' work.

Next up for Raymylette was the Betterware Gold Cup back at Ascot in December. We were into the big league now, racing against proven class chasers, like Dubacilla, a really high-class mare who had won the Timeform Hall of Fame Chase (better known as the Pillar Property) and the Comet Chase the previous season and who had been sent off as favourite for the Hennessy just a couple of weeks previously. The other unknown was that we were stepping up in trip. The Cathcart and the First National were both run over two and a half miles, but the Betterware was a three-mile race.

We were thinking that he wouldn't have to improve a whole lot to have a chance in the Cheltenham Gold Cup – there weren't that many top-class staying chasers around at the time – but the Gold Cup is run over three and a quarter miles, so if Raymylette was going to stay three and a quarter miles at Cheltenham, he was absolutely going to have to get three miles at Ascot.

I rode him like I had always ridden him, aggressively from the front. That was how he liked to be ridden, that was how he had won the Cathcart and the First National, stride on in front, have a clear sight of his fences and use his fast and accurate jumping to put the others under pressure. There is a school of thought that says that, if you are unsure about whether a horse will have the requisite stamina to stay the distance of a race, you ride him quietly in behind, ride him to get the trip. I don't fully subscribe to that notion. You still have to cover the same distance as the other horses, you still go at the same pace as the horses in front of you by and large, unless they are going bananas in front, which I wasn't going to do. But if I had tried to anchor Raymylette, I wouldn't have been playing to his strengths and, anyway, if he was going to be a Gold Cup horse he was going to have to stay.

He was brilliant again in the Betterware. He led the whole way, jumping like a gazelle again, until the last when Dubacilla came at us and actually headed us, but I asked Raymylette for everything that he had, and he responded, getting back up to get past Dubacilla in the last 100 yards.

That was a fantastic feeling, to get back up after being passed, after looking like we were booked for second place, and win the race. The win meant everything, both for the win itself and for the fact that it dragged us kicking and screaming into the Gold Cup picture. The bookmakers put Raymylette in at 10-1 and 12-1 third or fourth favourite for the Blue Riband after that win, and that seemed to be a fair reflection of his chance.

Everyone was thrilled after that race, Nicky, me and Andrew and Madeleine Lloyd Webber. Andrew was quite new to racing, but Madeleine, a renowned horsewoman in her own right, was really over the moon, and that appeared to make him happy. They were good owners, and they were very lucky with the horses that they had with Nicky. They would own Bacchanal later, on whom I would win a Stayers' Hurdle, a Reynoldstown Chase, a Feltham Chase, and on whom I would finish third in two King Georges.

If you had told us then that Raymylette would run in just one more race, we would have been fairly distraught, but that was the case. The Betterware was the penultimate race of his life. The last was in the Peter Marsh Chase at Haydock the following January on bottomless ground. When it got soft at Haydock, it got very soft, less so now since they have done away with the old steeplechase course and brought in the portable fences, which they put now on the hurdles course, but it used to be the case that, when it rained at Haydock, a three-mile chase took some getting.

I got to the course early on Peter Marsh Chase day and walked it, as I always do. I rang Nicky, who wasn't at Haydock that day, and told him that the ground was desperate, that we should consider not running Raymylette. Nicky wanted to run. The Lloyd Webbers were there, they wanted to run, and we needed to get this run into the horse anyway as part of his preparation for the Gold Cup. I said fine, I would look after him and I wouldn't be too hard on him if it looked like he wasn't going to win the race.

We led to the third-last, but Raymylette was never really happy on the ground. When Earth Summit, that soft-ground lover who would go on to win the Grand National in bottomless ground a couple of years later, powered past under Tom Jenks, I took it easy on Raymylette. We popped over the last two fences and I just pushed him out to the line. It had taken a lot out of him, but we were still on track for the Gold Cup.

Raymylette was never a good eater. He could only eat small amounts at a time, so Nicky used to go out to the yard last thing at night and give him a small bowl of feed. He seemed to eat better when it was quiet. What we didn't know was that his digestive system had been damaged by worms when he was a young horse, with the result that the food wasn't getting to his stomach. He was digesting everything in his intestines, which were rotting away. That March, when we were preparing him for the Gold Cup, he got a bad bout of colic. In an instant, dreams of winning the Gold Cup were in tatters and the primary objective was to save the horse's life. They operated on him on March 14, the first day of the 1995 Cheltenham Festival, but he died on the operating table.

I was riding out at Nicky's that morning, full of hope, another Cheltenham Festival about to begin, when I heard the news about Raymylette. I was gutted, just stunned. It was difficult to believe, such a young horse with so much talent and a glittering career in front of him. I tried to put it out of my mind when I got to Cheltenham, tried to concentrate on my big ride that day, my big chance of another Cheltenham Festival winner, Rough Quest in the Ritz Club Chase. You have to be forever looking forward in this game, always looking for the next big horse, the next big winner. It may be callous but, while I was desperately sad for poor Raymylette, there is nothing to be gained from dwelling on what might have been.

# CHAPTER 12

## ROUGH JUSTICE

I loved Rough Quest from the first moment I sat on him. It was just a routine phone call from Dave Roberts to trainer Terry Casey that had got me the ride on him in a handicap chase at Nottingham about four weeks before the 1995 Cheltenham Festival. He was a proper horse to sit on, a real racehorse, an absolute tank and a fantastic jumper. I just dropped him in, and moved up going to the last, probably looked like we were going to win, but he was running on empty at that stage and he just had nothing left to give. He hadn't run since the previous October, three and a half months beforehand, and he had just blown up. Terry was delighted. He had left plenty to work on. Nottingham wasn't his target, he was just getting ready for Cheltenham.

He had one run before Cheltenham, at Wincanton at the beginning of March. Terry was a great man for hold him up, make your ground steadily, jump the last and away you go. That was the way that Rough Quest liked to be ridden, although I didn't really realise how strong his preference for being held up was until that day at Wincanton. I held him up, made ground steadily, jumped the last upsides Menebuck and kicked him on to win his race. But he tried to pull himself up on the run-in. He hit the front, thought he had done enough, then shied to his left and tried to stop, with the result that Eamon Murphy got another run out of Menebuck and they got up to do us on the line.

I was disappointed. It would have been worse if it had been Cheltenham, but it was still disappointing. A winner is a winner and I thought I had the race in the bag. Still, it was a learning experience. I determined that I wouldn't let him pull up on me again like that.

I was really excited about this horse going to Cheltenham. Exit Raymylette, enter Rough Quest, that's the way this game goes sometimes.

Actually, Rough Quest had travelled so well with me at Wincanton that I thought he would have had a chance in the Gold Cup that year. It looked like the ground was going to come up soft, and Rough Quest loved soft ground. Apart from that, the staying chasers that year really weren't a vintage bunch. Master Oats was going to be favourite, but he had been just a handicapper the previous year. Actually, he had fallen in the Grand National the previous April, and it is highly unusual for a Gold Cup favourite to have run in the Grand National the previous season these days.

The Gold Cup was never on Terry's radar for Rough Quest, not that year. The Ritz Club Chase was the race at which he was aiming him, and Terry had trained him to peak for that. It wasn't that he wasn't trying at Nottingham or Wincanton, or that I didn't do everything that I possibly could to get him to win, it was just that Terry hadn't tightened the screws. When he lined up before the Ritz Club Chase on the first day of the 1995 Cheltenham Festival, however, he was as tight as whichever simile you want to choose yourself.

Of course, it is easy to say that a horse who would subsequently go on to be second in a Gold Cup was seriously underrated on a handicap rating of 132, but even at the time we thought he was thrown in. He had finished fourth in Miinnehoma's Sun Alliance Chase three years previously, he was a classy chaser and, as a bonus, the handicapper had even dropped him 5lb since his run at Nottingham. That left him set to carry 10st 3lb in the Ritz. I could do 10st 3lb fairly easily those days. I wouldn't have been stuffing my face with cream and spuds the night before, but 10st 3lb was easy enough. The bookmakers rated him a 16-1 shot, but we rated him much better than that.

That race went like clockwork for me. I kicked him off in the middle of the pack and he jumped like a dream the whole way. When he was meeting a fence on a long stride, he took off, when he was meeting one on a short stride, he shortened up nicely and popped over it. We moved up effortlessly at the top of the hill, joined in just behind the leaders going down the hill towards the home turn, moved up to join David Bridgwater and Grange Brake just before the last, winged that and he just took off.

It was amazing how much he found. He loved the soft ground and he loved to come off the fast pace that they invariably go at Cheltenham. I was surprised at how much he picked up after we touched down over the last, but I wasn't looking around for dangers or trying to give him an easy time of it. Remember Wincanton? I just put my head down and asked him for all that he had, I kept pushing and kicking and smacking and driving. You can't see it on the television screen, but it is a hell of a pull up the hill at Cheltenham from the last fence to the line. You give a horse any excuse not to come up it and he will take it. I didn't give Rough Quest one. I just kept asking and he kept responding all the way to the line, which we reached nine lengths clear of Antonin.

Everybody was on a high in the winner's enclosure afterwards, it didn't matter that we were all soaking wet. Andrew Wates, the owner, a real gentleman, was over the moon, and Terry was elated. I'm sure he had had a few quid on. It was really big for me as well, my second Cheltenham Festival winner. It probably wasn't as special as the first one (when is the second time ever as good as the first time?), but it was still up there with the very highest points of my career. So the first one wasn't a fluke then. To put the icing on the cake, the following month we went to Punchestown and won the Castlemartin Stud Chase.

*

The summer used to be a relaxing time for a National Hunt jockey. These days, with summer jump racing, it's difficult for jump jockeys to take a break. It's different on the Flat. Although you have all-weather racing now, the turf Flat season ends in November and doesn't begin again until late March, which gives Flat jockeys a fair break if they wish to take it. Some of them don't. Some of them go to Hong Kong or Dubai or India, but the option is there for them.

Until recently, National Hunt racing took an eight-week break during the summer. It is a winter game, it is safer for horses and jockeys to race over jumps when the ground is soft. I never really did that much during the eight-week break, just hung around with the other jockeys and drank lots. I did start playing golf during the summer of 1994. Shane Donohoe, my good friend in Ireland, introduced me to it when I was home that summer, and I was immediately hooked.

Shane and I were conditional riders at the same time when I came over to England first, he was with Chris Popham when I was with Ron Hodges, and we just hit it off straight away. Shane is one of the all-time good guys. I got him the job with Jackie Retter when I left there. Then he was head lad for Paul Nicholls for a couple of years and his wife was travelling head girl. Shane's wife and my ex-wife Jane were very good friends. Even after I split up with Jane, Shane and I remained best friends. He is godfather to my eldest son Zac, and he was best man at my wedding to Chloe.

So my interest in golf is down to Shane, and it is a huge interest. It is the only thing that ever came close to rivalling racing for me. I used to practice every day, I'd go down to the driving range and hit balls for hours, buckets of them, thousands of them, just whack them out there, high in the sky with a big draw, until it became second nature. Within two years I was playing off six. With all my injuries now, my neck, my ankle, my knee, my game has gone backwards, I play off 12 now, but it doesn't stop me going over to Ireland and taking a few quid off Shane. I call him my Irish ATM. It's great, I never had to take any euro with me if I was going over to Ireland to play golf with Shane, although he has got better recently. He's not the dead cert for a few quid that he used to be.

The 1995-96 season was a big one for Rough Quest. Terry was talking about the Gold Cup, and I wasn't trying to talk him out of it. Master Oats had won the Gold Cup the previous season by a street. He had relished the soft ground while other horses had floundered in it. Dubacilla had finished second, which made me think a lot since Raymylette had beaten her in the Betterware Gold Cup just three months previously. Also, Rough Quest had got to within half a length of Dubacilla in the Comet Chase the previous season, albeit getting a pile of weight. There could have been a Gold Cup there for the taking that year.

Rough Quest fell with me on his seasonal debut in November 1995. I couldn't believe it, it was the last thing that I expected, he was such a good jumper. We were travelling well at the fourth-last in the three-and-a-half-mile chase at Cheltenham's November meeting when he just clipped the top of the fence and came down. He kind of tripped over it rather than fell, but I suppose it's the same thing.

The Hennessy Cognac Gold Cup at Newbury at the end of November was his early-season target, but I had managed to get myself suspended, so I couldn't ride him. I was disgusted. The Hennessy was always a race that I really wanted to win. I can remember watching Burrough Hill Lad and Brown Chamberlin and Bregawn and Diamond Edge all winning the Hennessy when I was younger, and the race always had a good resonance with me. Newbury is Nicky's local track, and he always wanted to win the Hennessy, the track's biggest race, so I was sucked right in there with him.

I thought that Rough Quest was a certainty, insofar as there is such a thing as a certainty in a three-and-a-quarter-mile handicap chase. Even though he had gone up 17lb since he had won the Ritz, I still thought he was well handicapped, and he only had 10st 9lb on his back in the Hennessy. Still, it didn't matter how well handicapped he was, I still couldn't ride him. I couldn't bear to watch it. Nicky had a couple of nice horses going at Newbury that day as well, so it was going to be a tough day for me all round. I gave Shane a shout to see if he was free to play golf, so I jumped on a plane and flew to Ireland. Out on a golf course, free of televisions and radios and mobile phones, I was able to relax at least a little.

That Hennessy wasn't without its controversy. Terry got Jamie Osborne to ride Rough Quest, Charlie Brooks had two horses in it, and Graham Bradley chose to ride Black Humour, which meant that Dean Gallagher was booked to ride Couldnt Be Better. Everybody knew that both Rough Quest and Couldnt Be Better liked to be held up, and that was the way the race began, those two held up out the back. But then, with a circuit to go, Jamie allowed Rough Quest to stride up to the leaders and take it up. He jumped like a buck the whole way down the back straight, stretching his field out, but once he came back around to the last fence, he was effectively a spent force, and Dean Gallagher and Couldnt Be Better were able to pick him up easily on the run-in.

It was a bold move by Osborne. Maybe he thought that the pace wasn't fast enough for his horse, maybe he thought that he would allow him to stride on and put his bold jumping to good use, maybe he couldn't hold him. He was a funny horse, he took a bit of knowing, he was usually free enough in the early stages of a race, so you just had to hook him out the back. Once you did that he relaxed, he was fine. Maybe Jamie just couldn't get him to relax and figured that he'd let him stride on. Whatever the reason, he rode contrary to Terry's instructions, and Terry was spitting fire afterwards. Jamie never rode the horse again.

I watched the video that evening when I got home. It's a strange thing, I can manage watching the video of a ride that I have missed later on. It's different to watching it live. Whatever any jockey tells you, when they are watching live when a horse they are supposed to be riding is in with a winning chance, they are hoping it gets beaten. Nicky had a winner earlier in the day as well, Conquering Leader in the Long Distance Hurdle. She just got home by a neck under Johnny Kavanagh. Then I watched the Hennessy and I couldn't believe what I was seeing when Rough Quest went on with a circuit to go. Maybe he would have fared better if Jamie had held him up or if I had been riding him. We'll never know.

I was back from suspension and back on Rough Quest for his next race, the Betterware Gold Cup at Ascot in mid-December, the race I had won the previous year on Raymylette. This time, not so good. I hooked Rough Quest out the back, the usual, and he travelled like a dream as they fell like flies around us. Sibton Abbey and Yorkshire Gale went at the second, Couldnt Be Better and Ghia Gneuiagh went early on the final circuit until the race had effectively developed into a match between me and Dunwoody on Unguided Missile. He actually clouted the fourth-last and should have come down, but the horse did well to find a leg and Woody did well to stay in the saddle. Actually, his saddle slipped almost all the way around so that one of his feet almost touched the ground. He put all his weight on the other foot and managed to straighten the saddle up again before he got to the next fence. It was a fine piece of horsemanship.

I just stalked him going to the last. He was under serious pressure and I hadn't asked Rough Quest for an effort at all at the time. It is a long old run-in at Ascot and it's uphill, not quite as uphill as Cheltenham, but it still takes a lot of getting, so I didn't want to hit the front too early on Rough Quest, given his propensity to down tools as soon as he gets there. My plan was to jump the last behind Unguided Missile, close on him up the run-in but not to hit the front until about 100 yards from the line.

Alas, the best-laid plans. Unguided Missile stumbled badly after the last. Dunwoody did well to stay on him but the horse lost ground and momentum. That left me and Rough Quest in front on the near side as soon as we landed, much sooner than I wanted, so I had to go for him then even though I knew he was in front too early. He thought his job was done. As far as he was concerned, he had hit the front, he had won his race, so why was I still pushing and kicking him?

He started hanging over to his left, away from the far rail. I didn't know it, but Woody had kick-started Unguided Missile again and he was rolling down the far side. I allowed Rough Quest to drift, I figured that if I tried to correct his drift I might check his forward momentum, such as it was. It seemed like a long way from the last fence to the line, up that hill, as my horse wandered over to his left and tried to pull himself up, and it was. It was long enough to allow Woody to get Unguided Missile back up on the far side and beat us by a neck.

I was disgusted, almost inconsolable. I hate losing any race in any circumstances, but to lose a race like that, a race as big as that, in those circumstances, when I was probably on the best horse, was desperate. I went home that evening and put on the video. Nothing like a little bit of self-flagellation to help you get over something. I watched the run down to the last fence and I watched the run-in over and over. I started drawing lines on the television screen to try to figure out how much ground I lost by allowing him to drift left. I'm not joking, that's how bad it was. I tried to work it out mathematically. I should have listened more intently when they were talking about Pythagoras in school, but I figured out that actually, he didn't lose that much ground by drifting.

You look at horses coming off a true course and you think they are losing a lot of ground, but actually they aren't. It's more to do with the fact that they are pulling themselves up as they are drifting. If a jockey actually rode a horse diagonally across the track, with no loss of forward momentum, the amount of ground that the horse would lose would be minimal. I suppose that's why you see a field coming wide into the straight at certain courses when the ground is soft, figuring that the ground they lose by coming diagonally across the track will be more than compensated for by the fact that they will be racing on better ground.

Anyway, it wasn't the drift that cost us the race, it was the fact that he was pulling himself up. Bastard. The realisation didn't make the loss any easier to stomach. It didn't matter that it was Dunwoody who rode Unguided Missile, that my loss was Dunwoody's gain. If Our Lord Himself had been riding Unguided Missile I still would have been disgusted. But I did have a little laugh to myself later that year when *Racing Post* readers voted Woody's ride that day as the ride of the season. It was the way he got his horse going again after such a bad mistake at the last that did it. The truth is that, if he hadn't made that mistake at the last, he probably wouldn't have won. Woody had given other horses better rides that year, but that's racing. Perception is often reality.

Rough Quest's next run was in the Pierse Chase at Leopardstown in January 1996, which was a bit of a bugger for me because it clashed with Victor Chandler Chase day at Ascot, a big day for Nicky, so I couldn't go over to Ireland to ride Rough Quest. Dunwoody got the ride, somewhat unsurprisingly. Terry was a big Woody fan, and he was always hanging around there in the wings ready to pounce when I wasn't available. Woody was retained by Terry when he was training for John Upson, so there was always a very strong relationship between the pair of them. Actually, I wasn't sure that Woody wasn't Terry's first choice and that I was only standing in while he wasn't available.

Rough Quest fell at Leopardstown. It was a tough ask, to carry 11st 11lb on heavy ground at Leopardstown, but he was travelling well when he fell at the fourth-last. As luck would have it, I won the Victor Chandler Chase at Ascot on Big Matt, just getting the better of Adrian Maguire on Martin's Lamp on the run-in. That was a big race to win, and a big pot to go with it, £26,000 to the winner. Big Matt was a lovely horse. He wasn't quite top class, and he had to go right-handed, but he would have run his lungs out for you, and he deserved a big handicap win like the Victor Chandler. Two years later I would win the Grade 1 BMW Chase at the Punchestown Festival on him.

I still had my eye on Rough Quest as my Gold Cup horse. Deep down I was happy that he hadn't won at Leopardstown. Success can do funny things to people. If he had won that race, a big handicap, under Dunwoody, who knows, Terry might have been thinking of putting him up in the Gold Cup. Dunwoody had just ridden One Man to win the King George, re-routed to Sandown in January following the abandonment of Kempton's post-Christmas meeting, and the big grey horse had been put in as a warm ante-post favourite for the Gold Cup as a result. One Man had been Tony Dobbin's ride, but Dobbs was injured at the beginning of January and Dunwoody stepped in.

The week after the Pierse Chase, it was announced that Dunwoody would keep the ride on One Man in the Gold Cup. That was desperate news for Dobbs, he had done nothing wrong on the horse. He had won the Hennessy on him the previous season and he had ridden him to beat Jodami at Ayr that November. But the owners pay the bills and it appeared that John Hales, One Man's owner, the man who brought the Teletubbies toys to the UK and would later own such top-class horses as Azertyuiop and Neptune Collonges, wanted Dunwoody. It's a fickle business.

That was a bit of a relief for me, but I still couldn't exhale fully. You never know in this game. Rough Quest was running in the Racing Post Chase in February, his last intended run before the Gold Cup, and I couldn't ride him. Nicky was running Amtrak Express in the race, and there was never a question of me getting off one of Nicky's in a big race to ride something else. I wouldn't even ask. Things were going well at Nicky's. It was only my second full season as stable jockey and I was still feeling my way, but gradually I was gaining the trust of Nicky's owners and, as a result, I was getting to ride more and more of the horses in the yard. Nicky was always pushing my case with the owners as well.

Remittance Man had been retired after two disappointing runs following Cheltenham, he just wasn't the same horse, and I had ridden Travado for the first time in the Tingle Creek Chase at Sandown in

December 1995. So that was more or less it. After that, I was stable jockey full stop, I was riding all the horses. The fact that I never won on Travado still sits a little uncomfortably with me. I was second on him twice, third on him twice, fourth on him twice, but I never won a race on him. It is true that I didn't get on him until he was past his best, but I still would have liked to have won on him.

So I'm riding Amtrak Express in the Racing Post Chase, and guess who gets the ride again on Rough Quest? No prizes. Amtrak Express had led nearly all the way when I had won the Agfa Diamond Chase on him at Sandown three weeks previously, so I decided that I would be aggressive on him again. We led or disputed the lead all the way around. Kempton, like Ascot, is triangular in shape. You go down the side, turn right-handed, come up the other side, then turn right-handed again into the home straight. As we made the second-last turn to race down the side before the home turn, there were two magpies sitting on the ground in front of me, and I thought, happy days. One for sorrow, two for joy. I'm quite superstitious like that. Then I thought, you muppet. There are eight other jockeys behind you and they can all see the magpies. We jumped the next fence well, but then he clouted the next, the open ditch, and got rid of me, dumped me on the ground. I was through with magpies after that.

To add insult to injury – and I was sore – Rough Quest won the race. I was in the ambulance coming back to the enclosures, looking out the window at the finish. Rough Quest was trying to pull himself up in front on the run-in, the usual, and Percy Smollett and Brendan Powell were coming flying at them. I was willing Percy Smollett up, but the line came in time for Rough Quest and Dunwoody. That was another kick in the balls.

In the lead up to the Gold Cup, I was all the while aware of the possibility that I would be jocked off Rough Quest in favour of Dunwoody. I knew that he was set to ride One Man, but you never know in this game. Something could have happened to One Man. If he had got injured or something in the lead up to the Gold Cup, I knew that Woody would be on the phone to Terry looking for the ride, and I knew that, if he did ring for the ride, there was every chance he'd get it. There was also the chance that Woody would decide himself that Rough Quest had a better chance. That was highly unlikely, but One Man was not a certain stayer. He had looked tired going to the line in the King George, run over three miles at Sandown. The Gold Cup is run over more than three and a quarter miles at Cheltenham, and that requires a whole lot more stamina. Bizarre the things you dream up.

I didn't ring Terry in the lead up to the race. That was never my style. If he wanted me, I was available, but I always waited for him to call me. One Man didn't get injured, Dunwoody didn't jump ship and, four days before the race, Terry called to ask me if I would ride him. I was very happy about that. The ground wasn't as soft as it had been the previous year when I have no doubt he would have given Master Oats a run for his money, but it wasn't lightning-fast ground, and that suited Rough Quest well. I knew what I had to do, kick him off out the back, creep and creep and creep, try to get him into contention without asking him to race, then try to deliver him at or after the last. There was no huge pressure on me, he was a 12-1 shot, fourth or fifth favourite.

The race went as well as it possibly could have. He was a real tank of a horse, but not a big slow boat, he was a tank with gears, he was fast and accurate over his fences and he had a huge engine. Going down the hill on the far side we were fourth and travelling well. One Man and Imperial Call, under Conor O'Dwyer, were disputing the lead and Couldnt Be Better was third. Brad moved Couldnt Be Better off the rail a little after the fourth-last, and I moved up on his inside so that I wouldn't have to go around him on the home turn. Creep, save as much ground as you can.

Up front, Dunwoody was busy telling Conor O'Dwyer how far they had to go.

'I wouldn't be going for home yet,' he was saying to Conor. 'There's still a long home straight and a huge hill to climb. There's plenty of time yet.'

Conor was wise to Woody's mind games though. One Man was running out of petrol and Woody could feel it. He was trying to get a breather into the grey horse before the home turn. Conor hadn't ridden a winner at the Cheltenham Festival before, he obviously wasn't nearly as experienced as Woody, but he has a head on his shoulders. He was riding a horse who was full of running, so he kicked for home going around the home turn. One Man floundered. I moved Rough Quest up on his inside on the approach to the second-last and tried to get in Imperial Call's slipstream. I thought, not yet, just let everything happen around you, be the last one to deliver your challenge.

We jumped the second-last well and I gave Rough Quest a little squeeze, but Imperial Call was finding plenty. We jumped the last and got up to his quarters, but we were coming towards the end of our tether and Imperial Call was really strong, he just pulled away from us up the hill and beat us by four lengths in the end.

We finished second, second in the Gold Cup, you'd think I would have been delighted. I wasn't, I was gutted. To get so close to winning a Gold Cup was gutting. Who remembers second? Who was second to Best Mate in any of his Gold Cups? Who was second in Shergar's Derby? Or Nashwan's? Or Grundy's? How many runners-up of any big race can you name? Nobody cares about second. Nobody remembers. I certainly don't.

You'll see jockeys congratulating other jockeys when they are pulling up after a race after finishing second or third. I just don't get that. If I'm beaten in a race, especially if I'm narrowly beaten, the last thing I want to do is congratulate the fellow who has just beaten me. Maybe that's mean-spirited of me, but that's how I feel. I will say well done to him in the weigh room afterwards, or over a beer later that evening, but I don't feel it in the immediate aftermath of the race.

We were in the unsaddling enclosure, in the space reserved for the runner-up, when trainer Fergie Sutherland and Imperial Call came back in with Conor on his back. A hell of a cheer went up from the crowd, Cheltenham's amphitheatre at work again. Imperial Call was the first Irish-trained winner of the Gold Cup since Dawn Run ten years previously. Everyone was congratulating me, saying well done on running so well, on giving him such a good ride, but my overriding feeling was one of jealousy. I was looking at Conor's smiley face and wishing that I was him. You'd think that I would have been delighted at finishing second, but I wasn't. I just wanted to win, I wanted to be experiencing what Conor was experiencing.

I couldn't have thought for a second that, no more than a couple of weeks later, I would.

# CHAPTER 13

## BETTER THAN SEX

There was never any talk of Rough Quest running in the Grand National. I'm not even sure why Terry entered him in the race in the first place. Maybe in case something happened to him to prevent him from running in the Gold Cup, or maybe in case he fell at the first fence at Cheltenham, but Aintree came just two weeks after Cheltenham in 1996, so there was no way that the horse would have had enough time to recover from his Gold Cup exertions, certainly not enough to be at his peak for a four-and-a-half-mile race. Even after the Gold Cup Terry told Andrew Wates that he wasn't going to run him in the National. Andrew was more circumspect. Just leave it for now, he said, we'll see how he is, keep our options open.

Rough Quest was very well after the Gold Cup. In fact, within a few days he was bouncing again. Terry had a little bit of a rethink. Here was a Gold Cup runner-up who was set to carry 10st 7lb in the Grand National. He might never have as good a shot at the Grand National again.

As the days went by, the National plan began to take shape. Because the Grand National is an early-closing race, the handicapper wasn't able to take Rough Quest's Gold Cup run into consideration when allotting him his weight for the National. If he had been able to, he would have given him another stone and a half to carry. This fact was not lost on Terry.

I was desperate that Terry would run the horse in the Grand National. I thought that he was an ideal National type, he travelled so well, he stayed well, he had gears, he was a big horse, he was a great jumper and, as a ten-year-old, he was the right age for the race. As well as that, he had run at Aintree before and he had run really well. He ran in the John Hughes Chase over the big fences in 1994, when he jumped very well under Graham McCourt, and he was going really well when he came down at the fourth-last.

As much as I was hoping that Terry would run him in the National, I was desperate that I would ride him if he did, because it wasn't certain that I would. Dunwoody was in the picture again. Just like everyone else and more than most, he could see what was going on, a Gold Cup runner-up with a feather-weight in the Grand National. I know that he was on to Terry, probably on the phone to him every day, him or his agent, just chipping away. He had a fair argument. Do you want Richard Dunwoody, widely recognised as the best rider of his generation, if not of any generation, vastly experienced, veteran of the Grand National, winner of two of them, riding as well as he has ever ridden and willing to offer his services? Or do you want Mick Fitzgerald, a still-wet-behind-the-ears Paddy who is only just getting going, who has ridden in just one Grand National before and got no further than the first fence on Tinryland a year ago?

It's always an anticlimax to fall at the first fence in any race, but to fall at the first fence in the Grand National, the first Grand National in which you have a ride, is just gut-wrenching. All the build-up, all the hype, my first ride in the Grand National, and I fall at the first fence. Tinryland was just going a stride too fast going into the fence and he over-jumped.

To make matters worse, he managed to stand on my balls as he tried to get to his feet. That was a nut-wrencher. I was there on my knees, opening up my breeches trying to see if all my private parts are still intact. It feels like there's blood, I'm not sure because everything is numb, but I'm putting my hand down fearing the worst. This fucker is after slicing the top off my cock!

Suddenly, a representative from the St John's ambulance arrives on the scene.

'Are you ok love?' she asks.

I'm still on my knees so all I can see is this lady's feet, flat black shoes and tights.

'I'm not sure,' I wince.

'Where are you hurting?'

She has an unusually deep voice, she's leaning down trying to help me when I look at her face and it's not a she at all! It's a he in tights and flat lady's shoes. I stand up fairly smartish, grimace through the pain, mumble something about being fine, thanks very much, and hightail it as fast as I can hobble off back towards the stands.

While I would have been absolutely distraught if I had lost the ride on Rough Quest to Woody, I'm sure that I would have understood the rationale behind it eventually. As it turned out, there was no need for me to be understanding. I think Terry wanted me to ride, I think he wanted to remain loyal to me, I had given the horse such a good ride in the Gold Cup, he figured. A week before the race Terry rang me to tell me that the horse was going to run and that I was going to ride him, if I wanted to. I did, more than he could have imagined.

Rough Quest was announced as a runner and he was very quickly installed as favourite, so we had all the hullabaloo that went with that. I loved it. When I started out in this game I wanted to ride the big horses, the favourites, in the big races. I wanted the attention that that attracted, I wanted the pressure that it brought. If you didn't want that, if you didn't thrive on it, then I figured you had no business being in this game at all. I had all the media looking for me, what's it like to be riding the favourite for the Grand National? What chance do you have? I loved that. I loved being in demand.

My dad used to come over for Aintree. He started coming over three years before Rough Quest and we'd always have the same routine. He loved being at Aintree, and I loved having him there, because it was just the two of us. Those Aintree trips are a huge contributor to the fact that we are so close today, that I regard my dad as one of my best mates.

He'd come over the day before the meeting started, he would stay with me at home on Wednesday night and then we'd head for Liverpool. I wouldn't want to be up all night out on the beer or anything, so we'd stay in Haydock or Runcorn, Haydock in the beginning, then Runcorn. We'd go racing early, beat the traffic, get to the course at about ten o'clock in the morning, and I'd dump him.

'Will you be all right now?'

'Yeah, I'll be grand.'

There was this guy that my dad knew from home, from Wexford, Mick Jordan, who would be over at Aintree putting up tents or marquees or something, and my dad would meet him there every year and go on the beer with him. Obviously this was when my dad was still drinking. Then he'd meet somebody else that he knew from home and he'd have a few pints with him. He'd have a couple of bets during the day and plenty of pints, and sure he'd be delighted with himself by the end of the day.

I'd meet him after racing and invariably he'd be pissed. Not bad pissed or messy pissed, just happy pissed, my dad with a big happy smile on his face. So I'd drive back to the hotel with him, we'd discuss the day's racing in the car, shite day or great day, we'd get to the hotel and go for supper. After supper I'd come back up to the room and do some work, go through the next day's fields and rides, have a bit of a sweat in a hot bath, and go to bed. Then, at God knows what time, one or two in the morning, my dad would come stumbling up the stairs, twisted. He'd come into the room, he wouldn't turn on the light because he'd be afraid of waking me, he'd think he'd be doing me a favour, but he'd be fumbling around in the dark trying to find things, he'd be kicking and falling over everything, of course I was going to wake up.

'All right dad?'

'Oh, yeah, all right, I thought you were asleep.'

Indeed.

So he gets into the bed and starts talking to me, making no sense at all, then next thing he's asleep. I know that he's asleep because all I can here is this snoring. I'm not joking a team of trumpeters wouldn't make as much noise. I'm thinking, here we go again. So I'm trying to relax, trying not to think about it, trying not to get myself wound up, 'right, just relax now and you'll fall asleep', but I never do. 'Ah, this is not happening.'

I get out of bed and shake him.

'Dad, dad!'

He wakes up and the snoring stops. Grand, so I sit back down, but as soon as I do he's off again. Ah no. I'd reach out and grab his bed with both hands and shake it as much as I can just to get him to stop, but nothing ever worked. So I'd be sitting up, this would be at two or three in the morning now, and I'd have been awake for an hour or two, thinking, 'This happens every year. Next year we're getting separate rooms.' But we never would. I never would have, because I love my dad and this was all a part of it, it was all part of me and my dad going to Aintree together.

Eventually I'd get to sleep, and I'd wake up in the morning at about half seven, wrecked. I'd put the kettle on in the room and make myself a cup of tea. Dad would start to stir.

'All right?' he'd say.

'Yeah,' I'd say. 'How'd you sleep?'

'Grand. You?'

'Fucking terrible,' I'd say. 'You were snoring like a pig.'

'Really?' he'd ask, all serious. 'I never heard a thing.'

'Funny that.'

So it would be the same thing on Friday. We'd head off early, get to the racecourse, he'd head off, meet Mick Jordan, see you back here after racing, grand, he'd have a skinful, back to the hotel, supper, I'd go upstairs to go through Saturday's runners, he'd stay downstairs drinking, stumble up the stairs at one or two o'clock, snore his head off, I'd lie awake going, never again, sleep for about five hours, up the following morning, how'd you sleep? Groundhog day.

I loved it though. I loved spending time with my dad. He's a great lad, even though he used to drive me around the bend with his snoring. I wouldn't have changed a thing about our Aintrees together, I didn't change a thing.

So we did this in 1996. I had a bit of an up-and-down Thursday. I fell at the first fence on both Tudor Fable and Sublime Fellow, and I finished second on Our Kris in the four-year-old hurdle. Friday wasn't any better. A distant third behind Addington Boy on Golden Spinner in the Mildmay Novices' Chase was the best I could manage. I wasn't that despondent, I knew that I was riding the favourite in the Grand National the following day.

Saturday dawned as every Grand National day dawned for me those years, my dad in the bed beside me, snoring for Ireland. I got up and made a cup of tea for myself and one for him. I wasn't having any breakfast so he went down on his own as I stayed up in the room to go through the fields before *The Morning Line*, Channel 4's weekly preview of Saturday's racing. My dad came back up and we sat on the bed to watch the programme.

John Francome was asked what he fancied in the Grand National and he said that he didn't fancy the favourite anyway. He's very good at making a case, Francome. He figured that Rough Quest wasn't a certain stayer, that he had fallen at the track before, that he would remember that unpleasant experience, that he had just run his lungs out in the Gold Cup two weeks previously and would hardly have had time to recover, and he was being ridden by an inexperienced rider, a fellow who had got no further than the landing side of the first fence on his only attempt at the Grand National. Jim McGrath thought that Rough Quest was a handicap certainty, Graham Goode gave him a chance as well.

I turned off the television, it was time to go. Fuck them, fuck Francome. I didn't care what they thought, what mattered was what I thought, and I thought my horse was a certainty if he jumped around. All I had to do was get him around, it was as simple as that.

I had a ride in the first race that day on Nakir for Simon Christian. I wasn't thinking about the National when I was riding Nakir, I wasn't thinking of minding myself, of not falling because I was riding the favourite in the National. You can't think that, you just go and ride your race. I rode Nakir up in the van, the way he liked to be ridden, but once he got outpaced and had no chance of winning, I thought, right, look after him now on the way home, look after yourself. We finished seventh. That was it then for me before the National. I counted down the minutes.

I thought that Terry was quite nervous when he came into the weigh room to get the saddle for Rough Quest, and he was even more nervous in the parade ring. Andrew was there with his wife Sarah, both seemed to be quite relaxed. Strange thing, but I didn't feel nervous at all. I don't know why, I just wasn't. It didn't bother me that I had fallen at the first fence the previous year on Tinryland, my only previous attempt at the Grand National. I had ridden over the big fences before, I had ridden in the John Hughes and the Becher Chase. Ok, so they are not the Grand National, but they are over the big Aintree fences, so I knew what was required.

I knew that I was on the best horse in the race at the weights, and that was more reassuring than nerve-racking. I just thought, keep it simple. You're on the best horse, so keep him out of trouble, make sure he gets around. You never can be sure of anything with the Grand National, a lot of what happens is out of your control, and that was reassuring as well, in a strange way.

Some of the best jockeys have never won the National. Jonjo O'Neill, John Francome, Peter Scudamore, AP McCoy, four of the top jockeys of the modern era and none of them has won the National. Jonjo never even got around. Events conspired against them. Even now, I keep telling AP that you can't control everything in the National. Things happen, you get idiots running in front of you or you get loose horses carrying you out, as a couple of them did to AP at Becher's Brook when he was going well on Clan Royal in 2005. Or you'll get your own horse doing silly things, like Butler's Cabin jumping to his left with AP at Becher's in 2008 and coming down. That's what makes it such a great race, the uncertainty. One day, God will smile down and say, all right, today AP McCoy, it's your day.

I had my game plan, settle him out the back, hunt around for the first circuit, get him relaxed, get him jumping, don't follow any kamikazes, stay middle to outer, there's no need to go down the inside where the fences are bigger, there's no need to be a hero, just keep it simple and play the percentages. When you are on the best horse you can afford to play the percentages. That said, there were plenty of dangers. Woody was riding a horse for Jenny Pitman, Superior Finish, who was well fancied, Bridgy was riding one of Pipe's, Encore Un Peu, who had been just beaten in the Kim Muir at Cheltenham, Chris Maude was riding Young Hustler for Nigel Twiston-Davies, who was one of my biggest dangers, I figured, and Carl Llewellyn was riding the 1992 winner Party Politics. My plan was to follow Carl and Woody. They knew what they were doing, they had no peers when it came to riding Aintree and I figured that if I was close enough to those two, I wouldn't be going too far wrong.

Rough Quest felt fantastic when we set off to canter down to the start. You would never have known that he had run his heart out in the Gold

Cup just two weeks previously. Terry had done a great job at getting him back. He was bouncing. The starter called us in and we were off.

I was relieved when we landed over the first fence. He was meeting it on a nice stride, I gave him a little squeeze, he took off and landed running, as sure-footed as a mountain goat. Perfect. I was on the landing side of the first fence in the Grand National and I was upright, I had never got that far before in the race. I always had it in my head from riding over the big fences in the John Hughes and the Becher Chase, that if you got over the first three fences in the National, you would know exactly what chance you had of winning the race. You can tell by then whether a horse is taking to the fences or not.

Rough Quest was loving it. The third fence is the big ditch, one of the biggest fences on the course. He danced over it. He just gobbled it up. He was unbelievable. I thought, keep him out of trouble now and he'll win. After jumping three fences of the 30, I thought we would win.

We were towards the outside and we were well back in the field, but I didn't care. I was where I wanted to be. The first circuit in the National is about survival. Hunt around for the first circuit, make sure you jump and avoid the melee, and then start to ride a race on the second circuit when the field has thinned out a bit. He flew the second-last on the first circuit, winged the Chair, jumped the water jump in front of the stands well, and suddenly as the crowd in the grandstand cheered and we headed out on the second circuit to do it all over again, we were about seventh or eighth. Too close. I tried to take him back, whoa, whoa, hang on there.

He ran into the one before Becher's Brook, the fifth fence on the second circuit, but he got away with it. That wasn't a bad thing, he was just getting a little bit above himself at that point, thinking he was God, so it was no harm that he got a bit of a scare before Becher's again, make him concentrate on what he was doing. He jumped Becher's well, jumped Foinavon, jumped the Canal Turn, around and over Valentine's Brook. He was in a rhythm, and the Grand National is all about rhythm.

You don't have much time between fences to adjust anything, so when your horse is in a rhythm you just let him flow. It's like the sound you get when you're in a train carriage, de-de-de-dum, de-de-de-dum, de-de-de-dum, de-de-de-dum. Stride-stride-stride-jump, stride-stride-stride-jump. You hear jockeys talk about rhythm a lot, you hear them talk about a horse getting into a lovely rhythm in a race. That's what they are talking about. That's what I always looked for when I rode and it is why, even now, if I see a jockey pulling and dragging at a horse, rousting him along and then tugging sharply on the reins, I feel like jumping up and ripping the television off the wall. It's like a car, if you are accelerating and braking all the time, you will very quickly run out of petrol, whereas if you are coasting along at a constant speed it is much more economical. Same with horses. You will use up all their energy if you are constantly stopping and starting. Rhythm is vitally important in every race, but it is especially so in the Grand National.

Going to the third-last fence, I thought, 'Wow, I only have three more fences to jump and then I have completed the course in the Grand National.' We jumped the third-last well and I thought, two more. Amazing. Here I am, traveling like a dream on the favourite in the Grand National and I'm only thinking about completing the course. That's what the Grand National does to you. Then suddenly, on the approach to the second-last, my brain clicked into gear and I thought, right, you're going to win this now.

I looked at everything around me. Young Hustler was there, Three Brownies was there, Paul Carberry up, but Encore Un Peu was traveling by far the best of anything that I could see.

'He's your danger,' I thought. 'Keep an eye on him. But you have to give yourself at least three or four lengths over the last. You don't want to hit the front too early.'

David Bridgwater kicked Encore Un Peu on between the last two fences, and he went about four lengths clear. Don't panic now, you have plenty of horse under you. I sat as still as I dared and just allowed Rough Quest to follow him, easy now. We passed Young Hustler and Three Brownies to our left, and got in behind Encore Un Peu, in his slipstream.

We jumped the last a little to the left, but fine. Bridgy hadn't gone for everything on Encore Un Peu either, and we still had three lengths to make up, but all the while I knew that my horse had plenty left to give.

When you jump the last fence in the Grand National, you have to edge to your right, the rail takes you around the Chair and the water jump that you jumped on the first circuit, and on up to the winning line. There is a big open space between the final fence and that rail, the Elbow they call it, and my intention was to nick up on the inside of Bridgy, get on to the inside rail at the Elbow, and then ask Rough Quest for everything he had left. Bridgy had a peek over his left shoulder and saw me coming. He edged to his left so that I had to switch around him and make my challenge on the outside, which wasn't ideal for Rough Quest, who didn't like to be out on his own for too long.

I switched in behind the leader for a couple of strides, then moved to the outside as soon as we hit the Elbow, a furlong to run in the most famous horserace in the world. I asked my horse to go on and he responded willingly, he had loads of energy left. When we got upsides Encore Un Peu, my horse began to lean a little to his left, on to Bridgy. I tugged a little on the right rein just enough to keep him off the other horse but not enough to halt his momentum. Suddenly we were a neck up, then half a length up, then a length up.

The crowd was roaring now. Once Rough Quest knew that he was in front, however, the usual, he began to lug to his left, over towards the far rail just as he had done at Ascot. I let him drift, I didn't want to disappoint him. I had a little glance between my left arm and my body and thought that we were far enough clear of the other horse so as not to impede him. We drifted over to the inside rail, I kept on riding, just punching and kicking, I could feel him coming back underneath me a little bit, but the line was coming up, I knew we were going to get there. I didn't hit him with the whip once, I didn't need to, and then we crossed the line, Grand National winners. Amazing.

It was all a bit surreal. I didn't know what to think as I pulled up. I had just won the Grand National. What did that mean? How big was that exactly? Rough Quest had given me a hell of a ride, he was brilliant. This was unbelievable. Jeff ran over to us, the lad who looked after the horse at Terry's, and he was just ecstatic, jumping around all over the place. Woody said well done to me, Maudey said well done, everything was just a blur, just one elated blur. Then I heard the klaxon, the dreaded klaxon. Stewards' enquiry.

My heart sank. If the stewards felt that I had taken David Bridgwater's ground by coming over on to the rail, if they felt that I had impeded him, and that the interference had been detrimental to his chance of winning the race, they could throw me out, they could relegate me to second place, or even last place. But I hadn't impeded him, I was far enough clear, surely I was far enough clear? I had won the Grand National, but had I really?

Terry was on his way over.

'Ah you'll lose that,' he said to me. I couldn't believe it. I've just passed the post first on his horse in the Grand National and the first thing he says to me is that I'll lose it. Mr Optimistic, Terry Casey, the most optimistic Donegal man in the world.

'I don't think so Terry,' I said, part because I believed it, part because I wanted to reassure Terry, part because I wanted to reassure myself. 'I was clear of him.'

'Ah you weren't that far clear.'

Then the doubts began to seep in. Was I that far clear of him? Maybe I wasn't, maybe Terry was right. Maybe I was barely a length clear and I cut him off. Jesus. Imagine they took this off me, imagine after all this that they disqualified me. I was led back down the walkway, back into the winner's enclosure. There was a huge buzz about the place, big cheers, but I couldn't enjoy any of it because in the back of my mind was the possibility that I would lose it. Deep down I thought that the chance of losing it was very slim, but there was still a chance, even if it was a 100-1 shot it was still a chance, and you never know for certain which way stewards are going to go.

We were both called into the stewards' room, Bridgy and me, and we were shown a replay of the run-in from four different angles. God, maybe I wasn't as far clear as I thought I was. I saw on the video that Bridgy had snatched up Encore Un Peu as we moved over on to the rail in front of him, but I suspected it was a bit of an Indian rope trick, a bit of a Jurgen Klinsmann dive. I wasn't impressed. We both said our pieces. I said that I

135

thought that we were clear of the other horse when we moved on to the rail. In fairness to Bridgy, he said that we were probably far enough clear as well. We were good mates, me and Bridgy, and I wasn't surprised that he was fairly straight up in front of the stewards.

They sent us outside for a couple of minutes so that they could decide what to do, then they called us back in. I held my breath as I stood there in front of these stewards who had the power to take a Grand National victory away from me. It was a weird feeling. I was powerless. Then one of them spoke. Result stands.

That was unbelievable. A wave of emotion started deep in my gut and washed over the whole of my body. Mainly relief, but there were elements of ecstasy in there, euphoria, absolute exhilaration. All my ambitions, everything I had worked for, from Richard Lister's to Gerald Ham's and Jackie Retter's to Nicky Henderson's, all the effort, all the dreams, had been building up to this. I'd just won the Grand National, and that was official.

I came out of the stewards' room in a daze. As I did, I could hear the announcement over the PA system, result stands. There was a big cheer, lots of backslapping, some well done Micks, then a guy from the BBC grabbed me and ushered me out on to the stand where Des Lynam was. They must have had to do some filling in as they waited for the official result and they were probably desperate to have their interviews now. I just stood there in front of Des, probably a big stupid Irish ear-to-ear grin on my face. I didn't care about very much at that moment, I was floating, high on adrenaline, I'd just realised every jump jockey's dream.

'Mick Fitzgerald,' said Des deliberately, 'you've just won the Grand National. How does it feel?'

I just bumbled something at first about how unbelievable it was. I didn't for a second think that there were millions of people watching, or that we were going out live on Saturday afternoon television, it was just me and Des, Uncle Des, having a chat.

'I've never enjoyed 12 minutes as much before in my life,' I said excitedly. 'After that Des, you know, even sex is an anticlimax.'

# CHAPTER 14

## NATIONAL CHAMPION

Des was a bit taken aback. I had watched Des Lynam a million times before on television, I had watched him on *Match of the Day* probably hundreds of times, I had watched him do *Grandstand* probably thousands of times, I grew up with Des Lynam in my living room, and to me he has always been the consummate broadcasting professional. I had never seen him flustered before. Until that moment. I went on.

'That was probably the most enjoyable 12 minutes I have ever had in my life.'

I don't think Des was even listening to me. There were probably people screaming in his earpiece. This was 1996, people weren't as daring or as accepting as they are today. Des was expressionless. Two hundred million people watching and this muppet, this Paddy muppet, says that it's better than sex. He laughed it away and then got Terry in fairly promptly.

The rest of the day is a blur. There were more television interviews, radio interviews, the press conference, photographs, I didn't know which way was up. I even managed to fit in a ride in the Cordon Bleu Hurdle later on. I had more interviews to do after racing, it was non-stop but it was brilliant. The one slight regret I have was that it all washed over me very quickly, I didn't manage to take the time to take everything in, to fully appreciate what was going on. Woody and Carl Llewellyn always said that, that the first time they won the Grand National it all passed them by, but the second time they won it was even better because they knew what it was all about, they knew what to expect and they had both determined that they would take the time to appreciate everything. I was only 26, relatively young, so it did all pass me by. I resolved to win the race again, that I would pay more attention the next time. Sadly, I never did. But I nearly killed myself trying.

Towards the end of the day it hit me – where's my dad? He could have been anywhere. I was doing my final interview, a sign-off for the BBC for their highlights programme, and I began to get worried. It was about seven o'clock in the evening. In all the frenzy I had forgotten about my old man.

When we had arranged to meet after racing, we hadn't really thought about what would happen if I managed to win the bloody race. So there I was surrounded by cameras and lights and all these television people, and I look over their shoulders, just beyond the bounds of the television stand, and there he is, Frank Fitzgerald, absolutely twisted but on top of the world. He looked back at me, big smiley head on him, and stuck up his thumb: 'You did it'.

There are moments in your life that live with you, moments that are as vivid in your head as the day that they happened, and that is one of them for me. I'll never forget it. I'll never forget the feeling that I had in that split second, the surge of pride and emotion that came with the feeling that I had done something that would make my old man so proud of me.

So I loaded him up into the car and we drove home. I was on cloud nine, Mick Fitzgerald, Grand National-winning jockey. I let the feeling wash over me, tried to take it all in, what it meant, what it would mean to me in the future. When we got home, my fiancée, Jane Brackenbury, had a big banner up at the house and there were loads of people around. That was a good party. During the evening I went into the kitchen to get a drink, Jane was there, she looked at me with a wry smile.

'I heard your interview with Des Lynam,' she said.

'Oh yeah,' I said a bit sheepishly. We were set to get married three months later. 'That, yeah, sorry about that, I suppose I got a bit carried away there.'

'I just have one question for you,' she said.

'Yeah?'

'How often is the Grand National run?'

The following morning I went out and got all the papers. I was bowled over. We were front-page news in almost every paper. I suppose I hadn't fully realised how important the Grand National was until that day. For me it was always the Gold Cup, that was the championship race, that was the race for the best horses, so it was the one that I wanted to win more than any other race in the calendar, more than the Grand National.

But I realised that morning that the Grand National was the race for the masses, the most famous horserace in the world. Ask the man in the street to name a horserace, and he will say either the Grand National or the Derby. Ask him to name a horse and he is much more likely to say Red Rum or West Tip. Ask him if he has a bet, and he will tell you that he bets once a year on the Grand National. The Gold Cup is the race for the professionals, the purists, but the Grand National is the one for the populace.

When I meet new people, people who aren't necessarily into racing, and they hear that I was a jockey, I'm often asked if I have even done the Grand National.

'Yeah, I have,' I reply.

'When you say done, now,' they ask, 'what do you mean exactly?'

'I won it.'

'You won the Grand National?'

'I did.'

'What's your name again?'

People probably know me as much for my remark to Des Lynam in the post-race interview as they do for me actually winning the Grand National. It used to bother me. 'Oh yeah, you're the fellow who told Des Lynam that it was better than sex?' Big deal. It was never: 'Oh yeah, you were the fellow who rode Rough Quest with balls of steel, who settled him out the back, who got him travelling and got him jumping, who charted a precarious path through the field, who arrived there at the right time and had the bottle to hang on to him until you reached the Elbow?' Not a bit of it. I actually regretted saying it for a while, but not any more. I said what I felt and that was what I felt. Exhilarated, the best feeling in the world, better than the best feeling in the world.

There is no doubt in my mind that winning the Grand National made a huge difference to me. I was never lacking self-belief, but it gave other people a reason to believe in me. Winning the Cathcart on Raymylette was one thing, that was a huge step up the ladder, winning the Ritz on Rough Quest was another rung, winning the Grand National was a couple more. It was part of a process that was taking me to the top of my profession. Success breeds belief, which breeds success. I wasn't just a young promising rider any more, I wasn't even just a young promising rider who had ridden two winners at Cheltenham, I was a Grand National-winning jockey, and that was huge.

Andrew Wates had a party at his place the following day, and that was great craic. Andrew is a true gentleman. His sons were around my age, maybe a little bit younger, and we used to sneak around the back for a cigarette. Well, this time Andrew came around and caught us. He had a right go at the lads. He was livid. He couldn't say much to me, but I still couldn't help but feel a little bit like a naughty child.

Rough Quest was the guest of honour at the party; we were merely hangers-on. All the lads from the yard were there, and a lot of the staff of Wates Leisure. I got chatting to Terry there. Terry was a bit of a rogue, but he was a really likeable rogue. He was still on a high.

'You know,' he said to me, 'you were always going to ride him.'

'Was I?' I asked, intrigued.

'Yeah, I always wanted you,' said Terry. 'There was never a chance of Dunwoody riding him.'

'Really?'

'No, never,' he said. 'He was on the phone though, you know, every day, him or his agent. But there was never a chance. I always wanted you.'

'Thanks Terry,' my lips said, but my mind was screaming: 'You lying bastard! If you had had your way, Dunwoody would have been riding him. It was only because Andrew wanted to remain loyal to me that I kept the ride. I know that, but I appreciate you taking the time to tell me this.'

'Thanks,' I said out loud again. 'That means a lot.'

The following week, Andrew had another party to celebrate the win, mainly for his staff who weren't able to go to the party on the Sunday. When I got there I thought that Andrew wasn't his normal high-spirited self. Sarah Wates was there and she seemed to be decidedly and unusually down in herself. It was only later on, when I met Terry and his wife

Joanne, that I found out that their son William, who had been traveling the world on a gap-year from his studies, had been murdered in Honduras earlier that day. I couldn't believe it. And yet Andrew and Sarah went ahead with the party for their staff. That's the type of people they are.

Jane and I got married that summer. It was quite a good time in my life, I had just won the Grand National, I was riding for one of the top trainers in the country, I was in demand with outside yards more and more, I had a few quid in the bank and I was getting married. We went to Florida, to Disney World on our honeymoon. I love Disney World. I've been to Disney World three times and I've never taken a child there, although there was a girl I took there once who almost qualified.

*Hello!* magazine got wind of the wedding and contacted us, wanting exclusive pictorial rights. I said no way, I didn't want my wedding splashed all over the pages of *Hello!* But Jane's dad and I were having a bit of a spat over who would pay for the wedding, he wanted to foot the bill, I wouldn't hear of it, so I said, tell you what, why don't we let *Hello!* pay for it? Sorted.

So the magazine's photographer arrived and he went about his business, taking all his photos, and they had a girl taking the names of all the guests. In fairness, they weren't at all intrusive, they were actually much less intrusive than the guy we had hired ourselves to take the wedding photos, and it didn't look that bad in the magazine afterwards. They featured Paul Gascoigne's wedding the week before they featured ours, so we were in good company. Regrettably, the curse of *Hello!* struck for both Gazza and me. The fact that our marriage lasted a little longer than Gazza's was no consolation.

# CHAPTER 15

## JUST SIT STILL

On Boxing Day 1991, I rode a horse called Its Nearly Time in a novice chase at Newton Abbot for John and Becky Brackenbury, small permit-holders who were based in Moreleigh in South Devon. I came in after the race, after finishing second, just run out of it on the run-in, and Chris Maude was looking at me, a big silly grin on his face.

'Well?' he asked, about to explode.

'Well what?' I asked, genuinely mystified.

'What did you think of the bird who was leading you up?'

'I didn't notice her,' I said honestly. 'Was she fit?'

A couple of tentative enquiries later, and it emerged that the girl was a daughter of John and Becky. Paul Nicholls had just got married to another daughter, Bridget, and he asked me shortly afterwards if I would go down to Moreleigh to ride another horse that they trained that he thought was better than the one I'd ridden.

'Right,' I thought. 'I'd better have a look at this bird.'

The horse was It's After Time, a novice hurdler. Later on I would ride him in a novice chase at Newton Abbot, he would fall on me and I would break my collarbone, but the horse wasn't my real concern at the time.

The girl was Jane, I got chatting to her when I was down at the house in Moreleigh, she seemed really nice and I asked her out. It just went from there really. They are really good people, they're a lovely family. Jane moved up from Devon and worked for Paul in 1993, then she worked for Henrietta Knight and she ended up with her own yard a few years later, doing livery and training a couple of point-to-point horses.

I wasn't a big believer in monogamy in my younger days. It's almost a cultural thing among jockeys. I'm not sure what it is, maybe it's because of the precariousness of the profession, you live on the edge all day when you are at work, you get this adrenaline rush when you ride at 35 miles an hour over fences, maybe you are out to replicate that adrenaline rush in real life.

I had a couple of funny instances when I was younger. I tended to go in for long-term relationships that were interspersed with a couple of other short-term ones, some very short-term. There was this girl I was going out with when I was riding for Gerald Ham, I'd be sitting at home with her, looking at the clock, willing her to leave because I'd have another girl due to arrive later on in the evening. That was a big adrenaline rush. It was stupid in many ways, laddish, but it was funny looking back on it now. I loved the precariousness of it all, the sense of danger, but there came a point when I thought it was time for me to stop all that craic and be a little bit sensible, and that point coincided with my relationship with Jane reaching a point where the next natural step was marriage.

It's easy looking back on it now, but I wasn't in a marriage state of mind then. My career was number one for me, my profession, getting on in racing, riding top-class horses in the big races, at the big meetings. Girls or girlfriends were very much on the periphery of my life, and that was how I wanted it to be. I told Jane this before we got married, I told her that my career was always going to be number one, so she understood what she was getting into to a large extent.

A couple of days before we got married, I thought to myself, right, this is it, you have to be able to put your hand on your heart, walk up there, stand in front of your man, the priest, and God, and say 'I do'.

'Forsake all others?'

'I do.'

You have to say it with conviction and you have to mean it. None of this yeah yeah, whatever, no fingers crossed behind your back, none of this yeah well, we'll see how it goes. No more other birds, no more shagging around.

'Forsake all others?'

'I do.'

And I did. I really did mean it, and I did forsake all others, for a while. But a year and a half, two years into the marriage, things weren't great, we were just going through the motions, and then one night I was out, a few beers, this nice bird, I start chatting her up, and before I knew where I was, I was waking up the next morning and thinking, 'Uh oh, I probably shouldn't have done that.'

Things were a bit slow career-wise as well. Nicky had a couple of quiet seasons, he just didn't have great horses. I won a novice hurdle at Folkestone on Rough Quest in December 1996. It was quite bizarre for a Grand National winner to be still a novice over hurdles, as in he had never won a hurdle race before, but he was. I really enjoyed that race. David Nicholson, The Duke, had a horse in it, Destin D'Estruval, a French import who was having his first run in England and from whom quite a lot was expected, but we crept the whole way through the race, got there at the last, made a mistake there which nearly scuppered it for us, but my horse picked up well on the run-in to win by half a length.

We were thinking Gold Cup and Grand National again with him. He was almost 11 years old and probably wouldn't have the pace to win a Gold Cup, but we were going to have another go anyway and go on to the National again. I finished second on him in the King George that December behind One Man. He didn't jump as well as he can, and we probably would have finished third had Mr Mulligan not taken a crashing fall at the last when he was second, but it was still a fine performance from a near 11-year-old to finish second in a King George.

After that, Rough Quest's leg problems, the ones that had kept him off the track for four months before I rode him that first day at Nottingham, came back to haunt him and he didn't make the Gold Cup or the Grand National.

The 1997 Cheltenham Festival was the one at which Nicky's horse Barna Boy, owned by the late Lynn Wilson, won the County Hurdle, the last race at the meeting, with me having chosen to ride Cheryl's Lad in the race instead, presenting the ride on Barna Boy on a platter to Dunwoody. Great. So no winners for me at Cheltenham that year, I didn't even get close, but I did win the Aintree Hurdle on Bimsey for Reg Akehurst and owner Aidan Ryan. I was delighted with that win, and for Reg and Aidan.

I had ridden Bimsey in the Champion Hurdle at Cheltenham for them three weeks previously, but Make A Stand had set so fast a pace there over two miles that poor Bimsey was always going a stride faster than he wanted to or was able to. I had said to Reg after the Champion Hurdle that he would be much better suited by stepping up to two and a half miles for the Aintree Hurdle, and that I would ride him there, so it was great to be vindicated. Make A Stand ran in the Aintree Hurdle as well, but he didn't seem to be the same horse as he was at Cheltenham, he could never get clear of us and he was beaten at the top of the home straight. From there it developed into a battle between me and Dunwoody on Pridwell, and we just held on.

I was riding Go Ballistic in the Grand National an hour later. He was set to carry ten stone, so I had been wasting to get down to that weight. It wasn't easy for me to do ten stone, but I did, I got down so that I didn't have to put up any overweight. Go Ballistic had finished fourth in the Cheltenham Gold Cup under Tony Dobbin, but Dobbs remained loyal to Steve Brookshaw's horse Lord Gyllene, the New Zealand-bred horse on whom he had won the Midlands National at Uttoxeter, so I came in for the ride.

I was good friends with Go Ballistic's trainer John O'Shea. John's a good lad. I rode my 500th winner on one of his horses, and I rode my last winner as a conditional rider for John, Mandalay Prince in a claiming hurdle at Fontwell in August 1992. He asked me to school Go Ballistic for him at Southwell one day in December 1996. The horse wasn't a great jumper at the time, he was ok, but he was finding it difficult to make the transition from novice chaser to handicapper and John just thought that a pop over a couple of fences after racing at Southwell would do him good.

It was a wet day and there had been quite a few fallers during the day, so I thought it wasn't ideal, but it should be fine. John had a young lad there who was going to ride the lead horse, a horse who was a decent jumper, just so that Go Ballistic would have something to follow over his fences. I asked the young lad if he had ridden much, he said he had ridden lots, he'd had a couple of rides in point-to-points, so I said grand, perfect, just go a nice even gallop on the first circuit and then we'll pick up the pace a bit on the second circuit.

So we set off at the start of the back straight at Southwell and jumped the first fence. Your man on the other horse in front of me nearly goes out over his horse's head, and I'm thinking this doesn't look too promising. Go Ballistic jumped the fence ok. We come down to the second and the lead horse is getting a bit of a run on to it, and I'm thinking, steady now, steady. Your man is winding this thing up as if he was going down to the last in the Gold Cup, and I'm thinking, oh no, then, bang! He takes the fence by the roots and does a somersault over it. I manage to get over the fence, avoid your man on the ground, pull up and come back around to see if he is all right. He's a bit dazed-looking on the ground. I'm thinking, I probably shouldn't be going on with this now, but we're over the far side of the track and John is in the stands, so I think I'll just jump a couple of fences on my own. It's not ideal, Go Ballistic jumping without a lead horse, but it's probably the best thing to do now. Your man picks himself up off the ground.

'You all right?' I ask.

'Yeah I'm fine.'

'Are you sure?'

'Yeah, grand now.'

'Can you get back up on him?' I ask.

'Yeah, no problem.'

It takes him a little while, but he manages to get back up. The next fence in the back straight is an open ditch, so I'm thinking, well it won't be ideal to jump that first, so I suggest we go back around to where we started, jump the first two fences again and then jump the ditch. I suggest we go together, side by side, ostensibly so that I can dictate the pace at which we go, but really because I don't want him bringing me down if he falls again.

So we're down to the first again and your man is drilling this horse down to the fence, he still hasn't learned, and he nearly falls out over him again.

'Look, just leave the horse alone at the next,' I shout over to him. 'Just sit on top of him and let him do it himself.'

We approach the second fence.

'Just sit still!'

Not a bit of it. He drills his horse into the fence again, same result, the horse clobbers the fence and your man is arse over tits out over him and lands flat on his back on the ground.

This is in the middle of winter now, it's after racing, it's getting dark and it's cold and wet and your man is covered in shit from head to toe, the horse is plastered in mud, and I'm thinking, ah look I can't be doing with this. I'm thinking we'd be best to call it a day, but I hadn't done enough with Go Ballistic, John had brought him to Southwell and he was going to learn nothing from it. So I ask your man is he all right, he says he is. I'm thinking he's not really, but he's saying he is. He scrambles back up on to the horse.

'What do you want to do?' I ask him.

'I think we should start at this one,' he says, 'then jump the ditch and carry on around to the home straight.'

'Right,' I say. 'Just stay upsides me and we'll just go steady until we get over these two and then we'll go a bit quicker in the straight. And look, this time, whatever you do, don't move on the horse, just be a passenger, just put your finger in the neck strap and sit up there.'

'Ok, ok, I'll do that.'

Down to the first, Go Ballistic jumps it really well, but your man can't help himself, he can't sit still, so I let a roar at him: 'Just sit still!' The horse gets over it in a fashion. The next is the ditch and I can see him out of the corner of my eye. I'm trying to concentrate on what I'm doing, my job is to get Go Ballistic jumping, yet my main concern is this guy beside me who is trying to kill himself and as many other humans and horses as he can bring with him. He's kicking him into it like he's Billy the Kid, and I'm thinking, oh no. Same thing, hits the fence full pelt, down he goes, arms and legs and hooves everywhere, and I'm thinking fuck this, I'm not stopping, so I just kept going all the way around, jump the three in the straight and pull up. John is there waiting.

'What happened?' he asks.

'I'm sorry John,' I say. 'I couldn't stop again. I think the young lad is all right though.'

The horse comes galloping up past us without a rider and they send a car back to get the young lad. He's a bit shaken but otherwise he's fine. Confidence and pride dented a little, perhaps, but all limbs intact.

'This horse jumped quite well,' I said to John, 'but I won't be putting my name down beside your man's for a couple of months.'

It was great to get to ride Go Ballistic in the 1997 Grand National. I had ridden him in races plenty of times before that, and he was really well handicapped on his Gold Cup run – similar to Rough Quest the previous year – but, even though they put him in as the 7-1 favourite, I was a bit concerned about how he would take to the fences.

I was in the weigh room getting ready for the National, having my cap tied by my valet, when the fire alarm went off. There was no major panic, fire alarms go off in all kinds of different places all the time and nobody take a blind bit of notice. I continued psyching myself up until a fire officer came into the weigh room and asked us to leave. I just ambled out with the other lads, everyone assuming that we'd be back in a minute or two. But it wasn't just a run-of-the-mill fire alarm or drill. It turned out that, just before the Aintree Hurdle was run, there had been a bomb warning received at Liverpool Hospital using a recognised IRA code word. We weren't allowed get our cars or change our clothes or anything, we were just all ushered out of the weigh room and off the track.

So there I was, out in the street, in my breeches and silks, no money, no car keys, I didn't even have a coat. At least we were all in the same boat, all the jockeys. Suddenly it hit me – my dad! Where the hell was he? Obviously all our plans to meet after racing were redundant, he didn't have a mobile phone so I had no way of contacting him. He could have been anywhere. We had checked out of our hotel that morning, so I had no idea how or when I would get to see him again. He probably had had a good few pints already, he could have been meandering around the course or the streets, he could have been anywhere, he was probably half-pissed somewhere, happy out, couldn't care less about bomb scares or anything. I just hoped he would be all right.

All the jockeys ended up going to this house that wasn't far from the racecourse. One of the lads from the racecourse knew the woman who owned the house, Edi Roche, so he said we'd go up there, it would be nice and quiet, and we'd have a drink. It seemed like everybody who was racing that day knew Edi Roche. It was jammers. You could hardly get in the door. So there we are, all struggling in, battling through the masses, dying for a drink. I struggle in the door, through a load of bodies, into the sitting room to where the drink is and, lo and behold, who is serving the drink, no fuss, my old man! Frank Fitzgerald, barman. He looked at me.

'All right?'

I burst out laughing. Typical of my old man, landing on his feet, just getting on with things. What crisis? He took a drink for himself and sat down.

We went into town that evening, into the nightclub in the Adelphi Hotel. Nobody really knew what had happened, if there had really been a bomb, and nobody had a clue what was going to happen with the Grand National. We were certain that it wasn't going to be run on the Sunday, so we all let our hair down a bit. I had won the Aintree Hurdle, so I was in celebratory mode. I'd been sweating my insides out to get down to ten stone, so I figured, what the hell, I deserve it, I'll go on a bit of a lash. I hadn't a clue where I was going to stay or what was going to happen the following day, I didn't really care, I was out on the town.

We must have been some sight, all the jockeys in a nightclub, bopping away in our gear, getting pissed, trying it on with birds, the works. Jamie Osborne went outside to look for a taxi and this scouser walked past, stopped, looked at him and said: 'Just getting home from work, are you?'

I crashed in a room in the Adelphi that night, and got up the next day to learn that the race was going to be run on the Monday, the following day. So I stood on the scales, oh dear, this is going to be a long day.

I managed to get back down to 10st 3lb, which wasn't a bad effort given Saturday night's excesses. Actually, because Master Oats was in the race keeping the weights down, a lot of horses were set to carry the minimum weight of ten stone. It was standing room only in the sauna on Monday morning. Nine of the jockeys had to put up overweight. Spot the ones who were in the Adelphi on Saturday night. Go Ballistic shit himself, he was scared out of his wits at the size of the fences, and I pulled him up before the second-last. He actually broke a blood vessel, but he was never travelling anyway. Dobbs won the race on Lord Gyllene, good man Dobbs.

\*

Every Christmas when Jane and I were together, from 1992 to 2001, I went down to Devon with her to spend Christmas Day with her and her family. There was never a question of me flying back to Ireland for Christmas. It was too risky. The post-Christmas period is one of the most important times on the National Hunt racing calendar, and I would never have risked flights being cancelled or boats being delayed back from Ireland for fear of missing rides in the King George or the Welsh Grand National or in other high-profile races.

It wasn't really a big deal for me, missing Christmas with my family. In fact, I haven't been at home with mam and dad for Christmas since I left home in 1987. We're close as a family, but special occasions were never that big a deal. My birthday comes and goes in May, I might get a birthday card or I might not, and if I did it would usually be late. It never bothered me. We just don't go in for those sorts of things as a family, it doesn't mean we think any less of each other.

I loved going down to Moreleigh. There was such a nice atmosphere in Jane's family home, real family-oriented, very relaxed, and there would always be a good group of us there. Paul Nicholls used to come down with Bridget when they were still together, and Jane's parents were great, and her father's brother Ian and a couple of friends of the family would be there as well. It would just all be a good laugh. I would be watching my weight, but I would always eat Christmas dinner, at least a little bit.

On Boxing Day 1997, I finished third in the King George on Rough Quest, and I won the Feltham Chase on Fiddling The Facts. Terry Casey had done a great job to get Rough Quest back to the racecourse, but he was getting on at that stage, he was almost 12, and third in a King George behind See More Business was just about as good as he was. Fiddling The Facts was one of the stars at Seven Barrows at the time, and she battled on really well to beat Forest Ivory in the Feltham. She was tough, almost like a gelding masquerading as a mare.

We had high hopes for her but, remarkably and regrettably, that was the last race she ever won. She would go on to be third in two Hennessys and second in a Welsh National, but she never won a race after that Feltham Chase. She was going well in the Royal & SunAlliance Chase at Cheltenham that season when she clouted a fence going up the hill on the far side, and I had to pull her up.

There weren't many highlights during the 1997-98 season, but there were a few. Sharpical winning the Tote Gold Trophy in February was a huge one. Newbury is Nicky's local track and he always likes to have winners there. The Hennessy and the Tote Gold Trophy are the two big National Hunt races run at Newbury and, before Sharpical, Nicky hadn't won either of them.

Sharpical was talented but he was a tricky bugger. We had tried him in blinkers on his previous run in the Ladbroke Hurdle at Leopardstown the previous month, and he had gone well. My plan in the Tote Gold Trophy was to drop him out, make ground steadily through the field and not allow him to hit the front until well after we had jumped the final flight. It was very easy in the end. I arrived at the last with a double handful, but I held on to him behind Kerawi until about halfway up the run-in. Go on! I gave him his head and he quickened away to win impressively.

I won the BMW Chase at the Punchestown Festival on Big Matt that year. That was big as well, it was great to go back home to Ireland and ride a big winner, and it was great for Nicky. He loved Punchestown and he needed a bit of a tonic after a terrible Cheltenham. Barna Boy was fourth in the County Hurdle – of course I rode him this time – and that was about as close as I got at the Festival, so it was good to ride a Grade 1 winner at Punchestown.

I rode Rough Quest in the Grand National and he ran his heart out. It was bottomless ground that year and it took an awful lot of getting. Only six of the 37 horses completed the course, and Rough Quest wasn't one of them. He travelled like a dream throughout, jumped really well, loved the place, but he just began to get tired after we jumped the Canal Turn second time. I held him together until the home turn, but by then we were miles behind Earth Summit and Suny Bay, who were duelling up front, and he was out on his feet, so I figured there was no point in trying to make him jump the last two fences. I pulled him up before the second-last, but he had done himself proud.

Sharpical and Big Matt and Fiddling The Facts were nice horses, they were talented animals, but they fell some way short of the Remittance Mans and the Travados and the Raymylettes of the world. It was a hugely competitive environment. Martin Pipe was flying, David Nicholson was part of the old brigade, still hugely successful, and Paul Nicholls was just getting going.

Even so, I stayed focused on my career. I focused on improving my riding, increasing my understanding of horses, I studied form and re-runs of races all night. I was doing a lot lighter weights in those days than I was towards the end of my career, and I was struggling to do them, with the result that I used to spend a lot of time wasting. When you are doing light, wasting a lot and not eating, when you are trying to maintain your body at a weight that is significantly lighter than its natural weight, you are generally more irritable than you are when you are able to eat what you like.

I certainly wasn't making any time for Jane. My marriage was actually one of the last things for which I was prepared to make time. I'd get home from racing and get into the bath and have a sweat. Jane would be up early the following morning so she would be in bed early. I would stay up watching replays of the day's racing, going through the following day's runners, so by the time I'd get to bed Jane would be asleep. Then I'd be up in the morning, ride work, whatever, go racing, and it would be the same thing all over again. I was on the go all the time, so we actually didn't see much of each other. We didn't make time for each other.

I was riding a horse at Plumpton on October 19, 1998, a horse called Hippios for Simon Dow in a claiming hurdle. It was a poor race, Hippios was a poor horse, he hadn't managed to win a race in 18 previous attempts, but I was at the meeting anyway and I said I'd ride it. I didn't get too far. Coming up to the first flight of hurdles, Hippios decided that he didn't fancy it and he jammed on the brakes. There was a horse coming behind us called Sweet Amoret, ridden by Robert Massey, who had a massive head. If there was a prize going for a horse with the biggest head, I have no doubt that this monster would have won it. So my fellow is jamming on the brakes, doesn't fancy jumping the hurdle, even though Simon had assured me beforehand that the horse had schooled well, and there's this massive head coming behind me. He butts me, hits me in the back with his head like a ram on one of those Disney cartoons, knocks me clean off my horse, over the hurdle and, I'm not exaggerating, about 20 yards the far side.

I'm lying on the ground there and I'm gasping for air. I literally can't breathe. I have a massive pain in my back but, more than that, I literally can't draw a breath. So I'm lying there, like a fish out of water, thinking, ok, you need to breathe now, any time soon, you need to draw a breath, but I can't. Eventually I manage to squeeze some air into my lungs as the paramedics arrive. 'Are you all right?' Give me a second so that I can breathe and then I'll tell you if I'm all right. No I'm not. Broken ribs is the diagnosis, another couple of weeks on the sidelines.

Things began to look up a bit after that. I rode Katarino to win a juvenile hurdle at Newbury in November, and I rode him to win the good juvenile hurdle at Cheltenham's November meeting four days later. Actually, we were lucky to get Katarino. I was at Nicky's schooling one day and Nicky shows me this little horse.

'He just arrived yesterday from France,' said Nicky. 'Anthony Bromley bought him for Robert Waley-Cohen, said he was a nice horse, said he was big enough. He said he was 16 hands.

'But that thing is not 15 hands! He told me that it finished third in a chase at Auteuil, but sure it wouldn't be able to look out over the fences here. It's too small, it's no good to me. Give it a school there and see what you think.'

There was no mix-up with horses or anything, this was the horse that Bromley had bought for Robert, he just thought that he was bigger. He said afterwards that he was pissed when he went to see the horse, but he did think he was bigger.

I took this little horse up over the schooling hurdles and he was electric. 'Don't send this back whatever you do,' I said to Nicky when I pulled up. 'This is a little machine of a thing.'

Phonsie O'Brien, the legendary Vincent O'Brien's brother, used to say that if size had anything to do with speed, an elephant would outrun a rabbit, and so Katarino proved. He would go on to win the Triumph Hurdle at Cheltenham that season and he would follow up by winning the champion four-year-old hurdle at Punchestown. Not only that, but in his later years, he carried Robert Waley-Cohen's son Sam over the big Grand National fences to win the Fox Hunters' Chase at Aintree twice, in 2005 and 2006, and to finish second in it in 2008 as a 13-year-old. He was just an amazing horse. To look at him there at Nicky's that morning, you would never have thought that he would have ever been able to climb over one of the big Aintree fences, never mind win over them.

I also won on Stormyfairweather at that Cheltenham November meeting as well as on Katarino, and some of Nicky's young horses were beginning to show a fair degree of promise. I was starting to ride a bit for Paul Nicholls as well. Timmy Murphy had been his stable jockey the previous season, but things hadn't gone too smoothly for them as a partnership, a fact that was highlighted, I suppose, by See More Business being carried out in the 1998 Gold Cup. There was nothing that Timmy could have done about it, he couldn't have avoided it the way it happened, but it didn't help the relationship and, probably under pressure from some of his owners, Paul had let Timmy go at the end of the season.

I was offered the job as stable jockey with Paul then, but Paul Nicholls then was not Paul Nicholls now. He didn't have a top-class horse poking his nose over every stable door. There was no Denman, no Kauto Star, no Master Minded, no Neptune Collonges. He did have some good horses, but so did Nicky, and I loved working with Nicky. It would have taken a crowbar to prize me away from Nicky's, and Paul didn't have one.

Joe Tizzard was installed as stable jockey at Paul's, but Joe was young and lacking in experience for the really big races. He was being asked to shoulder huge responsibility. So Paul would ask me to ride some of the higher-profile horses sometimes when my commitments to Nicky allowed, and that suited me great.

I rode four winners at Kempton on Boxing Day. That was amazing. One of the biggest days on the calendar, and I win four of the six races – Grecian Dancer in the opener, the novice hurdle, Serenus in the handicap hurdle, Eagles Rest in the two-mile novice chase, and Melody Maid in the handicap hurdle.

I didn't have a ride in the Feltham Chase won by Lord Of The River, so my only losing ride on the day was on Imperial Call, who finished third to Teeton Mill in the King George, but there was even a silver lining in that. The horse ran well, he just didn't fully stay the distance for me on the testing ground. More importantly, I was delighted to have been asked by Fergie Sutherland to ride him in front of a host of other top jockeys.

I always wanted to be up there with the Dunwoodys and Maguires and Osbornes and Swans for those top spare rides that invariably came up. I wanted to be among those jockeys, I wanted to be thought of as one of those. Maybe now I was. One more rung up the ladder.

# CHAPTER 16

## TOP OF THE WORLD

I loved Get Real. He was one of those horses who would have walked through a wall for you. He was a monster of a horse, a fantastic jumper, and he'd give you every sinew of energy that he had in his body, then he'd go back and check to see if he had more if you wanted more. Unfortunately, he only just stayed two miles, the minimum distance for any National Hunt race, and he had to go right-handed, and those two factors prevented him from being a truly top-class horse.

Get Real loved Ascot. Even though Ascot has an uphill finish, he was at his best when he was winging over the Ascot fences, and I really fancied him for the Victor Chandler Chase to be run there in January 1999. I thought that he was well handicapped, he was going to be racing right-handed at his favourite track, and he was going to have a lovely racing weight of around 10st 1lb or 10st 2lb. We got to Ascot, fog and frost, we couldn't race, so they postponed the race until the following week. Two bad things about that – the race was switched to Kempton, where Get Real wasn't as proficient, and it allowed Paul Nicholls to enter Call Equiname, a lightly-raced grey horse who hadn't been in the original race at Ascot.

Get Real ran his heart out in that Victor Chandler, as he always did. He led from early, jumped brilliant and I asked him to kick on again at the top of the home straight, which he did. But Chocolate Thornton on this grey horse came at us and took it up from us on the stands' side over the last. Once he did, however, he began to idle. Get Real rallied, stuck his head out and battled, and I'm sure he actually got his head in front again, but once Call Equiname was passed again, he came back at us and won by a neck.

I was thinking that it was a good performance by the winner. He was giving us about a stone, he looked big enough, in that he would improve for the run and, although he only beat us by a neck, he did idle in front, so he probably had a fair amount more in hand over us than the winning margin suggested.

Charlie Mann's horse Celibate finished third in that race. Charlie wasn't long training, and I was riding a few for him. I had ridden Celibate to finish second to Arthur Moore's horse Jeffell in the Victor Chandler Chase the previous year. I quite liked Celibate, he was a decent honest-to-God horse, but he was always lacking the gears to be a truly top-class two-mile chaser. Even so, I had committed to riding him for Charlie in the Queen Mother Champion Chase that year. Nicky didn't have a championship two-mile chaser for Cheltenham. Get Real was the closest he had, but he had to go right-handed and Cheltenham is left-handed, so he was skipping Cheltenham and going to Punchestown instead, so I was happy to commit to Celibate.

A couple of days before the Game Spirit Chase in February, Celibate's last intended run before Cheltenham, Charlie rang me.

'Woody has been on,' he said. 'He wants to ride Celibate in the Game Spirit.'

'I thought I was riding Celibate,' I said, a little taken aback at what might be coming. Woody was riding a lot for Charlie as well at the time, they were quite good friends.

'You are, you are,' said Charlie, 'but you've got to promise me that you'll ride him in the Champion Chase as well.'

'I will,' I said. 'Of course I will.' What else was I going to ride?

'Ok,' said Charlie, 'you ride him so.'

We won the Game Spirit. It was a fine performance by Celibate. Ask Tom and Mulligan set a fast pace, which we just sat off, we took it up early in the home straight and Celibate battled on tenaciously to withstand the late renewed challenge of Adrian Maguire on Mulligan, who was back for more after having disputed the lead early.

I was delighted. That run put Celibate right into the Champion Chase mix. The Game Spirit Chase is the last real trial for Champion Chase aspirants before Cheltenham, so it was a good one to win. Celibate loved Cheltenham, he had won there twice before and finished third in an

Arkle, so I was quite hopeful about his chances. A phone call from Paul Nicholls on the Saturday evening before Cheltenham changed all that though.

Joe Tizzard was getting on ok at Paul's but not brilliantly. It was hard for him, it's hard for any young jockey to establish himself in a top yard. The owners pay the bills and they often want the best jockeys available. Why would you have an unproven youngster ride your horse in a race when Dunwoody was sitting in the weigh room? It can be difficult for the trainer to remain loyal to the stable jockey.

'What do you ride in the Champion Chase?' Paul asked me.

'I ride Celibate, why?' I answered.

'Will you ride Call Equiname?'

Now Celibate is one thing, a fine honest horse who could run well, but Call Equiname was quite another, a really progressive two-mile chaser with speed to burn who had put up a hell of a performance under a big weight in the Victor Chandler and who would probably improve significantly for that run. He would nearly be favourite for the Champion Chase. Celibate would have been at least a division below him. I didn't even have to think about it.

'Ok I'll ride him.'

Then I had to figure out how I was going to break the news to Charlie. Three days before Cheltenham, four days before the Champion Chase, and I'm ringing him to tell him that I'm not going to ride his horse, after me telling him that I would. I didn't feel proud of myself, it wasn't a nice thing to be doing, and I certainly wasn't looking forward to that phone call. I made it the following morning, Sunday morning.

'Charlie I'm really sorry,' I said, 'but I can't ride Celibate in the Champion Chase.'

'Why not?'

'Paul has asked me to ride Call Equiname and I'm going to ride him instead.' There was no point in beating around the bush.

'You fucking wanker,' said Charlie with feeling. Obviously Charlie didn't believe in beating around the bush either. Say what you feel Charlie.

'I'm really sorry Charlie,' I said meekly, 'but I think he'll win.'

'Ah fuck you,' he said. 'You'll never ride for me again.'

With that he put the phone down. Just hung up on me. I've had birds hang up on me before, but I think that was the first time a bloke had ever hung up on me. He was well within his rights, but this was just too good an opportunity for me to turn down. The Champion Chase is one of the five majors of National Hunt racing. Where golf has Augusta and tennis has Wimbledon, in National Hunt racing it's the Gold Cup, the Grand National, the King George, the Champion Hurdle and the Champion Chase. If you get a shot at winning one of those races, you have to grab it with both hands and make the most of it. I thought that Call Equiname could have been the best two-mile chaser in training. To turn down the opportunity to ride him in the top two-mile chase in the country would have been crazy. I hoped that Charlie would understand. I didn't expect that he would immediately, but in time I hoped that he would see it from my point of view.

Paul Nicholls was just beginning the metamorphosis into the champion trainer that he is today. He had never had a winner at the Cheltenham Festival before, but it looked like he was sending a strong team that year, Call Equiname was going to be nearly favourite for the Champion Chase, Flagship Uberalles was going to be nearly favourite for the Arkle and he had two in the Gold Cup, Double Thriller and See More Business, who had been carried out the previous year.

As stable jockey, Joe Tizzard had the choice in the Gold Cup. It was strange that he had the choice in the Gold Cup, and that he was set to ride Flagship Uberalles in the Arkle, but he was being jocked off Call Equiname in the Champion Chase, although he had never ridden him in a race before, so you probably couldn't really call it being jocked off. Perhaps they just felt that Call Equiname was a trickier ride and maybe needed someone with more experience. You couldn't hit the front too soon on him, they saw how he tried to pull himself up at Kempton, and maybe they thought that Joe might not have the balls or the experience to hold him up until the last possible moment. There was a big bonus going for winning the Victor Chandler and the Champion Chase, and Colin

Lewis, one of the co-owners, was having a few quid on as well, so maybe they just wanted to maximise their chances.

Joe chose Double Thriller in the Gold Cup. He was the logical choice, he was lightly raced and progressive, an ex-hunter chaser, he had won both of his starts under rules by a distance, and he was a lot shorter than See More Business in the ante-post market. See More appeared to be going the other way. He had been pulled up when favourite for the King George earlier that season, and he had been well beaten by Cyfor Malta in the Pillar Property on his latest run.

After Joe had committed to Double Thriller, Paul asked me if I would ride See More Business – it was better than watching the race from the weigh room – and I went down to Paul's place at Ditcheat to school the horse a couple of weeks before Cheltenham. I couldn't believe it when I got on him. He was a small, narrow little horse, you were almost chewing his ears when you were sitting on him, he was a horrible little thing, not at all what I imagined he would be.

When I got there, Paul told me that they were thinking of trying him in blinkers. Let's have a look. I schooled him over three fences without blinkers first, two plain fences and a ditch. He kicked the two plain fences out of his way, just walked through them, but he jumped the ditch really well. They put the blinkers on him then, I gave him a couple of cracks around his arse and we went again, jumped the same three fences, and he winged them, all three of them.

Paul Barber and John Keighley, the joint-owners, were there watching with Paul Nicholls. I came back in and told them that they had to put blinkers on him, that he was like a different horse in blinkers. John Keighley wouldn't hear of it. There is a bit of a stigma attached to blinkers. You see a pair of blinkers on a horse and you immediately think that it is ungenuine, that there is something wrong with it mentally, that it doesn't want to go on past horses. John didn't want to put the badge of ungenuineness on See More Business. He had won a King George for them, he had been a great servant, and the last thing he wanted was for the horse to suffer the ignominy of having to wear blinkers. I didn't get it. With blinkers, he would have a genuine chance of going close in the Gold

Cup, without them he might as well be at home in his box. I told Paul as much afterwards.

'Leave it with me,' Paul said.

I don't know what Paul said to John, but when I went to ride See More in a racecourse gallop at Wincanton the week before Cheltenham, there he was kitted out in a brand spanking new shiny pair of blinkers. He felt great. Paul Barber was there.

'If this thing jumps,' I said to him, 'I'm telling you it will not be out of the money.'

I was getting quite excited about my book of rides at Cheltenham. It had been three years since I had last been led into the winner's enclosure at the Cheltenham Festival on Rough Quest after winning the Ritz, and I had missed that feeling. I desperately wanted to experience that feeling again, just one winner at the Festival, I would have given up all my other rides for just one winner, just to get back into that winner's enclosure.

I drew a blank on the first day. Makounji in the Arkle was my best ride on that day. She had won her last three races before Cheltenham, including the Pendil Chase at Kempton, which is often a good pointer to the Arkle. But she just ran far too freely in her first-time blinkers and I ended up pulling her up before the second-last. It later transpired that she was in season, but she was no world-beater anyway. Flagship Uberalles won the race doing handsprings. That was great for Paul and Joe. I did finish second on Melody Maid for Nicky in the final race of the day, the Stakis Casinos Final, but we were never really in with a chance of winning.

March 17, 1999, St Patrick's Day, Champion Chase day. In the race before the Champion Chase, the Royal & SunAlliance Hurdle, the first race on the day, I finished second behind Barton on Artadoin Lad for Jenny Pitman. Again, I was never in with a realistic chance of winning the race. Barton was head and shoulders above everything else in it. I hoped this wasn't going to be a week of nearly.

Call Equiname felt brilliant on the way to the start for the Champion Chase. I had never sat on him before, I hadn't schooled him when I was down at Paul's. He was a fragile beast, he had glass legs and they found out later on that he had a fibrillating heart. But he could travel, he could jump and he had speed to burn.

If Cheltenham is the Olympics of National Hunt racing, the Champion Chase is the 100-metres final. Two miles is the sprint distance of National Hunt racing, you go almost flat out from beginning to end. Everything happens so fast, you have to fence accurately and quickly, one mistake and it is impossible to recover, you have to travel well and you have to be able to quicken up the hill at the end of it all.

Call Equiname was electric. AP McCoy made the running on Edredon Bleu, Henrietta Knight's horse, who had won the Grand Annual the previous season. I just sat still on Call Equiname and let the race develop in front of me. He travelled and jumped so well that I just left everything to him. I got up the inside of Joe Tizzard on Paul's other horse Green Green Desert going around the home turn and that left us just behind Edredon Bleu going down to the last. I was probably there too soon, but the horse had been travelling and jumping so well, and the gaps had appeared, we had just got there with no effort.

I sat in AP's slipstream when we straightened up for home, then pulled Call Equiname off the rail on the approach to the final fence so that he could have a clear view of the obstacle. That was a good feeling, sitting on AP's outside, me motionless, taking a pull even, him as animated as a Tasmanian Devil. We were almost upsides at the last, but we got in a little tight, landed flat-footed and suddenly we were a length and a half down. Direct Route and Norman Williamson came up on my outside. I hadn't wanted to get there too soon, Paul had said take it up halfway up the run-in, no earlier, I hadn't wanted to wing the last and land in front, but suddenly, from coasting into the last fence we now had a big battle on our hands.

I went for my horse and, thankfully, he responded. He picked up impressively to keep Direct Route at bay on our outside and then went and picked up Edredon Bleu on our inside. We got to the front a hundred yards out, which was perfect, and I just kept him going to get home by a length and a quarter. I punched the air, just to myself, not a big exuberant yee-hah for the cameras. It wasn't a punch for the cameras or the stands, it was just an outward expression of my inner feelings. Yes!

Strange thing, I often think that too much is made of the jockey at times in the celebration of a win. You are the contact point between the punters and the horse. The jockey almost always receives more adulation than the horse, and surely that isn't right. That is the main reason why I never went in for these histrionics when I rode a winner, even a big winner. I don't get these Christophe Soumillon antics, the waving to the crowd and all that carry on. What's that all about? Most of his winners are steering jobs anyway. It's not like he is the one who has run his lungs out or dragged his bollocks over 24 fences. How difficult can it be driving a Ferrari against a Mini? How difficult can it be for a Ferrari to beat a Mini in a straight line? Yet you don't see many Ferrari drivers whoop-whooping out the window when they go past. One of these days, a horse is going to jink and Soumillon or one of the others is going to go flying before the winning line and lose the race or, worse still, get injured.

I couldn't stop smiling as I was led back in. Back down the chute in front of the grandstand, up the walkway between the racecourse and the parade ring, into the parade ring and down the middle of it, down through the hordes and on into that golden circle, the winner's enclosure at Cheltenham, with the crowds packed deep on the steps behind creating that amphitheatre of sound, a gladiator returned. When we got into the circle I punched the air again, the crowd cheered, they were cheering for us, for me and Call Equiname, not for Richard Dunwoody, not for Conor O'Dwyer.

You won't find many sad people in the winner's enclosure at Cheltenham. Paul was on cloud nine. Flagship Uberalles was brilliant for him, but Call Equiname was his banker at the meeting so he was over the moon about this one. As well as that, the Arkle is a great race to win, but this was the Champion Chase. Different gravy.

After the presentation and the photographs, and the interviews with Channel 4 and the radio stations and the journalists, I was walking back into the weigh room, ear-to-ear grin still on my face, when I met Charlie Mann. I didn't know what to say to him. Dunwoody had ridden Celibate in the race, but he was never a factor. Charlie spoke before I could.

'I suppose you were right,' he said. 'Well done.'

It was very magnanimous of him. Fair play to Charlie. And I did ride for him again.

At the beginning of the week, I would have settled for one winner, no question. When I looked at my book of rides beforehand, I looked for the horse who was most likely to provide me with that winner. It's so difficult to ride even one winner at Cheltenham, it's so competitive, I knew it well having drawn a blank for the previous two years. There were only 20 races at the Festival then, and three of them were restricted to amateur riders, so you could only ride in a maximum of 17 races as a professional. You hoped for one winner at the beginning of the week, that was all. If you hoped for any more, you were just being greedy.

But after you have one winner, after you have entered the record books as the jockey who has ridden the winner of one of the races, you do get greedy, you look for another one. They can't take that winner away from you, it's in the bag, worst-case scenario you go home with one winner, so then you look for the next. It's like everything in life, the more you have the more you want. I had some very good rides on the final day of the Festival, Katarino was favourite for the Triumph Hurdle, See More Business had a chance of sorts in the Gold Cup, we quite fancied Stormyfairweather to run a big race in the Cathcart Chase, and Premier Generation had a better chance than most in the County Hurdle, so I was beginning to feel a little greedy.

Katarino wasn't a slow horse, but he was timid in those days, he didn't like being crowded, so I wanted to bounce him out and race handy, but Nicky was adamant that I shouldn't. He reckoned that it wasn't possible to make all in a Triumph Hurdle. So I jumped off among them and he never travelled. He wasn't carrying me and he hit the first flight, with the result that I had to get after him going away from the stands with a circuit to run. I was sure there was something wrong with the horse, but there wasn't, it was just that he didn't like being in there among the others.

We were still well behind at the second-last, but Ruby Walsh kicked for home on Balla Sola, and once Katarino got in the clear with no other horses around him and got out after Ruby, he began to pick up. It was amazing. He winged the last and devoured the hill, he caught and passed

Balla Sola and had put eight lengths of ground between us and the runner-up by the time we reached the line. This was amazing, my second winner of this meeting, my fourth at the Cheltenham Festival. I was delighted for Nicky and for owner Robert Waley-Cohen. It was only my second winner for Nicky at Cheltenham, my first since Raymylette, this was great stuff.

I was still on a high from the Triumph Hurdle when Paul gave me the leg-up on See More Business before the Gold Cup an hour later. He felt great going down to the start in his blinkers, just took a nice tug. He travelled great through the race, and jumped more than adequately for him. I had to get after him a bit on the way down the hill going to the third-last. My old mate Go Ballistic had gone on under Tony Dobbin at that stage and Dunwoody was cruising on Florida Pearl. See More Business picked up.

We turned for home and headed down to the second-last. I sat down to drive See More on. Dunwoody got lower in the saddle on Florida Pearl, but I noticed that he didn't pick up as well as it looked like he would. When we jumped the second-last See More Business began to get stronger. He had such an engine, there was nothing flashy about him, he just put his head down and galloped. Florida Pearl wilted on the inside, he had no more left to give. The only two things between me and winning the Gold Cup were in front of me – the final fence and Go Ballistic. I looked over to my left at Dobbs on Go Ballistic: 'Well I'll beat you anyway.'

We jumped the last almost as one, me and Dobbs, See More Business and Go Ballistic, but the momentum was with us. Go Ballistic had been in front for a while and he was coming towards the end of the line. He never really enjoyed being in front. See More Business was just getting going, he was just moving into overdrive. It took us a little while to get past Go Ballistic, but we always had his measure, we were always going to beat him. I could barely believe it. This was the Gold Cup, we were climbing the hill to the winning line in the Gold Cup. We were a neck up now, now a half a length, the roar from the grandstand was deafening, the roar from deep down inside my gut was louder. The Gold Cup. Incredible.

It is difficult to compare that feeling with the feeling that I had when I won the Grand National, but I'm sure that it was better. This was the pinnacle for me. For other jockeys it is the Grand National, it was the Grand National that they watched when they were kids, it is the Grand National winners that are etched in their childhood memories, it was the Grand National that they were winning when they were playing in the fields at home, but for me it was always the Gold Cup. The Grand National is a handicap, any horse can win it, but the Gold Cup is the purists' race, it is the race for the best staying steeplechasers in the world, and it is usually won by the best horse in the race on the day. Ask any racing enthusiast who the best steeplechaser of all time was, and he will tell you, Arkle. Triple Gold Cup hero Arkle. He won't tell you that it was triple Grand National winner Red Rum. Red Rum was a Grand National freak, an Aintree phenomenon, but Arkle was the best there has ever been.

I was floating. If you had asked me when I was 16 what would the pinnacle of my career be if I could achieve it, I would have said winning a Gold Cup, and here I was, Gold Cup winner, back into that sanctified winner's enclosure. People have dreams, aspirations that don't come within screaming distance of what had just become reality for me. It is difficult to describe. Think of something that you would wish for if you happened upon a genie, something that is so far removed from reality that it is almost embarrassing to tell somebody that you wish for it to happen. Scoring the winning penalty in an FA Cup final? Sinking the putt that wins the Ryder Cup for Europe? Well, that was winning the Gold Cup for me. That was how good this was. Really it was. You couldn't say that it was the realisation of a childhood ambition, because ambition implies that you think that there is a reasonable chance of it happening, it was more the realisation of a dream. This was dreamtime.

There is a picture of me coming into the winner's enclosure that hangs in my hallway in which my expression, I think, gives some kind of indication as to how I am feeling. Ecstatic beyond belief.

My head was still spinning when I went out to ride Stormyfairweather in the Cathcart. I didn't really appreciate it at the time, but I was leading rider for the Festival up to that point with three winners. McCoy and

Williamson both had two, but they had a fancied ride each in the last two races, McCoy was riding second favourite Potentate in the Cathcart and Williamson was riding the favourite Decoupage in the County Hurdle. None of this had really registered with me. I had just won the Gold Cup and everything else was secondary, anything else was a bonus.

I rode Stormyfairweather with the confidence that comes from sitting on top of the world. It was an unbelievable feeling, the feeling of near invincibility. I went out knowing I was going to win the race, I rode him knowing I was going to win it, I kicked him off in front, winged just about every fence, never saw another rival, and came home in front. To this day I still haven't seen a recording of the race. I never watched the winners, I only ever watched the losers and tried to learn. I rode him for all I was worth up the hill, and we got home by two lengths from Robbie Supple on Niki Dee.

This was surreal. My fourth time into the winner's enclosure at one Cheltenham Festival, my third time that day. They didn't make dreams like this. Another winner at Cheltenham for me, another for Nicky. That win ensured that I would be crowned top jockey at the 1999 Festival. As well as that, Channel 4 was running a jockeys' competition in which you accumulated points for winning races that they broadcast live, with bonus points going for the big races. The prize was a glass trophy and the use of a Saab for the year. Going into Cheltenham, AP was miles clear, but my four wins meant that I got up and pipped him on the line. Anything that was going, I was winning it.

When I walked back into the weigh room after winning the Cathcart, I was almost embarrassed. All the lads were great, everyone was congratulating me, but it was almost too much. Four winners was almost overkill. The fact that I had been in the winner's enclosure four times meant that there were three fewer lads in there who had experienced that feeling, and I was a bit embarrassed about that. You're taking the piss now Fitzy.

We have a drinks party in the weigh room every year at Cheltenham after the last race, and this year I was the star of the show. The party was just swinging into action when I had a call from Jane that sparked a pang of something, deep down buried under the feeling of immense self-satisfaction, guilt or regret that she wasn't there. She hadn't been at Cheltenham that day, she hadn't wanted to come up, which was as much a reflection on me as it was on her. It was a reflection on our relationship. I wasn't the ideal partner at the time and I certainly wasn't the ideal husband. She didn't feel a part of it, she didn't feel that she should be there. She was working that day instead.

That morning I didn't care whether she went to Cheltenham or not, and I'm sure she knew that. I couldn't have cared less what she did, to be honest. She just wasn't a factor, she was largely irrelevant. I was going to Cheltenham with four good rides on Gold Cup day, and that was massive. What my wife did that day was not even a green dot on my radar.

But that evening I felt that she should be there. Here I was, the hero of the week, top jockey, better than McCoy and Williamson and Maguire and Swan and Dunwoody, more winners at Cheltenham than any other jockey, Gold Cup-winning jockey, Champion Chase-winning jockey, on top of the world, and I felt that Jane should be there, my wife should be there. She was at home on her own as I celebrated. There was something wrong there.

All the lads were going out on the town. I was intending to head out with them, but Jane wasn't happy about it. Eventually I decided that I would go home. The pinnacle of my career and I wasn't going out on the town to celebrate, but something clicked with me, something was wrong. It's strange now looking back on it. I regret not going out that night, I really do, I regret not properly celebrating winning the Gold Cup and riding four winners at Cheltenham. But at the time, I felt that the right thing to do was to go home and be with my wife. The lads couldn't believe it. I left the party, got into my car and drove home.

# CHAPTER 17

## SPECIAL WEEK

I finished off the 1998-99 season with 121 winners. That was my highest total ever and it saw me finish third in the jockeys' championship behind AP McCoy, who rode 186, a moderate total for AP, who has just won his 13th title in a row. Quite incredible.

I never won the jockeys' title, I was never in with a shout of winning it. Of course it would have been nice to win it, but it was never something that I got too worked up about. The jockeys' championship is all about numbers. It is quite remarkable that, since 1980, in almost three decades, there have been just four different champion jockeys in the UK.

Fair play to AP now and Dunwoody and Scudamore and Francome before him, they are all worthy champions, but I never was in a position to ride the number of horses in a season that you need to ride in order to win it. Dunwoody abandoned his roles with Nicky and The Duke, both of whom had some top-class horses, to join Pipe simply so that he would be champion. At that time it was almost a given that whoever rode for Pipe, given the number of runners that he had, would be champion, and being champion was what turned Woody on. I was much more interested in riding top-class horses in top-class races, and there is no way I would have made the move that Woody made.

The first time I rode Marlborough was in a novice chase at Kempton in January 1999. Henry Daly was training him for Sir Robert Ogden at the time. He was a clumsy awkward bugger, a front-runner, to look at him you would think that he should have been a good jumper, but he just did silly things, he probably wasn't the sharpest tool in the box. Henry told me just to let him bowl along in front, which I did. He was cumbersome at a couple of his fences, but he managed to stay upright, and we won easily. I also rode Kingsmark to win the novice hurdle for Sir Robert half

171

an hour beforehand, so it was a good day for me, another good day for me at Kempton.

Bacchanal made his racecourse debut five days later at Huntingdon. We quite liked Bacchanal, who was owned, like Raymylette, by Andrew and Madeleine Lloyd Webber, but I went to Wincanton on the day instead to ride a novice chaser who we thought was nice called Waynflete. Johnny Kavanagh went to Huntingdon to ride Bacchanal, who ran a cracker to finish second.

Johnny is a great lad, he's a really good mate. He was my best man when I got married to Jane. Johnny is as honest a person as you will ever meet, straight down the line, there's no messing with Johnny, and he was a brilliant schooling jockey, one of the best schooling jockeys I've ever seen. He was always focused on getting the horse to jump well, he was always concerned with teaching the horse, with what was best for the horse, he was never looking to find out something new that he could use in a race, or to find out how good the horse was, or just what he would jump, and he never got involved in any antics like racing over the schooling fences. Johnny just did whatever he thought was best for the horse, and he was brilliant at it. He was with Adrian Maguire when Adrian set up training in Ireland for a little while, and he was with the BHA for a time, but he's with Jonjo O'Neill now and he's loving it.

The autumn is an exciting time at Seven Barrows. All the good horses start to come in in August and September, all the novice hurdlers, last year's hurdlers who are going novice chasing, last year's young chasers who are going to be competing in the big league during the coming season. It was always my favourite time of the year, seeing how the horse had progressed, if the youngsters had matured over the summer, schooling the youngsters, riding the class horses from the previous season again, and the autumn of 1999 was particularly exciting.

Bacchanal was there. I had won two novice hurdles on him before the end of the previous season, he had been very good in both even if he was never a real natural jumper of hurdles, but we had taken him to Punchestown in April to run in the Champion Novice Hurdle there, and he had finished lame. He had made a nice recovery over the summer, though, and Nicky was thinking about the Gerry Feilden Hurdle at Newbury's Hennessy meeting in November for him.

Marlborough had joined Nicky from Henry Daly's yard. Sir Robert Ogden and his racing adviser Barry Simpson had had a look at all their trainers and decided that they wanted to have horses with Nicky, so they decided to send Marlborough to him. I was excited about that. He was a bit clueless when it came to jumping fences, he had fallen on his last two runs of the season after I had won on him at Kempton – both times ridden by Woody, including at the final fence in the Reynoldstown Chase at Ascot that day when Woody and I had our little altercation in the weigh room – but I liked him. I thought he was a classy horse who could have been well handicapped if we could get him to jump properly.

Stormyfairweather was back in, Katarino was back – Nicky was preparing him for a Grade 1 hurdle at Auteuil in France in November – and we also had Tiutchev. Tiutchev had been trained by Roger Charlton on the Flat, he had joined Henrietta Knight to go jumping and then he had joined David Nicholson. Adrian couldn't ride him in the Lanzarote Hurdle at Kempton the previous January, so I rode him and won on him. Then they made him favourite for the Tote Gold Trophy at Newbury the following month, 6-4 favourite which was a crazy price in such an open handicap, even though he was 12lb well-in, in theory. Adrian was back on him, but I couldn't have him. I didn't think he had a chance in such a big field and he got well beaten.

Adrian was out injured for that Cheltenham Festival, so The Duke asked me if I would ride Tiutchev in the Champion Hurdle. Nicky didn't have a runner, so I was delighted, but this was during the Istabraq era, nothing had a chance during the Istabraq era, and we did well to get within ten lengths of him. But Tiutchev always shaped like a chaser to me. However good he was over hurdles, I always thought that he would be better over fences.

I got off him in the unsaddling area after the Champion Hurdle and I told the owners that he would win the Arkle the following season if they sent him over fences, and that, if they did, I would love to ride him for them. Next thing I knew, they had sent him to Nicky's. I don't think The Duke was too happy about that.

On top of all of Nicky's horses, I had Call Equiname and See More Business to look forward to that season. Unfortunately, Call Equiname was never the same horse again. They sent him off as favourite for the Murphy's, the feature race at Cheltenham's November meeting, but he was never travelling and he finished distressed. That was it for him really. He did run again in December, but it just wasn't happening for him again, which was a real shame, he was such a talented animal, he had such gears. Horses like him don't come along very often.

By contrast, See More Business was only getting going again, rejuvenated in his blinkers. He ran in the Charlie Hall Chase at Wetherby in October, and he sluiced in, breaking the track record by about five seconds. Looks Like Trouble was our main danger, he was the up-and-coming youngster, trained by Noel Chance. I had actually ridden him to win at Doncaster and Sandown the previous season, but I couldn't ride him in the Royal & SunAlliance Chase at Cheltenham as Nicky ran King's Banker in the race. Paul Carberry came in for the ride, and won on him in a race that was marred by the desperate injury to Edward O'Grady's exciting young staying chaser Nick Dundee.

I had the choice between Looks Like Trouble and See More Business in the Charlie Hall, but I couldn't have deserted the horse who carried me to my first (and only, as it turned out) victory in the Gold Cup. I was never going to get off See More, he was so tough, he just relished his racing. His win in the Charlie Hall meant that he was the first Gold Cup winner to win his next race in years. He put so much into that race that I thought that it would take a lot out of him, that it would take him a while to recover, but not a bit of it. He was as tough as nails, and Paul Nicholls was the right man to train him. Paul worked him hard and the horse thrived on it. To be able to keep him sweet and on song for that long was an amazing training feat.

See More's next race was in the King George at Kempton on Boxing Day 1999, and he was better than ever there. We disputed the lead with Dr Leunt and Double Thriller most of the way, but we were always travelling better than them, and when I urged him on at the end of the back straight the race was over very quickly. He was numb, absolutely numb, he would just keep on galloping, keep on finding more. He galloped on up the home straight, ambled his way over the last three fences and won by 17 lengths, eased down. He was just an unbelievable horse, an absolute beast, and this was an annihilation.

This was another star on my cv, another one of the majors. I had now won the Grand National, the Champion Chase, the Gold Cup and the King George. The only major missing from my trophy cabinet was the Champion Hurdle, and I wasn't yet 30 years of age. No jockey in modern racing has won all five. The Grand National is usually the one that gets them. Francome never won a National, Scudamore never won a National, Jonjo never won a National (actually he never completed the course in eight attempts), AP hasn't won a National yet. Dunwoody won the Grand National twice, and he won the King George, the Gold Cup and the Champion Hurdle, but he never won a Champion Chase. He rode Champion Chase winners Remittance Man, Viking Flagship, Klairon Davis and One Man, but he wasn't on board any of them when they won the Champion Chase.

I was now in a fantastic position to become the first rider to complete the set. Surely I would win a Champion Hurdle before the end of my career.

Sadly, I didn't.

The closest I came was on Blue Royal that season, in 2000, when we finished third behind the ubiquitous Istabraq.

Blue Royal was a remarkable horse, a supremely talented individual. Nicky got him from France for Lynn Wilson and he was dynamite at home. He was a big horse, he was always going to be better over fences, but I thought he was a certainty on his debut for us in a Class 3 juvenile hurdle at Sandown in January 1999. The favourite in the race was Norski Lad, a Paul Nicholls horse who had won four or five handicaps on the Flat for Mark Prescott, and he had won his only race for Nicholls by a distance. I didn't care, I thought our fellow was a machine. We took it up at the second-last, the favourite came at us over the last, then just when I was about to get stuck into my fellow about 100 yards out, I dropped my whip. I couldn't believe it. Even without the whip Blue Royal still rallied and nearly got back up, just went down by a short head. I couldn't believe it, I should have won, but at least it was a good performance and he was only going to get better.

Katarino was our outstanding juvenile hurdler that year, and I thought that Blue Royal would be better than him. Nicky was thinking Triumph Hurdle, but we had Katarino for that, he was much more battle-hardened. There was a danger that a horse as inexperienced as Blue Royal could have got lost in a Triumph Hurdle, he was still a bit weak, and it could ruin him mentally. We decided to hold on to him for Punchestown, Lynn really wanted to have a runner at Punchestown.

I rode him in an egg-and-spoon race at Towcester in early April and he won it doing handsprings at long odds-on. Then we were set for Ireland, not the champion four-year-old hurdle there, but another race, a lesser juvenile hurdle. I phoned Shane Donohoe to tell him to be sure and back this horse at Punchestown. Shane wasn't convinced, he's a little cautious like that.

'Weld has a horse in that race,' he said, 'Francis Bay, who wasn't beaten that far by Balla Sola at Fairyhouse.'

'I don't care,' I said, 'this horse is very good.'

'How can you be so sure?' he asked me.

'Look,' I said. 'Put it like this. If this horse was running in the champion four-year-old hurdle the day before, the Grade 1 race, instead of Katarino, I'd fancy him to win it.'

If Shane wasn't convinced, he was when I won the champion four-year-old hurdle on Katarino. The only problem was that the rest of the world seemed to be convinced as well. They backed him all the way down to 11-8 favourite and we won easily.

We were thinking Tote Gold Trophy for him in 2000. Even though we had won the race before with Sharpical, Nicky was only just beginning to think about handicaps. He was always a conditions race man before then, he was always looking to train horses for the big Graded races in which everyone carried the same weight. To win those big handicaps, you have to play the game, you need to have a couple of pounds in hand. You don't need to do anything dishonest or anything, but you just don't show your full hand. You need to have a horse who is capable of putting in a run that is better than his handicap rating, and to do that you have to make sure that he is unexposed.

Blue Royal was unexposed. He had only run three times for us. Even so, the handicapper gave him a rating of 138, which I thought was fairly harsh for what he had done, for the quality of races that he had won, but I still thought it underestimated his ability considerably. I told Nicky this, I told him that I thought he'd win the Tote Gold Trophy off that mark. He said ok, but he wanted to give him one run first, primarily for the experience but also in order that he might go up a couple of pounds and would be certain to get into the race.

He ran him in a conditions race at Ascot in December 1999. The horse was fit enough to run in a race, but Nicky had left a little bit to work on, a couple of screws that he could tighten before the Tote Gold Trophy. Jim Old ran Sir Talbot in the race, the horse who had won the County Hurdle at Cheltenham that year and was rated 156 as a result. We would have been getting 18lb off him in a handicap, but we were meeting him that day at level weights.

We beat him. Disaster. We beat him by two lengths, easy. It meant that the handicapper was going to have to give Blue Royal a serious hike in the ratings. They started talking about him in terms of the Champion Hurdle after that run, they started quoting prices of 20-1 and 25-1 about him for it. They say that handicappers don't read papers, but they do, and all this talk was doing his handicap mark no good at all.

Nicky tried to dilute some of the talk, he said that he had an awful long way to go before you could begin to think about the Champion Hurdle. I did my bit, I said that he was a chaser in the making, that he wasn't really a hurdler at all. I feared the worst. The handicapper obviously wasn't listening to me or Nicky, and he gave him a new rating of 150, a 12lb hike. Tote Gold Trophy hopes out the window.

Nicky still wanted to run him in the race. He figured that if he was as good as we thought, if he was a Champion Hurdle horse, which we thought he was, he would still have a chance in the race even off a rating of 150. I wasn't so sure, I wasn't so sure that he had enough experience under his belt to cope with the hurly-burly of a Tote Gold Trophy. Nicky was also intending to run Geos in the race, a young horse who was coming through. I loved Geos. He was a little demon, a little terrier. He was always just below top class, but he would later finish fourth in a Champion Chase and a Champion Hurdle.

I had finished third on Geos in the William Hill Handicap Hurdle at Sandown that December, and the handicapper had put him up just 3lb for that. But he wasn't fully fit that day, he needed a lot of work, typical French horse, and I knew that he would come on for it. He then went to Leopardstown and finished second in the Ladbroke Hurdle, but the weights had already been published for the Tote Gold Trophy so the handicapper couldn't put him up any more for that.

'You'll ride Blue Royal, won't you?' Nicky said to me the week before the race.

'I'd like to ride both of them work, if I could,' I said, 'and then decide.'

So I went down to Seven Barrows the Tuesday before the race. I rode Blue Royal in a piece of work first, then I pulled up, got off him, got up on Geos and did a piece of work on him.

'You'll ride Blue Royal now won't you?' said Nicky when I pulled up. He loved Blue Royal. All the lads loved Blue Royal. It wasn't a debate. They were amazed that I was taking so long to make up my mind.

'No,' I said, 'I want to ride the other horse.'

'Are you sure?' he asked, astounded.

'I am.'

'What's wrong with Blue Royal?'

'There's nothing wrong with Blue Royal,' I said. 'It's just that, at this point in time, the way the two horses are progressing, the way the weights are, Blue Royal will have about 12 stone, Geos will have about 11 stone, the way the race will be run, I just prefer Geos.'

'Fair enough,' said Nicky. 'On your head be it.'

The morning of the race, the following Saturday, I was in at Nicky's riding out, as I was almost every Saturday. Saturday was a work morning at Seven Barrows, Tuesday and Saturday, which was unusual. Most yards' work mornings are Tuesday and Friday, because Saturday is such a busy racing day, but Nicky always did fast work on Saturday, we worked the horses who were going to be running the following weekend on the Saturday beforehand. I quite liked that system. It meant that if you had a bad day at the races, you could always drive home thinking about the one you had ridden that morning who was going to be running the following weekend.

Corky Browne, Nicky's head lad, would hardly talk to me that morning.

'You're some fucking eejit.'

He was annoyed with me for not wanting to ride Blue Royal. Corky thought he was the Second Coming. All the lads were slagging me. 'You're on the wrong one Fitzy you know'; 'Nice of you to let Noel Fehily ride the Tote Gold Trophy winner'. Nicky had asked me who he should get to ride Blue Royal, and I recommended Noel, Charlie Mann's claiming rider. He was claiming 5lb at the time, so it meant that Blue Royal would carry just 11st 9lb instead of 12 stone. Those 5lb can be a huge help when a horse has so much weight to carry. He had a real chance off 11st 9lb. I had lingering doubts. I wondered if I had made a big mistake.

I was doing my weekly column for the *Daily Star* on Friday, and the guy who did it with me, Rob King, a really nice guy, was just as curious as everyone else.

'The talk is that you're on the wrong horse,' he said to me after I had done my column. 'They say that Nicky wanted to claim off Blue Royal, so he put Fehily up, so you had to ride the other one.'

'Let people think what they want,' I said, 'but you make sure and back Geos tomorrow. He's the one. The other horse will run a big race, I'm sure of it, but Geos is more likely to win the race.'

He did. He pissed up. The little bit of rain that they had had on the Friday helped him, but he was great on the day, he gave me a great ride, I was always where I wanted to be throughout the race and he quickened away on the run-in with me impressively. Blue Royal ran out of his skin to finish seventh. It was a great result for the yard.

'You were right,' said Nicky to me as I dismounted. 'Well done. Well done.'

'I promise you,' I said to him, almost before I hit the ground, 'the other horse is the better horse.'

Blue Royal proved as much when he finished third in the Champion Hurdle the following month, a remarkable performance for a five-year-old. But he had problems with his pelvis and he never reached his true potential, which was a real shame. He could have been anything, a Champion Chase horse, a Gold Cup horse, he could have been that good over fences. Alas, we never got to find out.

I won the Aon Chase on See More Business the same day at Newbury, and we were all set for another go at the Gold Cup. The other Cheltenham guns were being loaded as well. Dusk Duel had won two of his three novice hurdles, we had a lovely bumper horse, Inca, owned by Trevor Hemmings, who had been really impressive when winning on his only start at Kempton in January, and I had won two out of two chases on Tiutchev. He was proving to be an exciting novice. Stormyfairweather wasn't looking so good, though. I had had to pull him up in the Tripleprint Gold Cup at Cheltenham in December, and Nicky was in a race against time to get him ready for another tilt at the Cathcart. Then there was Marlborough.

Marlborough was getting better. We were doing a lot of work with him with Yogi Breisner and he was beginning to get the hang of jumping fences. We were also holding him up in his races. He had always been a front-runner with Henry Daly, but I suggested to Nicky before he ran in a handicap chase at Kempton in January that I hold him up out the back, that he might just settle better and jump better in behind horses. Nicky left me to it. He was great like that, he trusted my judgement.

We won that race at Kempton impressively, and he jumped impeccably. He went up 12lb in the handicap for that, but I still fancied him to win the Racing Post Chase back at Kempton in February, I thought that he had about a stone in hand of the handicapper now that he was getting his jumping together. Well, if he had a stone in hand, Gloria Victis had two stone in hand.

Gloria Victis was an amazing horse. A French import of Martin Pipe's, he had burst on to the scene, winning the Fulke Walwyn Chase and the Feltham Chase, and now here he was, a novice, a six-year-old with top weight of 11st 10lb, giving a stone to Marlborough, leading us all a merry dance in the Racing Post Chase. Marlborough travelled well, he jumped well for me, he pulled well clear of the rest of the field, but he just couldn't get near Gloria Victis, no excuses.

Nicky was a bit disappointed when I came back in to unsaddle, he said that he thought that Marlborough would pick up better than he did. But he did pick up. Just the other horse picked up more.

There was a lot of debate then about whether they should run Gloria Victis in the Gold Cup, pitch him in against the best staying chasers in the business, or in the Royal & SunAlliance Chase, the championship race restricted to novices. Pipe and owner Terry Neill decided to go for the big pot, the Gold Cup. He was right there in contention, still in with a winning chance and in the front rank when he fell at the second-last and broke his leg. Dead. It was a terrible shame for such a young horse with his career in front of him. Pipe was castigated in the press afterwards for being greedy, for running him against battle-hardened rivals when the SunAlliance Chase was there for the taking, but unfairly so, I thought. He could have fallen and broken his leg in the novice race, in any race. It was just one of those things. Regrettably, these things are a part of racing.

The race for Marlborough at Cheltenham was the newly-named William Hill Chase, the old Ritz that I had won five years previously on Rough Quest. The handicapper had raised Marlborough another 5lb to a mark of 141 for his Racing Post Chase run, which I thought was quite lenient actually. He was getting his jumping together now and, as he was, he was growing in confidence and improving at a rate of knots. I really rated the Racing Post Chase form, I really rated Gloria Victis. Marlborough could end up with a very low weight in the William Hill, especially if his owner Sir Robert Ogden also ran his French import Pain Royal, who was trained by Ian Williams and who was rated 166. If he was left in the race and carried top weight of 12 stone, that would mean that Marlborough would only have 10st 3lb to carry. I could get down to 10st

3lb no problem, and Marlborough would be a certainty off that. I told Barry Simpson, racing manager of Sir Robert Ogden, as much.

Yogi Breisner came to Nicky's on the Monday, the day before Cheltenham, to do a little bit of work with Marlborough, just to sharpen him up, get his mind on jumping for his big test the following day. Nicky wasn't there at the time. Yogi took the boots off Marlborough and sent him over a few poles, let him rub against the poles. He used to do that if he really wanted a horse to pick his feet up. Anyway, I rode Marlborough over these poles, clatter, knocked into the pole, took two strides and pulled up sharply, lame.

'Ah fuck,' said Yogi. 'What's happening with this thing?'

I couldn't believe it. A real shot at a Cheltenham winner gone, right there under me, and it was partly my fault. Shite. I was gutted for myself, but worse than that, Nicky wasn't going to be happy. What were we going to tell him? What would we tell the press? That we took the boots off the horse to make his legs more sensitive and he hit a pole and he's now lame?

Just as I was trying to get my head around the enormity of the disaster, Marlborough took a step forward, then another, then another, sound again. I couldn't believe it. He had just hit a nerve and there was no permanent damage. We had got out of jail, but it was a lesson. I never told Nicky.

Cheltenham dawned the next day. I love getting to Cheltenham on the Tuesday morning, just getting there early, just taking it all in, wallowing in the anticipation, walking the track, just relaxing into it before the hullabaloo begins. Dusk Duel was a bit disappointing in the first, the Supreme Novices' Hurdle, finishing well down the field behind Sausalito Bay and Best Mate, but Tiutchev was brilliant in the second race, the Arkle. He jumped impeccably, he bounced off the fast ground, and he scooted up the hill to break the track record by almost two seconds. And there I was, back in the winner's enclosure at Cheltenham again. It was just an amazing feeling.

The Champion Hurdle was next. Blue Royal ran his five-year-old heart out to finish third behind Istabraq. I kicked on after the second-last on him, trying to draw the sting out of Istabraq's turn of foot, but nothing that I could have done would have got Istabraq beaten that day, and Hors La Loi just did me for second place on the run-in.

The fourth race was the William Hill Chase, time for the real Marlborough to step forward. There was plenty of pace in the race, Beau, Star Traveller, Village King were all front-runners, so I told Nicky in the parade ring beforehand that I was going to be taking my time on Marlborough, that my plan was to switch him off completely for the first circuit, get him jumping, then make my ground through the pack and arrive there no earlier than the last fence. Nicky was happy enough with that. It made sense.

The race went like clockwork. They flew up front in the early stages, but Marlborough was unconcerned, he just relaxed, jumped nicely, minimum of effort. I made some ground down the back straight final time and got in just behind the leaders before we jumped the last ditch on the far side. He travelled like a dream down the hill over the third-last and second-last. Carl Llewellyn kicked for home on Beau off the home turn, he had taken the measure of Star Traveller, but I just stalked him through on the inside down to the final fence. He left a small gap on his inside so I didn't even have to switch off the rail. I actually took it up just before the last, winged the fence and landed running. I sat down to drive him on and he quickly went away from Beau. I gave him one crack of the whip, that was all he needed, that was how easily he was doing it. He powered up the hill to run out an impressive winner.

That was amazing. That win was probably the most satisfying of my career. It wasn't the biggest prize, it wasn't the most high-profile, but it was hugely satisfying for a number of reasons. The fact that it was Cheltenham, the fact that it was for Nicky and Sir Robert Ogden, the fact that the horse had been so clueless about jumping fences and that I had played a role in improving his jumping technique, the fact that I had suggested holding him up instead of allowing him to bowl along, and the way the race panned out. Bar a slight mistake at the ninth fence, it was the perfect race for me.

I drew a blank on the second day. I ended up riding Celibate for Charlie Mann in the Champion Chase, but he was never really at the races. I finished second on Inca in the bumper. He travelled really well and kicked for home a furlong out. But just after we hit the front, Charlie Swan came flying past me on Willie Mullins' Joe Cullen.

I won the Stayers' Hurdle on Bacchanal on Thursday. He had been beaten a neck by Lady Rebecca in the Cleeve Hurdle over two and three-quarter miles on his last run before Cheltenham, his first try at a distance in excess of two miles, but he had always shaped like a stayer to me, and I felt that he would improve for the step up in trip to three miles. Lady Rebecca was favourite for the Stayers', but I thought we had a chance of beating her at the distance. A bigger danger I thought was the Irish horse Limestone Lad, trained by James Bowe and his son Michael down in Gathabawn down on the Carlow/Kilkenny border in deepest southern Ireland, where they have significantly more sheep than horses.

Limestone Lad tried to lead the whole way, as was his wont, but we joined him between the last two flights of hurdles and his engine kicked in from the last. Limestone Lad and Shane McGovern came back at us inside the final 100 yards, but we were always holding him.

See More Business was favourite for the Gold Cup, but it just wasn't his day. He was a dour galloper who didn't have that many gears and the lively ground was all against him. Even so, he plugged on really well for me to finish fourth. Looks Like Trouble won the race, which was a bit of a sickener as I could have ridden him. Norman Williamson, who had been riding him all season, including when he won the Pillar Property by a distance, had been jocked off the horse inexplicably. I had the chance to get on him again for the Gold Cup, just as I did for the Charlie Hall, but there was no way I was going to desert See More. Dickie Johnson got the ride and they won well.

On the Monday before Cheltenham, the day that Yogi and I nearly ended Marlborough's Cheltenham aspirations, when I was down at Seven Barrows just putting the final touches to the horses who would be running at the Festival, Nicky asked me which of our horses was most likely to bring us into the winner's enclosure.

'Marlborough,' I said without thinking. 'You?'

'Stormyfairweather,' he said.

'You're joking.'

'I'm not,' said Nicky. 'I'm telling you, this horse has just come to himself, he is in the form of his life.'

Cantering down to the start on Stormyfairweather before the Catchcart, I understood what Nicky had meant. The horse felt great, a totally different animal to the one that I had pulled up in the Tripleprint three months previously. He just seemed to feel good about himself. Nicky Henderson has performed wonders with racehorses in his career as a trainer. He trained See You Then, he of the fragile legs, to win three Champion Hurdles, the first horse to do so since Persian War, he harnessed Remittance Man's speed, he has this innate ability to get thoroughbred racehorses to fulfil their potential, yet getting Stormyfairweather to the races that day in the form that he was in was one of his greatest, and least heralded, achievements as a racehorse trainer.

I bounced Stormyfairweather out of the gate and set out to make all. He was fantastic. He jumped like a stag the whole way round. Joe Tizzard on Fadalko loomed up to challenge us going to the second-last, but my fellow winged it while Fadalko just met it wrong. Same story at the last, I winged it, Joe just got in a little tight, and he kept going up the hill to win by about two lengths. Poor Joe got blamed for losing the race on Fadalko. Sir Robert Ogden owned Fadalko, and he said that Joe would never ride for him again, which was unfair, it wasn't Joe's fault.

So I was back in the winner's enclosure at Cheltenham for the fourth time in three days, my eighth Cheltenham Festival winner in two years. It was mind-blowing stuff. It put me clear in the riders' championship at the meeting again. Charlie Swan had two winners, Dickie Johnson had two, Norman Williamson had two, so there was a chance that I could have been caught before Stormyfairweather won the Cathcart, exactly the same scenario as the previous year.

I was a very proud man that day. I felt very proud of what I had achieved. I had ridden four winners again, I was top jockey at Cheltenham again. I found it difficult to get my head around that, the hallowed ground that I had revered from afar as a kid, on which I had watched Dawn Run and Burrough Hill Lad and Buck House and Bobsline and Sea Pigeon and Monksfield, and Jonjo and Francome and Scudamore and Dunwoody, and now I was top jockey, top dog, for the second time. My head could have exploded. And this time it was even better because all four winners were for Nicky. The following week we had a photograph taken up at Seven Barrows of all four horses, Tiutchev, Marlborough, Bacchanal and Stormyfairweather, with their regular riders.

That's a special photograph, a reminder of a truly special week.

# CHAPTER 18

## THE STROKE OF A PEN

I was going out on Gold Cup night, that was for sure. I had missed celebrating with the lads the previous year when I had gone home to Jane, and I certainly wasn't going to miss out for a second year running now that I was top jockey again. Jane wasn't there in 2000 either, same reasons as 1999, she didn't want to go, she didn't feel like she was a part of it and, if I am honest, she wasn't.

The craic was great at the weigh room drinks party, everyone was there, all the jockeys and their partners and close friends, all the trainers, a couple of journalists. Bridget was there, Jane's sister. Bridget and Paul Nicholls had just split up and she was there with a friend of hers. I'm not sure if it was because I got talking to Bridget, but I began to get pangs of guilt again that Jane wasn't there, or that I wasn't with her. She was my wife, the person with whom I was supposed to be sharing my life, and now, on the evening of one of the greatest achievements of my career, yet again, I wasn't with her.

The party began to break up at about midnight and the boys were going into town. I was fully intending following them in, I really was, pangs of guilt or no pangs of guilt. I hadn't had that much to drink, so I said I'd drive my car into town and meet them there. So I got into my car, the Saab that Channel 4 had given me use of for a year after I had won the Channel 4 trophy the previous season. I was due to give it back three weeks later. I was looking for somewhere to park, somewhere I could leave it overnight where it would be safe, while at the same time struggling with these pangs of guilt. The pangs won out. Don't be a dick, go home.

So I got on the road for home with mixed feelings. I was missing the craic with the lads, but I was sure that I was doing the right thing. I was driving along the A40 and I came upon some temporary traffic lights, roadworks, traffic restricted to one lane. There was a truck in front of me, about 100 yards away, that was pulling out around the lights, so I was following him, doing no more than 50 miles an hour (honestly officer). I don't know what happened then, if I dozed off or if I was thinking about something else, if I was reliving my win in the Cathcart or thinking about the boys in the nightclub, but the next thing I knew the truck had stopped in the middle of the road and I was heading straight for it. Bang! Straight into the back of him. Bye bye Saab. Airbags, the works, it was a real mess.

Thankfully I was all right. Imagine, after riding about 15 horses, each one a half a ton worth, full pelt over big black birch ditches on the fastest ground that they had had in years for the last three days, if I were to go and kill myself in a car driving home. The irony. But I opened the door and walked away from the car. The truck driver came around, not happy, said he was going to have to call the cops. What could I do? I wasn't going anywhere.

Then I began to get worried. How much did I really have to drink? The cops came, said they were going to have to breathalyse me, so I blew into the bag, red. Disaster.

'I'm sorry sir, but you're going to have to come with us.'

So they brought me to this police station and took my details. This was about three in the morning and I didn't know which way was up.

'Right,' said the policeman. 'You blow into this tube three times, if the average is over 40, we have to do you, if it's under 40, you're free to go.'

'Right.'

I blew in it the first time. 40. Not so bad. No-score draw. There's hope. Blew in it the second time, 38. Blew into it the third time, 37. Phew.

'You're free to go.'

'Great, thanks,' I said. 'How do I get home? Where am I anyway?'

'Stroud. You'll struggle to get a taxi.'

Stroud is only about 50 minutes from my home, but the taxi didn't arrive until about half past four. I had three rides at Folkestone the following day which I couldn't miss. How unprofessional would that look? Three rides booked the day after Cheltenham, but he's top rider at the Festival and he gets so hammered that he just doesn't bother showing up for work the next day.

I gave the taxi man directions, made sure he knew where he was going, and then I fell asleep in the back of the car. I woke up, still in the car, but it was getting bright. I looked at my watch, half past six.

'Where are we?' I asked your man.

'I'll show you now,' he said, 'I think we've gone wrong.'

He had basically been driving around in a loop while I was asleep.

I got home at about a quarter to seven, just as Jane was heading out the door to work. I hadn't rung her, there was no point, it was too late to call when I knew I was coming home, and it was too early when I was in the police station.

'Oh and where have you been?'

'Where the fuck do you think I've been?' I asked. I didn't explain. I didn't have the energy. I just went in the door and got into bed.

Then I got thinking, I had to cop myself on. I had got away with that. I had had a few drinks and I had got away with it. Imagine I had lost my licence? How would I have coped? What would the papers have said? It wouldn't have been good. Maybe now it was time to settle down and concentrate on being the loving husband for a while, stop acting the bollocks. Thankfully nothing had happened with any other bird at Cheltenham, so I felt reasonably guilt-free, but it could have.

Three months later, though, when I was driving home from Exeter, I realised that things with Jane had been going downhill rapidly since Cheltenham, even worse than they had been beforehand. I started thinking, I don't know this girl. I don't love this girl. If this carries on, I'm going to get caught shagging something, and that would be the end of it anyway. That would kill her. Time to do the decent thing and pull the plug.

I pulled into a lay-by to mull all this over, and I got fairly sad. I didn't want to go home. I wasn't looking forward to going home, but I knew what I had to do. Are you a man or a mouse? So I went home and told her that I thought it would be best if we split up.

She didn't see it coming. I was amazed. I had been agonising over this for ages, and she was oblivious to the whole thing, just trundling along in her own little world as if everything was rosy. I hadn't been happy for a long time, actually since very soon after we got married, but she thought I had just come up with this notion all of a sudden. It confirmed my suspicion that I didn't know this girl at all. I suggested that she should go to America for a while, over to friends of hers over there, which she did.

Jane had got very upset by the whole thing, which upset me a lot. It's amazing how much hurt you can bring on one person just by your own doing, when you actually think that you are doing the right thing. You think you're being selfish, but actually the difficult thing to do is to break up. You are probably being more selfish if you stay in a relationship that you know is going nowhere. Selfish and cowardly. Shortly after Jane had gone to America, no more than a couple of days later, I knew that this was the right thing. I was so much happier on my own than I had been with Jane. I was happy that she was gone, I was happy that we were apart, and I knew that that was the way that it had to be. As time went on, that realisation grew stronger.

Jane came back from America about three months later. I'm not sure what she expected, I think she expected that we would just get back together again and pick up from where we left off, live happily ever after, but we couldn't. I couldn't. This was it, I rented her a house, and away we went.

I loved living on my own. I love my own company. I could come home in the evening, watch the day's racing, study the following day's runners, watch the American golf on television, watch MTV, do what I wanted without having somebody else in the house to worry about, have birds around, whatever. I loved it.

I was trying to get the divorce sorted for months. It seems to me she went from 'I don't care who divorces who, you divorce me if you like, and I don't want any money', to 'I'm divorcing you, and I want a house and I don't want to have to pay a mortgage, and I want all this other stuff as well.'

So we ended up in a preliminary hearing – the high court would have been the next step – where she's in one room and she's making all her demands to me through her solicitor, who is coming out of the room and sitting down with me and my solicitor, Bente Nielsen. I was just recovering from a bad ankle injury at the time. I had broken it when a horse, Rock'n Cold, had spooked with me and dropped me on the way to the start at Market Rasen. It was actually touch and go whether I would be able to ride again, so I wasn't in the best of form anyway. But the figures that the solicitor was coming in with, the demands he was making, were just astronomical.

I was afraid that when I saw her I would still fancy her, and if I still fancied her I would have been in trouble, I would have been thinking, well, maybe this is not the right thing to be doing at all. But I didn't. And then these demands her solicitor was coming out with. I got quite annoyed.

'Look,' I said. 'You go and tell her, I will not give her a fucking cent if she keeps on pushing it like this. I'll give her that, that amount, the amount we agreed, and that's it. If she looks for any more than that, she'll get nothing. You go and tell her that.'

Your man scarpered. My solicitor was telling me to calm down. Threatening behaviour is not good in divorce proceedings, but I didn't care, I just saw red. As far as I was concerned, her demands were unreasonable, in one sense she was entitled to nothing. So we went in to the judge and the judge was fair towards me, said we've agreed this much, that's it, she's getting no more, thank you very much.

I drove away from that courthouse fuming. You realise that, all you've worked for, all the effort you've put in to getting where you are, and you've given away more than half of it in the stroke of a pen. Gone. I was bitter about it all for a few months, but then I figured, what's the point? Wave it away, good luck, lesson learned, and I actually became quite good friends with Jane for a while after that. Sometimes when I was going out with the boys, there were a few girls we used to hang around with as well, I used to give her a call and see if she wanted to come out with us.

When I met Chloe and started going out with her, Jane was grand. Even when Chloe got pregnant, Jane was cool with that. She never wanted kids; I always wanted kids. I'm sure that if she had wanted them, we would have had them. That was a huge silver lining on our break-up, that there were no kids involved. So I think she was actually happy when Chloe got pregnant.

But then there was the dog. We had had this dog, me and Jane, her name was Chloe actually, quite bizarrely. Jane kept the dog initially after we split up, but after a couple of years she wasn't sure that she would be able to look after her properly, with her work commitments, so she asked if Chloe and I could take her. I was a bit nervous about having the dog around a new child, but I said I'd take her, see how it went, do Jane a favour, see if the dog would be ok with the new child. So Zac was born and the dog was great with him. The dog loved him.

Everything was fine until we were going to AP's wedding in Majorca about a month after Zac was born, and I asked Jane if she could look after the dog while we were away. When we got back I sent her a message to say that we were back, that I could come and pick up the dog whenever she wanted. No response that evening, no response the following day. So I ring her, no answer, no reply for a day, no reply for about a week. I'm thinking, hold on a minute now, what's happened to the dog? I ring her the following day and she answers.

'Eh, how's the dog?' I ask.

'Grand,' she says.

'When can I pick her up?'

'Yeah, well, I'm going to keep her,' she says.

'You're what?'

'Well, you know,' she says, 'she came back to me a little bit fat, so I'm going to keep her.'

'You are joking me.'

'No, I think she'd be better here with me,' she says.

I couldn't believe it. After all this.

I put the phone down. That was two years ago now. I haven't spoken to her since.

# CHAPTER 19

# WHAT, NO IRISH?

Sometimes you wondered what it was all about, what was it all for, all the chasing around the country for rides, all the groundwork with trainers, all the early mornings and late nights, all the driving, the precariousness of the profession, two ambulances following you as you worked, the knowledge that any time you left the weigh room there was a chance that you could be carried back in. What drove you on? The desire to make your name as a jockey, to be recognised, to be remembered, to win the big races, to set records. Why?

I always thought that I would like to ride a winner at every National Hunt racecourse in Britain. I thought that I did it as well when I won a novice chase at Musselburgh on Carbury Cross for Jonjo O'Neill in January 2001. I had thought beforehand that Musselburgh was the last of the 42 tracks at which I hadn't ridden a winner. Then somebody asked me about Newcastle. How many winners had I ridden at Newcastle? I'd forgotten about Newcastle. None.

I didn't go to Newcastle that often, but I had it in the back of my mind that I would like to have a winner there, just to complete the set. Then one day I was sitting in the weigh room when Graham McCourt came in looking for a girth. Graham had been retired for a good few years, but he was one of my idols when I was getting going, he was a great jockey, tough and as strong in a finish as they made them. He won the Champion Hurdle in 1992 on Royal Gait and he won the Gold Cup on Norton's Coin in 1990. Fantastic jockey.

After he had left the weigh room that day, Tom Doyle, one of the young lads, turned to me and asked: 'Who's your man?' I couldn't believe it. Who's your man? That's Graham McCourt, that's who that is, one of the top jockeys of his generation. Something hit me then. Was all of this really that important, all this chasing for records, chasing for fame? Was it really that important for me to ride a winner at Newcastle? Did I really want to drive up so far north that go any further and you're in the North Sea? I figured if it happened, it happened, but it wasn't a burning ambition. I never did ride a winner at Newcastle.

Chalkie Run was just an ordinary horse running in an ordinary novice hurdle at Newbury in November 2000. He was one of those horses who could be very good over his hurdles or could totally miss. This day I decided, right, you're doing it my way. I gunned him over his hurdles and he picked up at every one. We went clear at the third-last, I gunned him down to the second-last, you're coming up, but he didn't. Chalkie didn't fancy it. He stepped straight into the middle of it and fired me to the floor. I landed awkwardly on my shoulder, fracturing it quite badly. The worst of it was that I was clear. I could have let him trampoline over the last two and he still would have won easily.

That was an expensive fracture. I missed the big Cheltenham November meeting and I missed the Hennessy meeting at Newbury. Marlborough was my intended ride in the Hennessy, and I was desperately trying to get back in time to ride him. I went down to Nicky's during the week, rode Marlborough one piece of work, and pulled up. My shoulder was killing me so I had to admit defeat.

I think that Nicky appreciated that. If I didn't feel up to it, I wasn't going to risk it, or ride at half pace. I didn't feel like it was fair. It would be like a football player telling his manager that he was ok when in fact his hamstring is killing him. It's not fair on the manager, it's not fair on his team-mates. You will get found out anyway so you're better off being straight up from the beginning. Nicky's owners were putting enough money into the game to expect a fully fit jockey to ride their horses in a race like the Hennessy. Marlborough didn't run in the Hennessy in the end, but Sir Robert Ogden's other horse Ad Hoc did, and I probably would have ridden him if I had been fit. He was travelling really well under Timmy Murphy when he came down at the cross fence, the fifth-last. You never know how he would have fared.

I also missed Bacchanal's chasing debut at the Hennessy meeting – he won by a distance under Dickie Johnson – but I was back well in time to ride him in the Feltham Chase at Kempton on Boxing Day. He hadn't jumped brilliantly at Newbury and he wasn't a whole lot better at Kempton, he was never a natural jumper of anything, hurdles or fences, but he had some engine, and he won the Feltham by a distance, beating Pipe's horse Take Control and the Nicholls horse, who was favourite, Shotgun Willy.

That was another really good day for me and Nicky. We won the juvenile hurdle with Fondmort, another French import who was having his first run for us, and who battled on really bravely to get the better of Impek and Jim Culloty, and we won the big two-mile novice chase, the Wayward Lad Chase, with Dusk Duel. I thought he was going to finish fourth of the four runners leaving the back straight, but he picked up really well in the home straight to get up on the run-in.

See More Business was a disappointing favourite in the King George that day, but he bounced back for me in the Pillar Property Chase at Cheltenham in January, beating Cyfor Malta and Beau and, even as an 11-year-old, he was all set to try to regain the Gold Cup that he had lost to Looks Like Trouble the previous year.

Landing Light was another horse that Nicky got off the racecourse in France although, strangely enough, he was bred in Ireland by Ballymacoll Stud. He had won his maiden hurdle in February 2000 but then fractured his pelvis the following month, so Nicky had done a super job to get him back to the racecourse as early as the following December. We knew that he had lots of ability, we were thinking that he might be well handicapped, we were thinking Tote Gold Trophy with him, so Nicky ran him in the same race that Blue Royal had won, the Brunswick Knights Royal Hurdle at Ascot. This time, Nicky had left plenty to work with, which was perfectly understandable given that it was his first run in ten months and his first since his fractured pelvis, but he still ran encouragingly, finishing third to a good horse of Pipe's, Valiramix. He was beaten 20 lengths, but he gave me a great feel throughout, and he just got tired in the home straight.

Inevitably, there was talk of the Champion Hurdle afterwards. Nicky just scoffed at that. 'I don't know where that talk of the Champion Hurdle has come from,' he said, his handicap rating very much in mind. He was rated 129 before the Ascot race, and he was rated 129 after it. The handicapper couldn't touch him. Perfect. Then Nicky set about training him for the Tote Gold Trophy. John Poynton, Landing Light's owner, a really good fellow, likes to get involved financially in his runners, and he had a decent bet on him then for the Tote Gold Trophy.

There is a good handicap hurdle at the Cheltenham meeting at the end of January, and Nicky figured that he'd run Landing Light in that. By then, the weights were out for the Tote Gold Trophy, so worst-case scenario he'd get a small penalty if he won the race, but the handicapper couldn't reassess him even if he won it doing handsprings, which he did, and was immediately put in as favourite for the Tote.

The 4lb penalty that he picked up for winning at Cheltenham was ideal. It meant that he was more or less guaranteed to get into the race and he would still only have close to the minimum weight of ten stone to carry. Nicky was concerned initially that he wouldn't get in, then he was concerned that he would have too much weight. To my mind, it didn't matter what weight he had to carry. He ended up with 10st 2lb, just 2lb above minimum weight.

There were two lads staying with me that weekend, two lads, Tony and Michael, who used to stay with us for the Tote Gold Trophy meeting most years. I was up early that Saturday morning, went and rode first lot at Nicky's, the usual, then came home to have a sweat in the bath, make sure I could do 10st 2lb, and the two lads are all spruced up and ready to go.

'You all ready lads?' I asked.

'Yeah, all set now.'

'Did you have showers?'

'We did yeah, thanks.'

'You didn't use all the hot water, did you?'

I turned on the hot tap. Freezing cold. The two lads went white, maybe because they knew that I was really pissed off, maybe because they were holding decent ante-post vouchers about Landing Light.

'Right, in the car, now!'

I drove to Newbury, broke all speed limits, dumped the lads on the grass, they could make their own way, and got to the sauna in the racecourse. My body always worked better in the bath. I never liked the sauna, it was much harder work for me, it took much longer and it wasn't enjoyable. Anyway, I made it, I weighed out at 10st 2lb.

They went a fair pace in the early stages of the Tote Gold Trophy in the soft ground, and I had to niggle Landing Light along a little just after halfway, but he kept on picking up for me. I was flat to the boards early in the home straight, but then a gap appeared and he picked up. We struck the front after the second-last and suddenly the race was over. We came home three lengths clear of our closest pursuer, subsequent Champion Hurdle winner Rooster Booster, even though he was getting a little bit lonely and looking for company on the run-in.

Everyone was desperately excited. Not only had Nicky and I won the Tote Gold Trophy for the second year running, not only had we landed a lucrative prize, not only had a long-term plan come to fruition, not only had John copped his bet, but the bookmakers put Landing Light in as second favourite for the Champion Hurdle behind the mighty Istabraq on the back of that performance. Now that was something to get excited about.

Alas, Cheltenham aspirations that usually burned like a furnace in February were mercilessly extinguished that year. You would never have thought that events at an abattoir in Essex would have any impact on Landing Light's bid to win the Champion Hurdle, but a week after the Tote Gold Trophy they found a case of foot and mouth disease at Little Warley. Four days later, they found another case in Northumberland, then another case in Devon, then Cornwall, Cumbria, there was even a case found in Scotland.

You can often only see these things from your own perspective, and the nightly news bulletins showing animal pyres were horrendous, and must have been devastating for farmers, but foot and mouth was also a disaster for racing. The authorities imposed a complete ban on the movement of livestock, with the result that racing was being cancelled at racecourses in areas where the disease had been detected. The Irish decided on a complete shutdown, which worked, as they managed to restrict the disease to just one small area in County Louth. Consistent with their shutdown policy, the Irish effectively decided that they wouldn't be sending any horses to Cheltenham. What, no Irish horses at Cheltenham? It was difficult to imagine that.

You could have looked at that in two ways. You could have thought that it represented an increased opportunity to bag a Cheltenham winner, no Irish equals less competition, happy days for the British horses. I didn't see it like that though. Cheltenham without the Irish would be like a World Cup without the South Americans. A Cheltenham victory without the Irish horses would have been hollow, it would have been like a gold medal at the Moscow Olympics with no Americans.

It was all a bit of a mess really. We weren't sure from day to day what racing would be on and what racing wouldn't be on. Cheltenham was going ahead, but they were keeping a watching brief. They closed racing down for ten days, which was actually a good thing because at least there was certainty in that. The following morning, myself and AP and a couple of other lads were on a flight to Dubai. We rang Michael Hills and he very kindly said that we could stay with him. I'm sure he regretted that. Michael doesn't drink and his place was all neat and tidy, lovely place. We were there on the piss, so tidiness and cleanliness probably wasn't at the top of our agenda. Actually, we hardly saw Michael at all. He'd be up early in the morning riding out, we'd be out playing golf during the day and out drinking at night with some of the other lads who were there, Ted Durcan and a few of the other Flat lads, and we'd be home late at night. We'd just basically put our heads down for a few hours in Michael's place every night and then we'd be off again. After we had left, Michael said he had to leave the windows open in his apartment for about three days.

We came home all set for Cheltenham, hoping that it would go ahead but fearing the worst. Our fears were realised. It didn't. They found out that there had been some sheep on the racecourse after the cut-off point according to the Ministry of Agriculture guidelines. The *Racing Post* ran a banner headline that day: 'Silenced by the lambs'. It was initially postponed until April, but then it was cancelled altogether after they found another case of foot and mouth five miles from the track. I'm not sure they ever would have allowed the Festival to go ahead without the Irish. At least the racecourse copped the insurance money of around £8 million.

Everyone was terribly disappointed. It was difficult to imagine that a season would pass without the quintessential test that is the Cheltenham Festival, the defining competition in every grade under every code and at every distance. Imagine training all year for an event, gearing up for one day, and then that day not happening. It would be like Kerry playing all season in the league, going through the championship, getting to the All-Ireland final, the entire focal point of the season, and then being told that the final was not going to be played.

I was gutted. I thought that I was in with a shout of being top rider at the meeting for the third time in a row. I consoled myself with a golfing trip to Ireland, but that wasn't without its hassles either. When I got to Cork the fellow on the gate wouldn't let me take my golf shoes into the country, no matter how much disinfectant I put on them, and made me sit there and clean all of my golf clubs, one by one.

They had some replacement races at the Whitbread meeting at Sandown to compensate for the loss of Cheltenham, but they weren't the same. I won the replacement Gold Cup on Marlborough. First Gold was long odds-on, but he unshipped Thierry Doumen at the fence in front of the stands. Marlborough should have beaten the rest of them easily, but he lost a shoe at the second-last and he just got up to beat 12-year-old Go Ballistic by a short head. I also won the two-and-a-half-mile novice chase on Ikrenel Royal earlier in the day.

The following day, Whitbread Gold Cup day, was not so successful. In the replacement Champion Hurdle I chose to ride Geos instead of Landing Light. Landing Light had run terribly at Aintree, he had been pulled up in the Aintree Hurdle. Geos was flying at home and he was fresh, he hadn't run in two months. It was a no-brainer. Lo and behold, Landing Light is a totally different horse to the one who ran at Aintree, and he and Dickie Johnson beat us by three lengths. I finish second on Geos, which made it even worse.

The Whitbread Gold Cup itself was crap for me as well. I was due to ride Ad Hoc in the race. He was owned by Sir Robert Ogden, like Marlborough was, and like Kingsmark, who was also running in the Whitbread. I had ridden Ad Hoc to finish second in the Scottish National a couple of weeks previously and I thought he would have a right chance in the Whitbread. The day before the race, the Friday, Barry Simpson told me that Ad Hoc wasn't going to run, that the ground was too soft. I said ok, I'd ride Kingsmark. Kingsmark was a decent horse, a good staying handicap chaser, but he just didn't have the touch of class that Ad Hoc had, and he wasn't as potentially well handicapped.

'Grand,' said Barry. 'If anything changes, you can switch to Ad Hoc.'

'What do you mean if anything changes?' I asked. 'He's not running, is he?'

'No, he's not, the ground is too soft.'

The ground didn't get any better overnight. In fact, it rained all day on the Saturday and it was so soft that they abandoned the last two Flat races on the card. Even so, Ad Hoc ran. I was amazed. I couldn't switch to him because he only had 10st 4lb and I wasn't able to do 10st 4lb without plenty of prior warning. I finished 13th of the 14 finishers on Kingsmark, Ad Hoc won the race by 20 lengths under Ruby Walsh. Absolutely danced in. I wasn't a bit impressed.

# CHAPTER 20

## CHELTENHAM BLUES

I was never one to shirk a challenge. I was never one for sitting in my comfort zone and being content with what I had. Not many jump jockeys are. Some people say that it is a failing of mine, and it is in many walks of normal life, but it also makes for an exciting existence. So when Jonathan Sheppard, the multiple champion jumps trainer in America, called me out of the blue in October 2001 and asked me if I would ride a horse for him in the Breeders' Cup Chase at Far Hills in New Jersey, I jumped at the opportunity.

It wasn't long after September 11, the attack on the Twin Towers in New York, and all the Americans were very nervous about flying. They cancelled the Ryder Cup that year because the Yanks wouldn't fly. I didn't mind it so much, I suppose you were a little bit more wary than you might have been flying to America, but it didn't really bother me.

I had never met Jonathan before, I had never even spoken to him. I'm not sure if he didn't try to get someone instead of me first, but I didn't care, it was a great opportunity. As it happened, Carl Llewellyn was going out as well to ride something for Jack Fisher in the race, so the two of us headed off together, happy days, landed in Philadelphia, were picked up at the airport and brought to our hotel. It was Friday night, the race was on the Saturday, so we decided that we'd head out on the town. I had just separated from Jane, so I was intent on trying out my new-found freedom. We walked into the first bar that we found. There was hardly anybody there, three or four people.

'It's Friday night, where is everybody?' I asked the barman.

'They're probably in town,' he said.

'Grand, we'll get a taxi.'

The barman looked at me strangely.

'How far away is town?'

'About an hour and a half.'

So there's me and The Welsh cooped up in this little place, no bigger than Camolin, and no action. We figured it might have been for the best, so we had a few pints and had an early night. Next day I'm up early, a car is coming to pick us up to bring us to the races, I'm a little bit heavy, about 10st 12lb, so I figure I'll get to the racecourse early and have a bit of a sweat in the sauna before racing.

As we're driving in the entrance to the racecourse, such as it is, I'm thinking, well this can't be it, there's not a whole lot here. Sauna? Some chance. It's basically a field. There are point-to-point meetings in Ireland that are better equipped. We got to the weigh room, a tent for all the world, and the guy there told us to put our gear down there, that it would be grand. No showers, no nothing, just a tent, and definitely no sauna.

So I was thinking, ah look, I'll be grand, I'm riding at 10st 12lb and I have a small saddle with me that I use when I'm doing light, so it should be ok. Then this guy comes up to me in the tent.

'Are you Mick Fitzgerald?'

'I am, how are you doing?'

'I'm good,' he says. 'You ride one for me later on in the three-year-old hurdle.'

'Oh do I now?' He's obviously got me mixed up with someone else.

'Yeah, you're a busy man today.'

'No, I'm just riding one for Jonathan Sheppard in the Breeders' Cup Chase,' I say smugly.

'Naw, you have about five rides.'

He picks up a racecard and shows me. He's right. I'm down for five rides. This is not happening. And here's this fellow telling me that I'm riding a three-year-old, a horse who has never run before. He probably thinks that he's doing me a favour by getting me to ride it, but there was no way. Ride a horse who I have never even seen before, an inexperienced youngster who has never been on a racecourse before, for a trainer about whom I had no clue? I'm sorry, I wouldn't do it in England, there was no way I was doing it in Far Hills, New Jersey. In fairness to the guy, he understood, he took it well.

I had a walk around the track, a nice track, a bit tight, a little downhill and a little uphill to the finish, but the ground was firm, not dangerous but definitely firm. It was amazing though, they had no real facilities and they still had 60,000 people there, all sitting around the track having their picnics, there was a really good atmosphere about the place. I met a couple of lads out on the track and they were marvelling at the ground, good ground, really good, they were saying. I told them that in England this would be firm. They were astounded, no way, this was beautiful ground, as good as it gets. Well I wouldn't like to be riding on firm.

I looked down the racecard and noticed that I was down to ride a horse for Sanna Nielson, one of the top jumps trainers in America, who was set to carry 10st 2lb. Well that wasn't happening either. The trainer came into the tent and I told her, look I didn't know I was booked to ride one with this weight, I won't be able to do any less than 10st 10lb or 10st 12lb. She didn't mind. She said that she really wanted me to ride it, that she just wanted someone to give it a strong ride.

I said fine, it was a $75,000 race, so I weighed out, 10st 10lb, not too bad. I kicked this thing out of the gate, drilled it at every hurdle, took it up at the last and just clung on to win by a head or a short head. It was nice to ride a winner in the States. My ride in the Breeders' Cup Chase, It's A Giggle, ran well enough, we finished fifth, one place behind The Welsh on Pinkie Swear.

I missed the Hennessy meeting at Newbury that year, which was a real sickener. Nicky didn't have a runner in the Hennessy, but Ad Hoc was one of the favourites, and I was in line to ride him. As well as that, Katarino was making his chasing debut and Got One Too, a decent novice hurdler from the previous season who had progressed well over the summer, was going in the Gerry Feilden. And as if that wasn't enough, Landing Light was running in the Fighting Fifth Hurdle at Newcastle on the same day. I'm sure I would have gone to Newbury, but that would also have been my opportunity to ride my winner at Newcastle. It was all irrelevant in the end.

I was riding a horse for Philip Hobbs, Surprising, in a handicap hurdle at the Cheltenham November meeting. It was a typical Cheltenham handicap hurdle, all in a heap going down the hill, all jockeying for position, lads weaving in and out all over the place like bumping cars, and I was doing the same. The only problem was that Brian Harding on Telemoss was directly behind me as I moved, he caught the back of my horse's heels and stumbled badly, almost came down. The stewards took a dim view, blamed me for the incident and banned me for six days. I appealed against the severity of the suspension in the hope that they would reduce it to four days, which would allow me to ride at Newbury or Newcastle, but they weren't for turning. I went to Ireland to play golf with Shane that weekend, and watched the video of the races on Saturday evening, watched Landing Light win the Fighting Fifth Hurdle at Newcastle under Johnny Kavanagh, and watched Norman Williamson win at Newbury on both Katarino and Got One Too.

Fondmort started jumping fences that season. Good as he had been over hurdles, he was dynamite over fences. I loved riding him over fences. He would put the fear of God in you sometimes, the stride that he would see and the point at which he would take off, but he very rarely let you down.

I won on him on his chasing debut at Kempton in October, we were right there with Seebald in the Grade 2 novice chase at the Cheltenham November meeting, and going well, when he just slithered on landing over the second-last. I'm not sure that we would have beaten Seebald that day, but we would have gone mighty close, and Seebald was put in as favourite for the Arkle shortly afterwards. Fondmort and I made amends, however, in the Henry VIII Chase at Sandown a month later. I used to love riding exuberant jumpers around Sandown and Fondmort was electric around there, possibly even better there than he was at Cheltenhem even though everyone knows him as a Cheltenham horse. Then we won the Wayward Lad Chase back at Kempton over Christmas, giving over a stone to the four-year-old Monkerhostin.

I was hoping that season was going to be Bacchanal's season. He was an unbelievable horse, he had such an engine, bags of stamina. It's amazing that we thought of him as a two-mile hurdler, a potential

Champion Hurdle horse, in his early days. He had never been a natural jumper of fences, but Yogi Breisner had done a lot of work with him and we were thinking Gold Cup with him, even though he was only a second-season chaser. I won an intermediate chase on him at Sandown on Tingle Creek weekend in December, and then we went to the King George.

I really fancied him in the King George. Best Mate was in it, he had been a really exciting novice the previous season and would have been a warm favourite for the Arkle had Cheltenham gone ahead. First Gold was in it, the previous year's winner and probably the best established staying chaser in the business at the time, and Florida Pearl was in it, although it looked like he was on the wane. He had been beaten in the James Nicholson Chase at Down Royal earlier in the season, and had just scraped home from Native Upmanship in the John Durkan Chase on his previous run. His trainer Willie Mullins was having trouble booking a jockey for him until Adrian Maguire became available.

When we turned for home in the King George, there were only three of us in it, Florida Pearl, who led into the home straight under Adrian, Best Mate, who was stalking him under AP, and Bacchanal. I used to love riding Kempton. I thought I understood the track better than most jockeys, and that that was why I was leading jockey there for a number of years. Everybody thinks that it's a tight track, but it really isn't. You really need to see out the trip if you are going to win at Kempton, but you also need to be prominent.

There is a long run around from the fourth-last fence out of the back straight, to the third-last, the first in the home straight. Ideally you will be prominent going over the fourth-last so that you can let your horse get a bit of a breather, fill his lungs, before the dash up the home straight to the line. But you can't be too far back turning for home. The three fences in the home straight come at you so fast, and the straight is so flat, that it is impossible to make up significant ground from the third-last to the line. How many horses have you ever seen coming from a mile back to win the King George? Very few.

I had ridden Bacchanal prominently, we had led over the first four or five fences, but Adrian had wanted to go faster than I could, so I let him off. As a result, though, he was able to freewheel around the home turn while I was just asking Bacchanal to do a little bit on the outside in order to make up the ground. Even so, I thought that, once we straightened for home, I would outstay the pair of them. Unfortunately, it almost turned into a battle of speed rather than stamina, and the other two had more of that than Bacchanal. I could never get to grips with them over the last three fences, and we ended up finishing third, a gallant third, but still third. No cigar.

That was a mixed day for me. I won the Christmas Hurdle on Landing Light, but I could only finish third on Katarino in the Feltham Chase. I lost out by a head on Montpelier to McCoy and Perfect Fellow in the handicap chase, after I thought I had taken his measure over the last, and then, just to crown the day, I chose to ride Clandestine in the final race, the handicap hurdle instead of Cupboard Lover. Clandestine finished ninth. You know how this one ends. Cupboard Lover won the race under Johnny Kavanagh.

The deck wasn't as well stacked going to Cheltenham in 2002 as it had been on any of the previous three years, including the Cheltenham that wasn't. There was no See More Business, no Call Equiname, no Stormyfairweather. I had horses with chances, but nothing that was really standing out. Going to Cheltenham in 1999 and 2000, I was hoping for one winner each time, I went thinking that I would be delighted with one winner, but I knew that I had several real chances, I knew that there was a chance that I could have had more than one even though I never said it out loud and was scared to even admit it to myself. Any time you can leave the Cheltenham Festival with one winner in the bag, you have had a good Cheltenham Festival.

In 2002, my book of rides was lacking substance, lacking conviction. Fondmort in the Arkle, Got One Too in the Supreme Novices', Landing Light in the Champion Hurdle, Iris Royal in the Pertemps, Tiutchev in the Queen Mother, Bacchanal in the Gold Cup – all good rides, all rides that you were delighted to have, but I couldn't have put my hand on my heart before the meeting and said that I really fancied any one of them to win. And none of them did. None of them even finished in the first four.

The horses that fill the first four places go into the winner's enclosure at Cheltenham, there is a spot marked for each one. Of course it is the winner who comes in last and receives all the attention and adulation, and it had been frustrating in the past being in there in the runner-up spot, but this year I never even got into it. When you don't finish in the first four you dismount and unsaddle on the grassy area beside the parade ring on the way in from the racecourse. That can be a very lonely place, and it can get a bit monotonous when you end up there after all 14 or 15 of your rides. I finished fifth on Wave Rock in the Grand Annual. That was the closest I came.

At the last Cheltenham Festival, that had been me up there, basking in the glow. Now here I was, unsaddling in relative obscurity, anonymous, away from public glare, away from public care. It's a fickle business. If I had never been in the winner's enclosure at Cheltenham, I wouldn't have known what I had been missing. If I had never experienced the elation, the feeling of absolute personal and professional fulfilment that starts in the pit of your gut and almost explodes out through the top of your head when you are led back into that winner's enclosure, I wouldn't have known what I was missing. I may have looked longingly at Jim Culloty as he was being led in on Best Mate after the Gold Cup, or at Richard Johnson as he was being led in on Flagship Uberalles after the Champion Chase, but I wouldn't have fully appreciated the magnitude of what they were experiencing. It would be like you see someone eating a bar of chocolate, but you have never tasted chocolate yourself. You have a fair idea that you were missing out on something, something good, but you don't know exactly how good. I had tasted chocolate before, boxes of it, and I missed it desperately.

I headed off to Spain for a holiday with AP that summer. He had had a poor Cheltenham as well. He had gone into the meeting with lots of fancied rides, and he didn't have a winner until the second-last race, the Cathcart Chase, when he kicked Royal Auclair out of the gate and virtually carried him around the track. He wasn't going to leave that meeting without a winner. He was a grumpy old bollocks all week actually. In fairness, he did suffer a real downer in the Champion Hurdle when the horse he was riding, Valiramix, a really exciting young hurdler of Martin Pipe's, was traveling like the winner going down the hill on the far side, but he fell on the flat and had to be put down. When he came into the weigh room after winning the Cathcart, he wasn't ecstatic like he should have been after riding a winner at Cheltenham, he was more: 'Phew, at last, at least I've got one.'

In Spain he wouldn't shut up about the terrible Cheltenham that he had had. Poor me, I only had one winner. Eventually he came around though, and realised that one winner was better than no winners, my impressive haul for the week.

Nicky decided to run Marlborough in the Grand National that year, but he fell at the first with me, and I injured my left wrist. Two weeks later, my wrist was still sore when I went out to ride Fadalko to beat Wahiba Sands in a three-horse race at Cheltenham's April meeting, and when I pulled up it was killing me. An x-ray showed that it was broken, so that was the end of the season for me, six weeks on the sidelines.

*

I learned a little bit more about Fondmort when I rode him in a handicap chase at Wincanton in December 2002. It was his first time trying two and a half miles for us, so I wanted to ensure that he got the trip. So I rode him in behind, he jumped with his usual flamboyance, we crept and crept and crept, but I was getting there too soon, so I hung on to him a bit, not yet, we got to the last, I said now, let's go, but he couldn't. I had got there, disappointed him, and then I couldn't kick-start him again. We finished third, three lengths behind Poliantas. I resolved that I wouldn't let that happen again.

So when, in the Tripleprint Gold Cup at Cheltenham three weeks later, I crept and crept and crept on Fondmort, and his jumping took him into the firing line as far out as the third-last, I let him go. Go on now, no worries about your stamina, show us what you've got.

He had lots. He flew the second-last and careered down to the final fence, Foly Pleasant in vain pursuit, the race in the bag if he only jumped the fence. I saw a long stride, but it was very long, especially at the final fence in a two-and-a-half-mile chase when the pundits had said that it was lack of stamina that had beaten him at Wincanton. I pushed him into it, one, two, up you come, and he did. He soared.

He came up off the ground as if he was on springs, not the last lunge of a tired horse, but the poised leap of one who had lots more to give and was prepared to give it willingly. I was up in the air for longer than I had ever been in the air on any horse over any fence. He didn't touch a twig, he could have been a Puissance horse. Clear, no faults. Mike Tucker, the showjumping commentator, said to me afterwards that he had never seen a racehorse jump a fence as cleanly as Fondmort jumped the last fence in the Tripleprint that day. Of all the times I rode Fondmort, of all my eight wins on him, that win in the 2002 Tripleprint Gold Cup was the most satisfying, the most exhilarating.

Two weeks later I rode a five-timer at Newbury. That was an incredible day, one of those days when nearly everything went right. Seven rides, five winners, Saintsaire, Calling Brave, Iris Royal, Caracciola and Royal Rosa. Saintsaire won the juvenile novice hurdle, just a Class D event, but they put him in as the 7-1 favourite for the Triumph Hurdle directly afterwards. It was a crazy short price, but we did think the world of him. News of how he was impressing us at Seven Barrows must have leaked to the bookmakers.

A couple of weeks before Christmas I got a call from Tony Martin. Harvey (they call him Harvey after Harvey Smith, one of the best showjumping riders ever to don a red jacket) is a serious trainer. He is a great man to get a horse to improve, to lay one out for a big handicap and to know exactly how much the horse has in hand. When the Martin-trained Dun Doire won the William Hill Chase at Cheltenham in 2006, he raced off a handicap mark of 129. Just four months previously he had won a handicap chase at Wetherby off a mark of 79. In four months Tony had found improvement of 50lb in Dun Doire and still managed to train him to win one of the most competitive staying handicap chases on the calendar.

'Will you be able to ride one for me in the Pierse Hurdle on January 12?' Harvey asked.

'I will,' I said.

He didn't tell me who the horse was, and I didn't ask. I really didn't need to know. If Harvey was ringing me three weeks before the biggest handicap hurdle in Ireland to ask me if I was free to ride one for him in it, I was free all right, that was for sure.

'You know I can't do much less than 10st 7lb,' I said.

'Yeah, no bother.'

I watched Xenophon go around the Leopardstown paddock before the Pierse. He looked like a nice horse, a big chasing type actually, not an obvious hurdler. He had won his maiden almost a year previously, and on his only run since he had finished second in a handicap hurdle at Punchestown. I ask Harvey how he wanted me to ride him.

'Just drop him out early,' he says. He's a man of few words, Harvey. 'Have one or two behind you.'

I'm thinking: 'One or two behind me? Are you crazy? You know this is a 28-runner handicap on the inside track at Leopardstown, which they will hurtle around as if it is a stampede of wildebeest, and in which nobody will give an inch?'

'You can't do that on an inexperienced horse around here,' I protest.

'Just do it,' says Harvey quietly. 'It'll be fine. Don't hit the front until you are going to the last.'

'Fair enough.'

I couldn't believe this thing when I took him out on to the racecourse and down to the start. He was like a Rolls-Royce. A gorgeous animal, a really smooth mover, bursting with power. I did what Harvey had said. I rode him out the back, we were about tenth jumping the second-last flight, the last before you turn for home, we moved up on the outside, took it up before the last, then kicked away on the run-in. To be honest, it wouldn't have mattered how I had ridden him or who had ridden him. He was so talented, Harvey had produced him so well and he was so well handicapped, he would have won if Peter Kay had been riding him.

When I dismounted in the winner's enclosure, I told Harvey that he was one of the nicest young horses I had ever sat on.

'Great,' he said. 'What do you think we should run him in at Cheltenham?'

'It doesn't matter,' I said. 'The County Hurdle over two miles, the Coral Cup over two and a half, it doesn't matter, he has the speed for two and I have no doubt he would have the stamina for two and a half.'

'Grand,' said Harvey. 'I was thinking about the longer race. Will you ride him?'

'I'd be delighted to,' I said, 'once Nicky doesn't have anything in it. And I'll try to make sure he doesn't!'

I had a chat with Nicky when I was down at Seven Barrows the following Tuesday. I told him that Harvey was going to run Xenophon in the Coral Cup and that nothing that we had would beat him. I also told him that I really wanted to ride him, as I thought he would win. The British handicapper had given him a mark of 130, 13lb higher than the Irish mark off which he won the Pierse. He only got home by three lengths, so you could have thought of it as harsh. I didn't though, Harvey didn't, we knew that he had much more up his sleeve than that.

Nicky didn't run anything in the Coral Cup. I rode Xenophon, Harvey had produced him ready to run for his life on the day, and we won easy. I was delighted, as I always was to have a winner at the Cheltenham Festival. It had been a long three years since Stormyfairweather had won the Cathcart Chase. Xenophon was my only winner at Cheltenham in 2003.

I had always felt that he would make an even better chaser than a hurdler, I thought he would be a Gold Cup horse, and I'm sure Harvey shared my view, but it just didn't happen for him. He was never a natural over fences. He had bad hocks and he didn't really want to leave the ground. I rode him in his first chase, a novice chase at Navan the following December, and we were bang there travelling like the winner when he clouted the second-last. We ended up finishing third to Colnel Rayburn. I never rode him again after that, but he never managed to win over fences. His last run was in the Irish National at the end of that season. He looked to be thrown in on 10st 9lb, and he was right there in contention when he hit the second-last fence, came down, and broke his back. It was a sad end for a really gorgeous horse.

We lost Bacchanal that year as well, January 2003 in the Pillar Property Chase. I was gutted about that, I loved that horse. He was never the most fluent of jumpers, he had a low head carriage, he probably wasn't the most attractive galloper in the world, but he was so willing, he would always give you his all. I was off at the time with my injured ankle, so Ruby rode him in the Pillar Property. I was over in Ireland when Ruby called me to ask me about him, as he had never ridden him before.

Nicky was trying him in blinkers for the first time, see if they would sharpen up his jumping a little. He was right there among the top-class staying chasers, I had finished third on him behind Best Mate in the King George a month previously, the second King George in a row in which he had finished third, so Nicky was just trying to find that tiny little bit more that would give him a chance of winning the Gold Cup. He had won the Long Distance Hurdle at Newbury that November, so the plan was, if he took to blinkers, if they improved him over fences, to go for the Gold Cup, but if they didn't, if we decided that he didn't have any chance of beating Best Mate, to go back over hurdles and go for the Stayers' Hurdle again. We never got the chance to make the decision. He fell at the eighth fence in the Pillar Property, the one coming down the hill on the first circuit, and was killed.

I have never seen that Pillar Property Chase. I didn't watch it live and I sure as hell don't want to see a recording of it.

# CHAPTER 21

## EIGHT GRAND OUT THE WINDOW

Jump jockeys get injured. That's what they do. It's like policemen encounter ruffians from time to time, teachers get chalk marks on their jackets, jump jockeys break their bones. I have broken my neck, fractured almost all my vertebrae, done both my collarbones, fractured my shoulder, broken my arm, broken my wrist and broken my ribs, but the pain that I felt when I broke my left ankle second time around was as bad as it gets.

It began with a fall at Taunton in January 2003. I was riding a horse for Stuart Kittow, Hoteliers' Dream, in a poor novice hurdle. This thing was a 100-1 shot, but Stuart is a good mate and I was going to Taunton anyway so I said I'd ride it. We were out the back with no chance of winning when the horse stepped at the fourth-last hurdle and came down. When you hit the ground, you instinctively curl into a ball, and make yourself as small as you can. You hear the thump-thump-thump of hooves hitting the ground all around you, you brace yourself for an impact, you hope you won't get caught by a following hoof, sometimes you do and you're ok, sometimes you get caught and you're not ok, but you are all the while wincing, bracing, hoping that you won't feel an impact. Then they're gone, you exhale, you love that sound, the sound of silence, no more missiles to dodge.

I did that, no impact, not too bad, I wasn't sore anywhere, everything seemed ok, relief. Every time you hit the ground there is obviously a chance that you will do some lasting damage to yourself. It's a game of percentages. The more often you fall, the greater the chance of sustaining injury, so when you can get up uninjured after hitting the ground, things aren't so bad.

Silence, happy days, I moved my limbs, everything is working, not so bad, I got away with it. Next thing, crash! Hoof on timber, another horse coming along so far behind that he was virtually not in the race and probably should have been pulled up long since, Anthony Honeyball coming on a yoke of Paul Nicholls', Aussi Don, who had been about 20 lengths behind me, even though I was well behind the leaders. He crashed through the hurdle and landed on my horse, Hoteliers' Dream, who was on the ground beside me, then he landed on me, most of him on my left ankle, all half a ton of him.

The pain was excruciating, I knew I was in trouble straight away. They examined me at Taunton Hospital, X-rayed my ankle and said that I was grand, nothing broken. Not so bad, it would be better in a matter of days, I thought. I went home, delighted with myself. The next morning, however, I could hardly get out of bed, so I took myself straight into the Ridgeway Hospital in Swindon to see Dr Michael Foy, told him what had happened, told him that this clown had sent me home saying there was nothing wrong with me. He said, you're right, it's broken, so he put me in a cast and gave me exercises to do.

As soon as I could, I was on my feet, on the bike, in the water, I was desperate to get back riding as early as I could. This was January, so the last thing I wanted was to miss Cheltenham, I was definitely going to be back for Cheltenham. But this was a slow injury. Usually with me, the harder I work at injuries the faster they heal. The more you get your blood flowing around, the better, the easier it is and the faster the healing process. So I worked hard on this one, but it just wasn't coming right. I had cortisone injections and everything to try to get it back, but it was taking a long time.

I missed the Tote Gold Trophy meeting, I missed the ride on Non So in that, who finished second to Spirit Leader under Marcus Foley, but I was back in time for the Racing Post Chase meeting in late February.

I never felt that it was fully right though. My ankle was still painful through Cheltenham and Aintree. Xenophon was my oasis at Cheltenham, Irish Hussar my oasis at Aintree, winning the Mildmay Novices' Chase for Nicky. That was a big deal for us. It had been a while since we had had a winner at Aintree, Nicky didn't really aim horses at Aintree until relatively recently. It used to be Cheltenham or bust, all duck or no dinner, but now he thinks about Aintree a little bit and he will aim one there if he thinks that Aintree will be more suitable for the horse than Cheltenham. Irish Hussar was such a talented horse. He had the ability to be a Gold Cup horse for sure, but he was plagued by sore shins all his life.

My own shins weren't so good, but it's amazing how adrenaline keeps you going. I hardly even thought about it, I thought that it was just something that would get gradually better with time. The dull pain that was there all the time became normality.

Then in June came the fall from Rock'n Cold at Market Rasen. He was running in his first chase and had a good chance of winning. The horse shied on the way to the start and dropped me. I landed on the ground, it wasn't a bad fall or anything, it would have been almost like jumping off a three-foot wall and landing on your feet, but my left foot took the impact and a darting pain went all the way through my body. It's difficult to remember pain. You can remember colours or sights or sounds or smells, but try to remember pain, try to remember what a certain pain felt like, and you will struggle.

I can't remember the pain that I felt at that time, but I do remember thinking that I had never felt anything like it before in my life, as if somebody had shot my ankle off from close range. I thought about getting back on the horse – no jockey likes to suffer the ignominy of getting dropped on the way to the start – but I couldn't stand up. It was futile. The horse had to be withdrawn and I had to be hauled off to the Ridgeway again.

Dr Foy told me that my ankle was gone, that I had done a proper job on it this time. As well as my ankle, I had broken my tibia as well. It was really bad. Because of the strain that I had been putting on it over the previous four months, there was a chance that the bone might not have fused back together properly. He told me that my chances of riding again were just 50-50.

I couldn't believe it. I couldn't imagine not being a jockey, not being able to ride horses. What would I do? What else could I do? The next four weeks were the most difficult four weeks of my life. As well as all this doubt, this wondering if I would ever ride again, was the pain and the debilitation. Michael Foy did a fantastic job in putting my ankle together again and in giving it every chance to recover fully. In fact, Michael Foy has been brilliant throughout my career. After every injury, all the injuries that I have listed and many more, he was there to sort me out, to put me back together again. And later on when my mobility and very life hung by a thread, it was he who turned the thread into a safety net.

They gave me these crutches when I was leaving the hospital, but told me that I had to try to put some weight on my ankle, that I had to try to step on it as much as I could. I remember going to bed that evening, not feeling too bad, not in too much pain. The following morning I woke up, got on my crutches, and went to the loo, went to step away from the loo and crash! Straight to the floor. I thought I would be able to put a little bit of weight on my ankle, but I wasn't. Not an ounce. I had to crawl on my hands and knees in from the toilet. It was horrific, I was thinking, what's happening here, what's going on? So I got back to the bed, took some painkillers, put some ice on it, and started to do some work on it, gently at first. By lunchtime it wasn't too bad. I got on the bike, did some pedalling, got on the cross trainer, did some work on that. When I went to bed that night I was thinking, this isn't so bad now, this is really working. Next morning I got up, stepped out of bed, smash! Straight to the floor again, hands and knees again to the toilet.

This went on for about six weeks, no kidding. I would go to bed every night after exercising during the day thinking that I was getting better, that I was making progress, then next morning, without fail, as soon as I would go to step out of bed I would hit the floor. It's like, you walk into a bar and someone gives you a belt in the face. Next evening you go back, he says he won't hit you a belt in the face, so you go in, then whack. Next evening the same. Until one day, you realise that he's going to hit you a belt no matter what he says, so you are ready for it. He hits you a belt, but at least you are braced for it. Then one evening you go back and he doesn't hit you. Now you're healed.

I was going through my divorce at this time as well, so it was all coming down on me like a house of cards. It's funny now, thinking of me sitting in that hearing with Jane's solicitor running over and back with his various demands and suggestions, and me sitting there, with all my expletives, as angry as a wasp with a hangover, with my crutch and my broken ankle, absolutely immobile, Bente Nielson trying to restrain me, telling him that she wasn't getting a cent. It wasn't funny for me at the time, that's for sure, but I can understand how a fly on the wall might have been pissing himself laughing.

I was back riding by November, and I really appreciated it. It's like anything, when you don't have it you want it desperately. I rode the 1,000th winner of my career on Orswell Crest in a handicap chase at Sandown on November 8, 2003, then proceeded to ride two more winners the same afternoon, thus equalling Peter Niven's career total of 1,002 and making me the joint ninth winningmost jockey in the history of National Hunt racing. That was a difficult one to get my head around. There were only eight jockeys in the world who had ridden more National Hunt winners than me, and all of my idols were among them, Francome, Dunwoody, Scudamore. Indeed, some of my idols were behind me. Not only that, but 1,000 winners. That was just as difficult to fathom. One winner was to be cherished. I remember Lover's Secret at Ludlow in December 1998 as if it were yesterday. I remember going a year and a half without a winner and mentally packing my bags for New Zealand, now here I was, 1,000 winners in the bag. It was all a bit mind-blowing.

One of my other victories that day was on Iris Royal in the two-and-a-half-mile handicap chase, and that sparked an unbelievable run of big handicap-winning Saturdays for Nicky and me. The following Saturday, we won the Paddy Power Gold Cup with Fondmort. The following Saturday I won the big three-mile handicap hurdle at Aintree on Calling Brave and Nicky also won the First National Gold Cup at Ascot with Iris Royal, whom Marcus Foley rode. The Saturday after that, we drew a blank in the Hennessy. We had big hopes for Irish Hussar, who was favourite, but he made a bad mistake at the cross fence and I pulled him up. He would have had to have been at the very top of his game to have beaten the novice Strong Flow that day anyway. We got back on track two weeks later, however, when Iris Royal and I just got home by a head from Risk Accessor in the Tripleprint Gold Cup back at Cheltenham.

He was a gorgeous horse, Iris Royal, a true gent and a super jumper. He was a really game horse, but his wind was bad in the end, which was what held him back, but to win a First National and a Tripleprint in the space of three weeks was a fine achievement. He's still in training with Charlie Longsdon now as a 12-year-old, still owned by Sir Robert Ogden, but it breaks my heart to see him running around gaff tracks, trying his heart out. He was a grand servant and the nicest, kindest horse you could ever ride. He deserves a happy retirement.

Nicky's father, Johnny Henderson, died just before Christmas that year at the age of 83. That was a sad occasion, Johnny was an absolute gentleman and hugely influential in Nicky's career. It was very sad for Nicky, he was very close to him. Johnny had led a hugely interesting life. He was ADC to Field Marshal Montgomery in the North African desert in 1942 and he remained in his post with Montgomery throughout the Italian campaign and the advance of the Normandy landings to the German surrender. Although even back then he apparently liked a bet. He reportedly spent a day plying Montgomery with cups of coffee, not because he wanted to curry favour with the Field Marshal, but because he wanted to win a bet on how many times he would relieve himself that day. Johnny was appointed MBE in 1945 and OBE in 1985, and he and Montgomery apparently remained the best of friends until Montgomery's death.

It was Johnny Henderson who, when there was a threat that Cheltenham racecourse would be sold to developers, put together a group of investors to buy the racecourse for £240,000. Shortly afterwards, he set up Racecourse Holdings Trust, whose sole objective was to ensure that racecourses that were under threat of closure remained viable. He was also instrumental in saving Aintree racecourse from developers. He was amazingly visionary.

He was such a nice man, so polite, never had a bad word to say about anybody. The best horse he owned was Mighty Strong. I rode the horse for him innumerable times, I managed to win on him five times, but there was one time I rode him in a handicap chase at Newbury in November 2002, I had taken it up between the last two, we were going to win the race, no question, when I gunned him down to the last and put him on the floor. I couldn't believe it. It was the third time I had put him on the floor in five starts. I came in full of apologies, I was disgusted at myself for letting him fall, but Johnny was brilliant.

'Never mind,' he said. 'It was one of those things. There was nothing you could have done about it.'

There was another time, Johnny Kavanagh rode a horse for him, Acre Hill, in a handicap chase at Kempton in 1992, he won on him, came into the winner's enclosure, and began explaining to Johnny Henderson how the race had gone for him. Johnny Kavanagh has difficulty with his r's, he's a little bit like Jonathan Ross, and when he gets nervous or excited or embarrassed, his r's get even more pwoblematic. So Johnny is talking away, lovely horse, did it very well, jumped super, the works, and Johnny Henderson is nodding away politely, yes, yes, great, then Johnny Kavanagh heads off in with the saddle to weigh in, and Johnny Henderson is left with Johnny Worrall, Nicky's traveling head lad and says: 'I did not understand a word of that!'

Fondmort didn't stay in the 2003 King George. We didn't fully believe him when he told us he didn't stay in the Racing Post Chase the previous February. He had had to carry top weight that day, and we thought that, maybe if he was competing off level weights, another ten months older, he might be stronger, he might have a better chance of staying, but he didn't. Fondmort was a two-and-a-half-miler, pure and simple. I made up for the disappointment the following day, however, by riding a four-timer at Kempton, the highlight of which was Caracciola's victory over the Paul Nicholls horse Thisthatandtother, who was odds-on to beat us and who had been favourite for the Arkle up to that point.

A week later, Nicky and I were back on the big handicap treadmill again.

Isio was a horse who I really liked and he was owned by great people, Sir Peter and Lady Gibbings, just such lovely, lovely people, old-style National Hunt people, the type of people that define the spirit of National Hunt racing. I remember riding Isio for them in a novice hurdle at Kempton in February 2002. Isio didn't really like going right-handed in those days, he had a weakness in one of his joints and he found it hard to go right-handed. He came wide into the home straight at Kempton and he was hanging all over the place over the final two flights. I couldn't give him a ride at all, I was just trying to get him balanced, and we went down by a head to Hitman. I was disgusted with myself, I was frustrated at the ride I had given him, to be all over the shop like that and just get done a head. Surely I could have found that head from somewhere.

I came in to unsaddle, the owners were there, and I just said I'm really sorry. What else could I say? But they were ecstatic, they were delighted that we had got so close, that we had finished second in a big race at Kempton Park. Here I was, like somebody had just told me that a close relative had died, and they were over the moon. That's the type of people they are, always glass-half-full people. I was still gutted for them. I rang Nicky later that evening to get their number so that I could call them and apologise again, but they wouldn't hear of it.

It's lovely to ride for people like that, and when I lined up on Isio in the Victor Chandler Chase in January 2004, I thought he had a hell of a chance. Azertyuiop was a warm favourite in the race, but he was carrying top weight of 11st 10lb, we were carrying 10st 5lb. He had to give us 19lb. In the Arkle Chase at Cheltenham the previous March, Azertyuiop had beaten us by 12 lengths off level weights. Strictly on the book, then, we had his beating, and Isio's homework suggested that he had improved significantly since then.

Not that Azertyuiop probably hadn't improved as well. John Hales's gelding would go on to win the Champion Chase and, together with Moscow Flyer and Well Chief, form a triumvirate that would light up the two-mile chasing division for years. Azertyuiop had run just twice since he had won the Arkle, once when chasing home Moscow Flyer in the Tingle Creek Chase in December, and once when he unseated his rider at the first fence in the Haldon Gold Cup at Exeter on his seasonal reappearance. It was the only time that he fell or unseated in a 22-race career, so the rider must have been mighty embarrassed to get unseated at the very first fence. He was. It was also the only race in which I ever rode him.

I rode Isio handy the whole way. We took it up at the fifth fence. Got One Too, Nicky's other horse, ridden by Barry Fenton, took it up off us at the third-last, just before we turned into the home straight, but I was happy enough, we had gone a hell of a pace and I was confident that we could pick Got One Too up. Got One Too was not my primary concern. I took it back up off Barry at the second-last, and suddenly Ruby appeared on my outside on Azertyuiop. From there, it was lung-bursting, neck-stretching, nostril-flaring battle all the way to the line. Going to the last I thought I had him. There was no way he was going to beat me here, not giving me 19lb. Over the last and on the run-in, I thought we were beaten. He went at least a head up, maybe a neck, and looked to be the stronger. But Isio dug deep again and found reserves of energy that took him up Ascot's incline, up back up to Azertyuiop eyeball to eyeball, level with him, past him, home by a willing neck.

This game has a funny habit of knocking you flat when you are in the ascendancy. Just when you think you have it sorted, when things are going well, when you are finding it difficult to remember the bad times, the injuries, the long barren spells, when you are getting a little bit cocky in yourself, when you are on the road to invincibility, getting a little above your station, it has a habit of bringing you right back down to earth with a thud.

I was riding See You Sometime for Seamus Mullins in the Scilly Isles Chase at Sandown on February 7. The Scilly Isles is an important race on the novice-chasing calendar and, although See You Sometime was a 14-1 shot, I thought he had a chance. We were bang there travelling well going down the far side when he galloped straight into the eighth fence, the one before the ditch. He was a bit numb like that sometimes. Jamie Moore was coming along behind on Tikram, and one of the horse's hooves caught me square on my left arm, smashed it. I knew it was gone straight away, a searing pain from my left thumb all the way up to my left ear. I was straight up to the Ridgeway again to see Michael Foy. I almost had my own seat in the Ridgeway. If the Ridgeway had had a loyalty scheme, I would have been a Platinum member. The diagnosis wasn't encouraging: four weeks minimum, possibly six.

Those weeks were frustrating, and they went by very slowly for an incapacitated jockey. They are important weeks on the National Hunt calendar, the weeks when a lot of the Cheltenham aspirants are having their final runs before the Festival. The following Saturday, Geos won the Tote Gold Trophy under Marcus Foley, incredibly, four years after I had won it on him. Two weeks later, AP McCoy won the Pendil Chase on Calling Brave and Marlborough won the Racing Post Chase under Ruby Walsh the same day. A week after that, Isio and Barry Geraghty won the Vodafone Gold Cup. If I had had a cat at the time, he would have got a serious kicking.

In one sense I was delighted for Nicky, delighted for the yard, and I wouldn't for an instant begrudge Marcus or Ruby or AP or Barry those big wins. Marcus in particular deserved a big-race win like that, he is a fine rider who doesn't get the opportunities that his talent deserves. But it was difficult looking on from the sidelines. I suppose it's a bit like an injured or a suspended football player looking on from the stands or the dugout, half-willing his team on, half-gutted that he isn't part of it. When Roy Keane was suspended for the 1999 Champions League final, he found it difficult to hide his disappointment even as he celebrated with the team after winning it.

I was working for Channel 4 when Marlborough won the Racing Post Chase. I watched him the whole way through the race, watched him come under pressure at the fourth-last but I knew he would stay on, I thought they had gone too fast up front, and he got up and beat Gunther McBride fairly easily in the end. That was a killer. That was the hardest one to stomach. I loved Marlborough. Even though he was 12 years old by then, a veteran in racing terms, he still had bags of ability. I almost regarded him as my horse, he was a special horse for me and I just loved riding him. We had fought so many battles together and I loved the way that he loved making ground through his field, picking them off one by one and arriving there at the last.

John Francome came to me live on air.

'That won well,' he said in that typical Francome drawl that you know is trying to elicit a response. 'How do you feel?'

'I feel like someone has just driven a stake through my heart,' I said. 'And I've just watched eight grand flutter away out the window.'

My goal was to get back for Cheltenham, which I did. I rode out at Nicky's on the Tuesday before the Festival, I race-rode at Sandown on the Saturday beforehand, and I was right as rain for kick-off the following Tuesday. I needn't have bothered. Fondmort finished third behind Tikram under top weight in the Mildmay of Flete, and that was as good as it got.

It was desperately disappointing not to have a winner at Cheltenham. It always was. You'd walk out of the place on a real downer. You could say, get over it, it's only horseracing, and in a sense you would be right, but in another sense you would be as far removed from reality as *Celebrity Dancing on Ice*. It was all about Cheltenham for me and for Nicky, the whole year would be geared towards Cheltenham, some horses would have been targeted at a particular Cheltenham contest for more than a year, and when you walked out the gate on the last evening, dusk descending, without a winner to show for your endeavours, it was soul-destroying. Because it wasn't just a week's endeavours or four days' endeavours, it was the work of a year, sometimes more, and it was all for nothing if you didn't get your head in front at least once.

Nicky decided that he wouldn't take Isio to Cheltenham that year, that he would keep him for the Melling Chase at Aintree. We figured that he wouldn't have had much of a chance of beating both Moscow Flyer and Azertyuiop at level weights, and we thought that the two and a half miles at Aintree would suit him better than the two miles at Cheltenham. Unfortunately, Moscow Flyer unshipped Barry Geraghty at the fourth-last at Cheltenham, so he hardly had a race, and his trainer Jessica Harrington decided that he was still fresh enough to go to Aintree. So that didn't work out either.

Isio and I tried to outstay Moscow at Aintree. He had never won over two and a half miles before and Isio had just won the Vodafone Gold Cup over the distance, so I kicked on early trying to draw the speed out of him, but Moscow stayed it well. He just ran away from us over the second-last. Nicky and Jessie are great mates, Nicky stays with Jessie for Punchestown and Jessie usually stays with Nicky for Cheltenham, but it counted for nothing. There was no question of Jessie leaving the Melling Chase to Nicky, not when she had a potential two-and-a-half-mile superstar

standing in his box, fresh as paint. Sorry Nicky, it's fair game. Now, for
how many days are you staying with us during Punchestown?

# CHAPTER 22

## DREAM TICKET

The BBC screened a *Panorama* documentary on race-fixing in July 2002 that caused a furore in racing circles. In it, Chris Bell, head of Ladbrokes, claimed that at least one horserace every day was fixed. Afterwards I was contacted by a couple of journalists and asked for my opinion. I told them that, to my knowledge, I had never ridden in a fixed race, nor had I ever heard about one.

It was an absurd claim for the head of one of the biggest bookmakers in the UK to make. Racing now is cleaner than it has ever been. You hear stories from old, from the good old days, of jockeys fixing races, you win today and I'll win tomorrow. There are stories of horses going into a fog or behind a mound in front and coming out 20 lengths behind, but even if you wanted to, there is no way you could do anything like that these days. There are cameras everywhere now, they have every angle covered, you're being watched all the time, not just by the stewards but by punters, with every single race run in the UK these days shown in betting shops and on At The Races and Racing UK. Every move that a jockey makes is dissected and analysed.

With the advent of Betfair and the other betting exchanges, you can now lay horses to lose. You could probably always do that with a friendly bookmaker if you wanted, but the presence of the betting exchanges makes it more accessible to the ordinary punter. Ostensibly, you used to have to be able to pick the winner of a race in order to make money, now it is enough that you pick one that isn't going to win.

But Betfair's policing methods are merciless. If you have an abnormal strike-rate at laying losers, it appears that you are immediately flagged up on Betfair's system, and they notify the authorities. A recent follow-up programme by Panorama highlighted that. You can see it from Betfair's point of view. They are being castigated by the bookmakers for encouraging skulduggery, for providing people with an easy solution if they know that a horse isn't going to win, so Betfair want to be seen to be squeaky clean, to bring any suspicious betting patterns to the attention of the authorities. If you knew that a horse wasn't going to win, I'd say that the last place you would lay it would be on Betfair.

There was a horse of Nicky's involved in a BHB investigation. It was a race at Leicester in February 2004 in which Tollbrae got beaten by Venn Ottery. I was off injured at the time so Marcus Foley rode Tollbrae. Venn Ottery beat him by six or seven lengths, Marcus gave Tollbrae a tender ride and the stewards had him and Nicky in afterwards to explain the ride. What most people didn't know was that Tollbrae had fallen when schooling that week. He wasn't a great jumper anyway, and Leicester's fences at the time were among the stiffest in Britain. Marcus was intent on getting him to jump around, so he rode him patiently out the back, maybe too patiently in the end, but that's with the benefit of hindsight.

Some people probably knew that he had fallen at Seven Barrows, stable lads talk, which is probably why people were laying him on the betting exchanges. The whole incident put a bit of a black mark against Marcus, which was really unfair, he's a good rider, but he's a sympathetic rider, a quiet rider, and his style can give the impression that he's not trying too hard, which counted against him that day. He was very upset by the whole thing.

Trabolgan made his debut over fences at Lingfield Park in November 2004. I loved Trabolgan from the start. He was always one of those horses who loved himself, he just thought that he was gorgeous, better than any other horse in the world. If he was a human being he'd be the quarterback.

Every time Trabolgan stepped up a level, he got better. He ran in three bumpers, and he finished second in the three of them, stepping up in class each time. I only rode him in one of them, his second bumper at the Kempton meeting that is just before Cheltenham, and I got him beaten. I hit the front too soon on him, I was just travelling so well on him that I let him go on about three furlongs out, and we got caught by Jim Culloty on a horse of Henrietta Knight's, Chelsea Bridge.

I didn't ride Trabolgan in the 2003 Cheltenham Bumper, I chose to ride Back To Ben Alder instead, which I thought was a fair decision given how impressive Back To Ben Alder had been on his only run at Kempton six weeks previously under Marcus Foley. He didn't perform at all at Cheltenham, we finished last of the 24 finishers. Trabolgan and Seamus Durack, on the other hand, finished second behind Liberman at 50-1.

We were hoping that Trabolgan's run at Cheltenham wasn't just a one-off. You know that a horse needs to have a degree of class to finish second in a Cheltenham Bumper, it is invariably a hot race, but sometimes they can't reproduce that level of form again. Obviously we were hoping that we would have a nice horse to go to war with over hurdles that season and over fences the following season. Trabolgan was always an embryo chaser, but we were especially hopeful because he was owned by Trevor Hemmings.

Trevor is a fantastic supporter, he loves his National Hunt racing, and he had recently sent a good few really nice young horses to Nicky for the first time. One of them was Inca, who had finished second to Joe Cullen in the 2000 Cheltenham Bumper and who looked a really nice prospect. Unfortunately Inca died on the gallops at Seven Barrows, just shattered his fetlock doing a routine piece of work. The previous week another really nice horse of Trevor's, who had yet to see a racecourse, shattered his fetlock as well. It was unbelievable, the two of them were just cantering on the gallop at Seven Barrows, which is like a carpet, both of them just went, just like that, shattered a leg and had to be destroyed. It was desperate luck for Trevor, so Nicky was really hoping that he would have a nice horse for him.

Trabolgan's hurdling career got off to a fairly inauspicious start. I rode him in a novice hurdle at Aintree in November 2003, we came to the fourth-last going well, jumped the flight well, then about three strides after the hurdle he just stumbled and came down. Things got better after that though. He won his next two hurdle races, progressing all the time, then Marcus rode him in a novice hurdle at Market Rasen in February 2003 when he went lame, and he pulled him up before the fourth fence. After that, Nicky decided to leave him off for the summer, and bring him back in the autumn to go steeplechasing, which was, after all, what he was bred for.

He was very good for me that day on his chasing bow at Lingfield. It was desperate ground, which he really hated, always did, but he got out of it ok, jumped well, joined the leaders at the third-last and went on over the last two fences to win impressively. I got off him beaming. 'This is some tool,' I said to Nicky.

He missed his next intended run because of the weather and suddenly the Feltham Chase at Kempton's Christmas meeting was upon us. Nicky decided that he would let him take his chance in the race, see how good he really was. That race was a disaster for us. Ollie Magern and Carl Llewellyn set a fair pace in front, Trabolgan made a mistake at the second fence, got fairly badly hampered when L'Ami fell in front of us at the first down the far side, then walked through the third-last, just walked through it, I have no idea how he stood up on the landing side.

I got him back going after that, jumped the second-last well, winged the last, and suddenly we had caught Ollie Magern and had gone a neck up. Happy days. Then he rallied, the bastard, and got back up to beat us by a short head. I felt sick, there was a race that I should have won. I shouldn't have let The Welsh get back at me once I had gone a neck up. I thought that this was the horse that we had been waiting for, the big horse who would go right to the very top, and here I was after losing the Feltham on him.

Looking back on the performance a couple of days later, it was actually a very good run. Despite those mistakes, despite the interference, on only his second ever run over fences, he had been just beaten by Ollie Magern, who had already run in five chases, and had finished second in the Hennessy Cognac Gold Cup on his previous run.

The Royal & SunAlliance Chase at Cheltenham in March was always going to be Trabolgan's target after that. Nicky was never a great man for the SunAlliance Chase, he thought that it could bottom horses out, and sure enough the race went through a period in the 1990s when it seemed that the winners of the race were taking a long time to recover from their exertions. But Trevor Hemmings was a big fan of the SunAlliance Chase, he loves his three-mile chasers and it didn't make sense to him to have a staying novice chaser who was as good as Trabolgan could have been and not run him in the SunAlliance.

We took Trabolgan to Haydock in January for his prep run for the SunAlliance. Trevor loves Haydock, it's his favourite track, his local track, but the ground was atrocious there, real pea soup. Trabolgan hated heavy ground, he could hardly even walk on it. The experience with Raymylette was in the back of my mind. I always thought that Raymylette never really felt the same after he had run that time at Haydock on heavy ground, the time that Earth Summit beat him in the Peter Marsh Chase. He had such a hard race that day that it could have bottomed him. So I figured that I'd look after Trabolgan if he wasn't handling the ground.

I held him up, made some ground into the home straight, closed up on the approach to the third-last, but Nicky Richards' horse, Jazz D'Estruval, who absolutely relished soft ground, just went away from us under Tony Dobbin. I accepted the situation, I wasn't going to beat Trabolgan up to have him just get a little closer, but when we jumped the last I moved him over to the middle where there was a strip of ground that I had noticed when I had walked the track earlier, about two horse-widths wide, that wasn't as chewed up as the ground was on the stands' side, and he picked up nicely. We were never going to catch the winner, but I was hugely encouraged by how well he finished the race once he got on to the better ground. And the big thing was that the horse came home not having had a hard race. Next stop Cheltenham.

Nicky and I discussed the race beforehand. It didn't look like it was going to be a very hot SunAlliance Chase. Ollie Magern and Lord Of Illusion, two of the top staying novice chasers that season, missed the race due to injury, so Trabolgan was going to be among the favourites. I told Nicky that I thought he needed plenty of daylight, there was no point in going down the inside, being a brave man, with a novice who had only run in three chases in his life. Better to go middle to outside, the ground that we would lose by going a little bit wide would be more than compensated for by the momentum that we would maintain and the space that he should have at his fences as a result.

Nicky was happy with that, so that was what I did. Trabolgan jumped brilliantly behind a fast pace that was set by Timmy Murphy on Comply Or Die, out of this world, better than he had ever jumped, until we got down to the second-last. There were a lot of fallers at the second-last at that Festival, and we were meeting the fence on a wrong stride, just a little too long for a long one at that stage of the race. So I thought, right, here's a situation where you do nothing. If you fire him at this fence and he doesn't fancy it, if he puts down, he'll turn a somersault that will probably kill the two of us. Just leave it up to him, let him go in and fiddle his way over it if he wants, he will because he's clever, and we don't need to fly the fence anyway, we are travelling well enough. So I sat still, and lo and behold he got into the fence so deep that I thought there was no way he was going to get over it. A kangaroo wouldn't have been able to get out and over the fence from where he went, right into the base of the fence. But he did. He's so athletic. Up he popped like he was on springs, landed on the other side, made a bit of a mistake, but I would have easily settled for that a fraction of a second earlier, and galloped on.

Comply Or Die was still in front going down to the last, but I knew I had him covered. I kicked Trabolgan on down to the last and I thought, here, you're not going to do that trick again, so I drilled him down to it, saw a stride and he flew it. That was it, race over, I punched him up the hill all the way to the line.

That was a great win. It was an important one for me – weren't they all? – and for Nicky, but it was especially important for Trevor Hemmings. He had never had a winner at the Cheltenham Festival before. Quite remarkably, two hours later he had his second winner, as Juveigneur went and won the amateur riders' race, the Kim Muir, for Nicky under Richard Burton.

Trabolgan was my only winner at Cheltenham in 2005, but what a winner. He was beginning now to fulfil the dreams and expectations that we had for him. SunAlliance Chase this year, Gold Cup next year, he was our dream ticket.

It was the year that the Festival was extended from three days to four, the Cathcart Chase was abolished and replaced with the Daily Telegraph

Chase, which was also run over two miles five furlongs, but was open to all, not restricted to first- and second-season chasers like the Cathcart was. That was ideal for Fondmort. That trip around Cheltenham was just what he wanted. I'm sure he was sick of carrying big weights in handicaps, so it made sense to step him up to Graded company.

I thought we were going to win the Daily Telegraph as well. He jumped super throughout, I took it up early in the back straight, Ruby Walsh on Thisthatandtother joined me at the third-last and the pair of us went all out from there all the way home. The upper-hand see-sawed between us a couple of times, I thought we were going to win at the bottom of the hill, halfway up it I thought we were beaten, then Ruby got in a bit of a tangle when he tried to change his whip, and we went ahead again, but he got it sorted in time and drove Thisthatandtother home by half a length. I was as disappointed for the horse as I was for myself. He deserved to win a race at the Cheltenham Festival. You don't always get what you deserve in racing, but a year later, he would.

Nicky decided to allow Fondmort to take his chance in the Grand National that year. There is an old theory that still has some resonance with some of the older racing people that what you need for the Grand National is a good two-and-a-half-mile chaser. It's a slightly bizarre theory given that the National is a real grueller these days, run over four and a half miles, the longest race on the British racing calendar, and it is probably founded on Gay Trip's win in the race in 1970. But whereas they hunt around for the first circuit these days and only begin to race on the second circuit, back then they hacked around for the first circuit and probably didn't start really racing till they were over the Melling Road on the way home, with the result that horses who didn't truly stay four and a half miles could run very well. Nicky had had two-and-a-half-mile chasers do well for him in the past at Aintree, Zongalero was second to Rubstic in the 1979 National, Classified finished third behind West Tip in 1986 and The Tsarevich was second to Maori Venture in 1987, so he was keen for Fondmort to have a go.

One thing that wasn't surprising was that Fondmort took to the fences. It was some thrill to ride such a good jumper over those massive fences.

He gave me an unbelievable ride, he just danced over those fences. I was trying to get him to go short, trying to get him to conserve his energy, but at the same time I didn't want to disappoint him. He wasn't listening anyway. He would just see one of those big green spruce mounds and he'd want to attack it, whoosh! Then it was hard to break his rhythm, the fences come at you so fast. At Becher's Brook, he stood off a mile, I thought there was no way he was going to make it, but he flew the fence and landed running. Eventually and inevitably, though, he began to falter at Valentine's Brook second time, and he totally ran out of petrol before we got back to the Melling Road, so I pulled him up at the third-last.

It was a real pity that he could never run in the Topham Chase. Two miles six furlongs over the Grand National fences, that would have been some spin, it would have been ideal. But up until 2007, you couldn't run in the Topham if you were rated higher than 150. Fondmort had been rated 150 or higher since he won the Tripleprint in 2002. It was a ridiculous rule and it kept him out of the race. I kept saying it to the handicapper, Phil Smith, about changing the rule and eventually, last year, they did, but it was too late for Fondmort. He got injured at home preparing for the 2006/07 season, and he never raced again.

He was a fantastic horse. I have been very lucky in my career to ride some horses who would lay down and die for you, and Fondmort was one of them. I rode him in all but three of his races since he came over to Nicky's from France, 30 times in total, and I won on him eight times, four times at Cheltenham and three times at Kempton. He was a grand servant, and he was part of my life for six years – much longer than most of my girlfriends.

*

Golf always did it for me. From the time that Shane Donohoe introduced me to the game, it is the only activity that ever rivalled racing for me, it is the only other sport about which I have ever got really passionate. I enjoyed playing football and hurling when I was a kid, I enjoy watching sport, I'm a Manchester United and a Swindon Town supporter, but golf was the only sport that ever got to within shouting distance of racing for me.

I was asked to play in the JP McManus Pro-Am at Adare Manor in Limerick in the summer of 2005. I was riding a little bit for Jonjo O'Neill at the time, and Gay Smith, wife of Derrick Smith, whose purple and white colours have since become synonymous with some of those top-class Ballydoyle horses on the Flat, had a few horses in training with Jonjo, so Derrick and Gay asked me if I would play in the Pro-Am. That was a big thrill and a great honour.

That was an amazing experience. I'm lucky that I have got to know some of the golfing lads over the years, Darren Clarke and Lee Westwood and all the lads who are involved with ISM, Chubby Chandler's organisation for which I still do some work on the racing side, but I was still a bit star-struck playing at Adare that weekend. Something like 15 of the top 25 golfers in the world were there, Tiger Woods, David Duval, Davis Love.

AP McCoy and I played with Michael Owen and Padraig Harrington on the first day, the second day we played with Justin Rose. It was a bit daunting standing up on the first tee with the fairways all lined with people. It was a huge event, one of the biggest sporting events to take place in Ireland that year. There were more than 50,000 people there over the weekend, and it was great just to be a part of it.

We were coming up the 18th fairway, AP, Michael Owen, Padraig Harrington and me. This was before Harrington had won his first Open, so he wasn't an international superstar at the time. Owen was playing for Real Madrid. So we've all driven off and we've all hit our second shots and we're all over the bridge on the green. We're walking up the fairway to the green when the crowd breaks through the barrier that is holding them back and comes rushing towards us. Harrington is walking up with me, so he stops and takes out his pen. All the golfers have their own pens with them all the time, apparently, it stops them messing around with autograph-hunters' pens. So he has his pen out, ready for the hordes of autograph hunters that are about to mob him. They all come charging up, straight past me, straight past AP, straight past Harrington and almost smother Michael Owen. Harrington has a little chuckle to himself and puts his pen back in his pocket.

'I won't be needing this then.'

I didn't play that well though, which was desperately disappointing because I had been playing fairly well before going over. I didn't go mad on the first night, the craic was great but I just had a few beers and went to bed relatively early because I wanted to be fresh and ready for the next day. I might have played better if I had been hungover, I certainly couldn't have played any worse. Some of the lads were asking me afterwards if I learned anything from playing with Padraig Harrington and Justin Rose – yeah, I learned that instead of walking across the bridge on the 18th at Adare Manor, I should have stopped and thrown my clubs into the water underneath.

There is a big difference between 50,000 people at Adare Manor and a summer afternoon at Market Rasen, even Summer Plate day at Market Rasen, but that's where I was three weeks later. I rode a 40-1 shot in the first, the handicap hurdle (finished nowhere), I rode a 66-1 shot in the second, the juvenile hurdle (nowhere), and got ready to ride Celtic Boy in the big race, the Summer Plate, for Peter Bowen. We were travelling well early on, but we got the fifth fence wrong and came down. Jamie Moore was coming behind on a horse of Philip Hobbs's, Royal Tir, and he caught me, came down and kicked me on the back of the head. I was knocked out cold for a minute or two, but when I came around I knew straight away that it was serious. My head and neck were sore, like a strange sort of pain, different to anything I had felt before, and it felt like my shoulder was smashed as well.

The racecourse medics obviously thought that it was bad enough to get an air ambulance, they put me on a spinal board and took me to Lincoln Hospital. My shoulder was in bits, in real pain, but they X-rayed me at the hospital and figured that it wasn't so bad.

'Your back is ok,' the doctor said to me, 'your neck is ok, so we're going to take you off the spinal board.'

'Are you sure?' I asked him.

'Yeah, yeah, I'm certain.'

'Hold on a second,' I said. 'I'm telling you now, there is something seriously wrong here. I've broken my shoulder before and it was nothing like as painful as this.'

'It's a really bad break,' said the doctor. 'You got a bang on the head, you were knocked out, we're going to keep you in overnight just to observe you, but trust me, your neck and back are ok.'

I slept very badly that night, even with painkillers, woke up in the morning and still felt terrible. I got home, still felt terrible. I couldn't lie down. The only way I could sleep was by propping myself up straight with cushions. I couldn't sleep for very long, I was tired all the time, and I could never get comfortable, I was in constant pain. AP was hosting a party at Kingston Lisle, I wasn't going to go to it, I was in too much pain, but I figured what the hell? I may as well be in pain and enjoying myself at a party instead of being in pain and feeling sorry for myself, a miserable git at home. I got absolutely twisted at the party, after which AP brought me home. I thought I'd sleep then in my bed, but I couldn't. It was like someone had driven a stake though my shoulder and my neck.

I went to Ridgeway Hospital the next day. Mike Foy was on holiday but they looked at the X-rays and said that there was no obvious signs of anything else except the shoulder. Four days went by, I still wasn't getting any better, so I went to see Rabbit Slattery at Newbury races, and she said that she wasn't happy with the way that it wasn't progressing. Mike came back from holidays a few days later, he sent me for an MRI back at Ridgeway, and I went to see him at his clinic in Marlborough.

'How did you get here,' he asked.

'I drove,' I said, slightly bemused.

'Right well you can't drive home.'

'What do you mean I can't drive home?' I asked.

'You've broken your neck,' he said, matter-of-factly. He could have been telling me that it was lunchtime. 'You've fractured C7 and T1. Normally around that area, if it's stable you're ok, we don't have to do anything, but it's not stable and it has penetrated your spinal cord case. If you were to get hit from behind in your car, you would be paralysed. You're a very lucky boy. If you fall over, wearing no neck brace as you are at the moment, you could be in a wheelchair for the rest of your life.'

This was 11 days after my fall. Lucky I didn't go and get drunk at any parties.

Jeremy Fairbank did the operation the following day. He put two titanium rods down into the damaged vertebrae, four screws and two bits of wire. I woke up after the operation and couldn't believe how little pain I felt. Even my shoulder felt fine. I was relieved in a way that they had found something wrong with me, that I wasn't just imagining it or finding it more difficult to bear pain as I was getting older, and I was delighted that that pain had gone.

I went home to relax and recuperate. I would have four months to do so.

# CHAPTER 23

## OVERWHELMED

I suppose it was natural for people to think that I might have retired at that point, that I might have thought that enough was enough. I was 35 years old, I had had a great innings and more than my fair share of time among the top echelons of National Hunt riders, and I could have walked away with all my limbs and all my faculties intact, but the thought never entered my head. I simply didn't even consider it as an option.

I couldn't say that my neck injury didn't scare me a bit though. Actually, it was more the fact that I had walked around for 11 days with a broken neck, driven all over the place and gone out and got drunk, and the danger in which I had therefore unwittingly placed myself, that scared me when I sat down to think about it. I think it frightened my dad a bit as well. He wasn't a bit happy about the whole thing. However, from a career perspective, it was just another broken bone, more serious than the normal broken collarbone or broken wrist all right, but the only implication of that for me was that I was going to be out for longer.

Strangely enough, when I was younger, when I thought about retirement, if I thought about retirement, I always thought that 35 would be a good age at which to do it. But more than that, I always said to myself that I wouldn't outstay my welcome, that I would quit before I started to go into decline, and that I would know when that was, when I was ready. I certainly wasn't ready in the summer of 2005.

AP says it now, he says that he will retire when he is 35. He won't. How will he? He will still feel the same as he does now, he will still have the same will to win, the same ability, the same fearless mentality. I felt the exact same mentally at 35 as I did at 25. Physically I felt different, I had had a few more knocks and bruises, and it was taking a little longer to recover from each one, but mentally I was exactly the same. I hadn't lost any of the verve.

Dunwoody retired when he was 35 and it killed him. He thought that he would ride on until he was at least 40, his dad rode a winner when he was 50. Woody just wasn't ready to give up when injury got the better of him, and he has struggled with that since. I'm not sure that he has learned to deal with it fully yet. Woody was obviously someone for whom I had huge admiration, someone that I looked up to as a jockey, because he was a brilliant rider. He has done so much for racing, he raised the bar for jockeys by setting such high standards himself. And now I see him, going on treks to the North Pole, conquering mountains, chasing around the world setting impossible targets for himself, and it irks me a little bit. When he achieves one impossible target he sets another. It seems to be never-ending.

He's still trying to fill the massive void that was there when he had to stop racing, he's still trying to recreate the adrenaline rush that he used to get from riding horses at 35 miles an hour over fences. He turned his back on racing in the beginning, and he is getting back into it a little now, but only a little. I still think Woody finds it hard to be around racing now that he is not riding, and that's a real shame.

Nicky was great during the time that I was out. Perhaps that is why retiring wasn't a realistic option. He kept on telling me that my job was waiting there for me when I got back, that all the owners were on wondering when I would be back. That was brilliant. My aim was to be back riding as quickly as possible. It soon became apparent that I wasn't going to make it for the Paddy Power meeting at Cheltenham in November, so the Hennessy at the end of November was the next big meeting, and that looked like a realistic goal.

Nicky was preparing Trabolgan for the Hennessy. It was a natural target for him. Second-season chasers tend to do well in the Hennessy, probably because they are improving at a faster rate than the handicapper can determine, and Trabolgan was almost certainly the best staying novice of the previous season.

I went down to Nicky's two weeks before the Hennessy to ride out for the first time since my accident. I have to admit, I was a little nervous, not about actually getting up on a horse again, it wasn't a fear of falling off and injuring myself or anything as self-preserving as that, but about how I would feel getting up on a horse again. Would I still get the same kick, would I still have the same feel? Fondmort, quite appropriately, was the first horse on whom I rode work when I came back and, when I got up on him, before I had my feet in the irons, he shied a little, but I caught a hold of him quickly and allowed him to settle down again. It felt good. If that was a test, I passed it with honours.

I was a little stiff though. When I adopted my usual sit on the horse, I was looking straight down at the ground, I couldn't lift my head to look forward. I was doing lots of exercises to try to loosen up my neck muscles, but it was taking a while. I thought I was going to get seasick riding out those first few days, all I could see was the ground bobbing up and down beneath me. I had to tilt my whole body back so that I could look out through the horse's ears. Nicky says he wondered if I could see where I was going.

Trabolgan looked and felt great. He was only seven years old, going on eight, an age at which staying steeplechasers can improve a huge amount, and he had really strengthened up well over the summer. It looked like he was going to be lumbered with top weight in the Hennessy. It had been 21 years since a top weight had won the Hennessy, but I wasn't too concerned about that. This fellow could have been anything.

I was riding him work for those two weeks, but then on the Tuesday before the Hennessy, Trabolgan's last piece of work before the race, I went in expecting to ride him out, but I wasn't down to ride Trabolgan. I thought that it was a mistake, but you don't question these things. But it wasn't a mistake. Nicky had taken me off him because he thought that I might try too hard on him, I might do more on him than Nicky wanted him to do because I might be trying to prove to myself or to Nicky that I was back, that I was up for the job. He just thought that there was a small chance that it would be as much about me as it was about the horse, and he wanted to remove that chance. That attention to detail is remarkable, and that is why Nicky Henderson has been one of the top trainers in Britain for decades.

I was back riding at Warwick during the week before the Hennessy, and I rode The Market Man to win a handicap hurdle at Newbury on the Friday, the day before the Hennessy. It was great to be back riding again, but it was even better to be back in the winner's enclosure. I had missed that feeling more than I knew I had.

I got a phone call from Andrew Franklin, head of Channel 4 Racing, on Friday evening to ask me if I would go on the *The Morning Line* on the Saturday morning, Hennessy morning. The bookmakers had made Trabolgan favourite, so I was the natural choice I suppose, just back from injury and everything, but I declined. I love going on *The Morning Line* and giving my opinions about races, but I thought that I should go in and ride out first lot at Nicky's instead. Hennessy day is a huge day at Nicky's, not only because it's the biggest day at the local track and Nicky is likely to have runners, but because the stable lads who aren't looking after runners want to get home early so that they can either go racing or go home and watch it on television.

The race went great, almost exactly as I had planned and as Nicky and I had discussed. I got my position a little off the rail and just behind the leaders. Trabolgan was still relatively inexperienced and there was no point in going down the rail. The important thing was to get him into a rhythm. I always try to get my position and maintain it, try to engineer a little bit of space for myself wherever I sit in the field. It is important that you have room to jump, that you are not all the while competing with other horses for space in the air, or jumping on to the heels of horses. Good jockeys can generally find that space in a race in much the same way as a good midfielder always seems to have lots of time on the ball. Watch Cesc Fàbregas play football these days, or Paul Scholes, or Deco, or Liam Brady back in the 1970s and 1980s, they always seem to have time on the ball to pick out a pass. You think: 'How come he has so much time? He wouldn't have been able to play that pass if they had closed him down sooner.' But he did have that time, he made it for himself. That's what good players do.

During the Shergar Cup at Ascot in 2008, I watched an interview with Russell Baze, the American jockey who is vying for the title of having ridden more winners than any other jockey in the world ever. He rode his 10,000th winner in February 2008. Quite incredible. But there was one thing that I took out of his interview, one thing that every young apprentice should be taught. He said that everyone wants to ride the perfect race. Everyone wants to sit last on the rails, bring his horse through the field, weaving and ducking, taking the gaps as they appear, land in front just on the line and win by a short head. That's all very fine, but if you want to ride lots of winners, you just have to be in a position where you won't meet with interference.

Trabolgan made a mistake at the second fence in the back straight, and he made a slight mistake at the cross fence, the fifth-last, just before turning into the home straight, but he was never in danger of coming down. Once we turned in, however, I felt sure that we were going to win it. There were quite a few horses who appeared to be travelling well around me at the top of the home straight, but I felt like I had a lot of horse underneath me, and that it was going to take a supreme effort from something else if we were to get beaten. L'Ami and David Casey took it up from Ballycassidy at the fourth-last, but we were very quickly out after him. We jumped to the front at the second-last, and we set sail for home. Trabolgan found loads. He winged that last and stayed on really strongly up the run-in, making light of the supposed steadier of 11st 12lb.

That was an extraordinarily emotional victory. I felt as emotional after winning the Hennessy on Trabolgan as I have ever felt after winning any race. It was a combination of lots of things. For starters, it was my first Hennessy win, it was Nicky's first Hennessy win, and that was huge, the biggest race of the season at our local track, one of the biggest handicap chases on the calendar. There was also the issue of me coming back, possibly in the face of some questioning from certain quarters, and the faith that Nicky and Trevor Hemmings had shown in me, and the fact that Trabolgan was such a horse for us for the future, potentially a real live Gold Cup prospect. And my brother was there, and his wife, and Chloe was there, my girlfriend at the time, now my wife, so there was a lot going on in my head that was ready to jump out and grab me if I relaxed my guard and allowed it.

I did. I crossed the line and it all hit me, all of a sudden, and it overwhelmed me. I have always been able to switch off my emotions like a tap, I have always been able to keep them under control, but I lost control a little after winning the Hennessy on Trabolgan.

Someone stuck a microphone in my face after I pulled up, I think it was Alice Plunkett from Channel 4, trying to get the sentiments of the winning jockey just after he had crossed the line in the Hennessy, and I just welled up. I couldn't speak. I almost burst into tears. It was quite extraordinary, quite inexplicable. And if I had, I would have had no idea why. I nearly did a Gwyneth Paltrow on it, and that would have been a disaster. It would have ruined a lifetime of creating a tough-guy image.

Nicky was ecstatic and quite emotional as well. It was brilliant for everyone, it was great for all the lads at Seven Barrows as well, a win like that in a big race lifts everyone in the yard. Corky Browne, Johnny Worrall, Trabolgan's lass Sarah. Trevor Hemmings mind was made up. It had been an amazing few months for Trevor. As well as Trabolgan providing him with his first Cheltenham Festival winner and winning the Hennessy, he had also seen his colours carried to victory in the Grand National in April by Hedgehunter. Staying steeplechasers is what Trevor Hemmings is all about, and now he had one who was capable of going right to the top, that was a real live Gold Cup contender. The bookmakers put him in at 5-1 second favourite for the Gold Cup after the Hennessy, and it was difficult to argue with that. Next stop, the King George.

A couple of days later I got a call from Paul Nicholls to ask me if I would ride Kauto Star in the Tingle Creek Chase at Sandown the following Saturday. That was some phone call to receive. Kauto Star was already being hailed as the new black. He had missed Cheltenham because of injury, but he had run a cracker to chase home Monkerhostin in the Haldon Gold Cup on his previous start, and he was already high in the betting for the Champion Chase. Ruby Walsh, his regular jockey, was injured, so Kauto Star's owner Clive Smith apparently wanted to get a good horseman to ride him. Obviously they couldn't find one of those, so they asked me instead. I resolved that I would get further than I did on the last top-class two-mile chaser I had ridden for Paul.

The ground was very soft at Sandown on Tingle Creek day. Ruby had told me not to get into a battle with Ashley Brook and turn it into a slog. Paul told me the same thing in the parade ring before the race, but in the race I just couldn't disappoint the horse. Ashley Brook just wasn't going fast enough for us, despite the fact that he's a real tearaway. Kauto was some traveller, Ashley Brook was flat out and still he wasn't going fast enough for Kauto. I didn't want to break his rhythm, so I let him go on over the Pond fence, the third-last. I'm sure Ruby was scratching his head looking at the television at home, I'd say Paul was screaming at me from the stands, but the horse was just travelling so well. We just kept going further and further clear, winged the last and won by an easy length and a half.

I dismounted in the winner's enclosure.

'He's a machine,' I said to Paul.

'What about the Champion Chase?' asked Paul.

'Yeah,' I said. 'There's not a better two-mile chaser in the country.'

That was some ten days for me, from sitting at home, wondering if I was going to be ok to ride Trabolgan in the Hennessy, to winning the Hennessy and the Tingle Creek.

I came down from my high the following week as news that Trabolgan was lame filtered through. It wasn't anything that was really obvious initially but, between Corky Browne and Nicky, they don't miss much. When they had him scanned, they discovered a little hole in one of his tendons. It wasn't a serious injury, but when you are talking about tendons in racehorses you really have to be very careful. Corky thought that it would be ok, that they would be able to push on and prepare him for the Gold Cup, but Nicky was more cautious. He was such a good horse and he was only seven years old, that he thought that it would be best to give him time off, let him recover, and bring him back for the 2007 Gold Cup. That wasn't an easy phone call to make to Trevor Hemmings, but Trevor was great about it. He has been in racing long enough to understand the fragility of the beast.

I was gutted, everyone was gutted. We were all looking forward to the King George with him and then the 2006 Gold Cup, for which he had been challenging the 2005 winner Kicking King for favouritism in the ante-post markets. As it turned out, Kicking King also got a leg after winning the King George at Sandown, so he didn't make it to Cheltenham either.

The long-term plan for Trabolgan didn't come to fruition either. Nicky was slowly building him up for his 2006-07 campaign when his leg went again. Then he was back in at the end of the summer in 2007 with a view to preparing him for the 2008 Gold Cup, and it went again. It is remarkable and fairly sad to think that he hasn't contested a race since he won the Hennessy off top weight in November 2005. It's the one thing about horses that is soul destroying: they get injured. People say that it only ever happens to the good ones. That's not true, it happens to the bad ones as well, but you only ever really notice the good ones, and it is desperately frustrating when it happens. It's just a waste of talent. I rode L'Ami to finish fourth in the 2006 Gold Cup and, given how far superior Trabolgan was to L'Ami when they were both novices and then in the 2005 Hennessy, although it doesn't always work out as you expect, you have to think that Trabolgan would have at least got close to War Of Attrition.

I won the Victor Chandler Chase again the following February on Tysou, who was owned by Fondmort's owner, Bill Brown. I'd had a few near-misses on Tysou, so he owed me one, and I suppose I owed him one as well. When he was on song he was a very good horse. He just zipped around Sandown that day, did everything right, arrived there at the last and nabbed Dempsey on the run-in. That was a very satisfying race.

It was a good year for Bill as Fondmort finally landed the Cheltenham Festival win that he so deserved in 2006. That was brilliant. It was his fifth appearance at the Festival and, after just getting touched off by Thisthatandtother in 2005, it was fantastic for him to get a win on the board. Impek was joint-favourite with Fondmort for the race, I took it up fairly early on Fondmort because I thought that Impek was a bit soft, and I put the gun to his head over the last two fences, may the best man win. He did.

That was also a very good day for me, day three of the 2006 Cheltenham Festival. I just got beaten by Reveillez on Copsale Lad in the first race, the Jewson Chase, then I won the Ryanair on Fondmort, pulled up Millenium Royal in the World Hurdle and then went out and won the Racing Post Plate, the old Mildmay of Flete, on Non So. That was another very satisfying win. Non So had fallen a couple of times in the past so had a reputation for being a bad jumper, but he wasn't bad at all, he was actually very good, but he was just a little awkward in the air sometimes, his legs used to get in his way.

Andrew Tinkler led the field on another of Nicky's horses, Saintsaire. He kicked on from the top of the hill and I thought, 'Where is he going, setting sail for home at the top of the hill? Much too early.' So I sat, took my time, allowed my horse to fill his lungs on the way down the hill. Saintsaire began to falter over the second-last, like someone had dropped anchor on him, and I went by him as if he was in a lay-by. I went down to the last, saw a stride, and flew it. I didn't know it at the time, but Non So actually crossed his legs in mid-air over the fence. Luckily he managed to straighten them up again before he hit the ground. We wouldn't have been returning to a hero's welcome back in the winner's enclosure, that's for sure.

I don't know if I would have felt any different if you had told me then that that would be the last time that I would be led into the winner's enclosure at the Cheltenham Festival. I don't know if I would have done anything different, if I would have done a flying dismount or thrown my whip or my goggles to the crowd, or any of those showbiz things. I doubt it. I definitely would have tried to savour it more though. My 14th time being led down the chute and around and through the parade ring to the hallowed circle at the end of it to be greeted by a cacophony of sound and the appreciation – near adulation – that is carried thereon.

It would have saddened me greatly if I had known, that's for sure. I might have been staring down the barrel of another Gwyneth Paltrow moment, so it is probably just as well that I didn't.

# CHAPTER 24

## CHANGING PERSPECTIVES

In September 2006, I announced my retirement from race-riding. It all came about quite suddenly in the end, but it made perfect sense to me. I had become friendly with Lee Westwood in 1999. I met him at a golf event and we just became friendly straight away. Lee is a really good fellow. He was exactly the same person when he was playing well and on top of the world as he was when he was in the doldrums and couldn't make a cut. He's playing really well again now and fair play to him. He is a really genuine guy.

It was through Lee that I met Andrew 'Chubby' Chandler. Chubby's International Sports Management (ISM) company manages Lee as well as other golfers Darren Clarke, Graeme McDowell, Paul McGinley, Ernie Els and now Rory McIlroy, as well as the cricketer Andrew Flintoff. He was setting up this club through which members had access to a lot of premier sports events, like a box at Old Trafford, seats at Wembley, the opportunity to go to the US Masters, all that kind of thing, and he asked me if I would head up the racing side of it.

Their intention was to buy a couple of horses, so I would be their Director of Racing. I would liaise with the trainers, sort out running and riding plans, and look after the members when they would go to the races. For me it sounded like a dream job for when I would retire. I would still be involved in racing, I would have a say in which horses were bought, I would have money behind me to buy some nice horses, and on top of all that I would have access to more top football, cricket and golf events than I could shake a stick at. And the package was good. It seemed like a no-brainer.

It was going to be a full-time job, for when I stopped riding, so part of the deal was that I would ride until the end of the 2006-07 season and then retire. I would do some work for ISM during the season before going full-time into it at the end of the season. I thought about it for a long time, and the only conclusion that I could come to was that it was too good an opportunity to turn down. I didn't have that many more years left in me in the saddle anyway and, crucially, I always said that I would retire before I began to deteriorate as a rider. I didn't want to overstay my welcome. The last thing I wanted was for guys to be looking at me in the weigh room and saying, 'Look at him, look at Fitzy, he used to be a good jockey.' I wanted to go out on a high, I wanted to be riding as well as ever when I retired, give it my all, go out at the top. I owed that to Nicky as well. I told Nicky and we announced my decision to the press.

So 2006-07 would be my last season riding. Perfect. I put the job to the back of my mind and just got on with riding. Nicky had some very nice young horses that season. I won two novice hurdles on Sir Jimmy Shand before Christmas, then we went and finished second to a top horse of Jonjo's, Wichita Lineman, in the Challow Hurdle at Newbury just after Christmas. Punjabi was a nice juvenile who was coming through, a horse who had won three times on the Flat and had schooled very well over hurdles. I won a bumper at Warwick on a really nice mare, Amaretto Rose, who then went on to win a novice hurdle at Ascot, and then a Grade 2 contest at Haydock in January. I won two novice chases on Jack The Giant, a decent young hurdler from the previous season who was built to jump fences, and Afsoun was around at that time as well. He was a really nice Aga Khan-bred horse who was trained by Alain de Royer-Dupre on the Flat in France and on whom I finished second to Fair Along in the juvenile hurdle at Cheltenham's November meeting before we beat Turko at Cheltenham in December. And then there was Duc De Regniere.

I loved Duc De Regniere from the first time I sat on him. He was another horse who Nicky got from France, a big scopey horse, a real chaser. The first time I rode him in a race was at the Newbury meeting just after Christmas in a novice hurdle, when he battled on well to beat a good horse of David Pipe's, Osana, who had already won over hurdles and who would go on to finish second behind Katchit in the 2008 Champion Hurdle, the pair of them clear. This was unbelievable. I couldn't remember Nicky ever having a group of young horses that had so much ability and so much potential all at the same time.

As I was coming back into the winner's enclosure at Newbury, it suddenly hit me, like Saul on his way to Damascus, I can't give this up, not when I have all these horses to ride, no way. This is what I have put my whole life into, to be able to ride horses like this and see them progressing. How can I turn my back on all this?

I got back to the winner's enclosure and the owners Sir Peter and Lady Gibbings were there. They were so delighted, so appreciative, they got such a kick out of their horse winning at Newbury. I couldn't leave. Unless something changed radically, I wasn't going to leave at the end of the season. I would just be giving up too much. Nicky was in the winner's enclosure as well.

'If you keep producing horses like this,' I said to him, 'I'm not going to be able to walk away.'

It was the first time that I had given him even the slightest hint that I wasn't going to retire, but he wasn't a bit surprised. I don't think he ever thought that I was serious about retiring.

He smiled back at me. 'Why do you think I'm trying so hard.'

Things were very good. Here I was doing a job that I loved. I was working as hard as ever, I was at Nicky's as often as I had ever been, and I was loving it, I loved working with the young horses, riding them work and schooling them and trying to help Nicky unearth their talent, fulfil their potential, and there was a huge amount of potential in the yard at the time. I felt good in myself, I thought that I was riding well, my weight was good, and lots of things were just starting to come together for me professionally.

My personal life was great as well. Things were going well with my girlfriend Chloe, and she had just given birth to our first son Zac the previous August. It hadn't always been a bed of roses with Chloe. I first met her in the Malt Shovel in Lambourn in 2005. The Malt Shovel was basically the Lambourn 'scene' pub. Sunday nights were always good nights in the Malt, especially if you were a single bloke, there were always plenty of women about.

249

So I went down the Malt this Sunday evening with AP and The Welsh and Seamus Durack, and I was chatting to Amanda Davy, a very pretty girl who was going out with Andrew Tinkler. I've known Amanda since she was 14 or 15, her dad used to be a starter with the BHB, she's a lovely girl. Amanda had a friend with her, a tall, good-looking girl who immediately drew my attention (I've always had a weakness for tall girls).

So I got chatting to this bird, she was new to Lambourn, she had just started working for Charlie Mann, we got on great, I asked her for her number, she eventually gave it to me. I rang her the following week and basically we started going out. We went out a couple of times, but it wasn't really progressing as I would have liked, or as most blokes would have liked. Basically, she wouldn't let me shag her. I suppose I had a bit of a reputation around Lambourn at the time, and her friends had warned her about me, said that she should have nothing to do with me. So I thought, ah here, this is not happening, she either starts playing the game or else I'm out of here. She didn't play the game, not by my rules anyway, so I was off.

A couple of months later, Amanda had a barbecue, and I met Chloe again there. So we got chatting again a bit, but I was chatting up these other birds who were there, and I don't think she was very impressed about that, so she got the hump and she was off. She says now that I followed her out to the car and asked her for a kiss, but I don't remember that at all. She says I was very persistent. Girls say that kind of stuff. Anyway, she sent me a text message after that and I thought, why not, I'll give this another go, so we started seeing each other again.

This was around the time that I broke my neck at Market Rasen, so I was spending a lot of time at home, convalescing, and Chloe used to come around quite a bit. She helped me through a lot of that, getting myself fit and mobile again. We got on great, I really liked her, she was good fun and she was a good person to be around. We just became really good friends and gradually we came to be pretty much inseparable.

Then, just after the 2005 Hennessy, Trabolgan's Hennessy, she arrived at the house one night and told me that she was pregnant.

Chloe was anxious about how I would react. It was probably well known that I was fairly keen on being single. Also, we had known each other for a relatively short period of time, we had known each other for just eight months, and we had been going out together for just four months. Against that, I had always wanted to have kids. I was obviously relieved that I didn't have kids from my first marriage, given how that one worked out, and I was probably getting to the stage where I thought that kids just weren't going to happen for me.

As you get older and you are not in a permanent relationship, you get to be fairly happy in your own company, you get to be fairly independent, selfish even. I loved going home in the evenings and watching racing or MTV or the American golf. I loved the fact that I had my sofa and no bird sat in it, I loved that there was no make-up in the bedroom and no cotton wool in the bathroom and that there weren't about a million different bottles of shampoos and conditioners and hair-care stuff in the shower. (Why do they need so many different products?) This is my life, this is how it is, this is how I like it, this is how it's going to be, so if you don't like it, there's the door.

I didn't really want a permanent partner, so I figured that I wouldn't really be able to have children then. I hadn't really thought about the prospect of having children with Chloe, I just hadn't thought that far ahead, until she sprang this news on me on that fine December evening. Chloe was worried about how this would look, she was concerned that I or the whole of Lambourn would think that she had got pregnant on purpose. She needn't have worried. I knew that she wasn't that type of person and, although it took me a little while to get used to the idea, I was delighted by the news. I thought the world of Chloe and, although it was seriously fast-tracked, we were probably heading down the kids road anyway.

We told our parents, but really nobody else, until the following June when Chloe moved in with me. I told her that she was moving in on a trial basis, and I was only half-joking. She was just as nervous about it as I was. We thought that, if we couldn't get on together when there was no child in the house, we had no chance when there was. But it worked out really well, we still got on as well as we always had after she moved in.

Zac was born in August 2006. That was amazing. It was a life-changing experience for me which I didn't see coming. I'll never forget it, being in the hospital with Chloe and watching her, someone you love, in such pain and you feeling utterly useless, completely powerless against it. It was an unusual situation for me. It is usually me who is suffering the pain and other people who are standing around not able to help me. To be honest, I would have preferred it if it had been that way around.

Anyway, he arrived, this little package, a little human being, a son, my son. He was amazing, a little miracle, our little miracle, and he turned my life upside down. Before it had been all about me, now it wasn't any more, it was about me and Chloe and Zac, about me and my family. Chloe was great, I was retiring, then I wasn't, then I was staying on. We talked about it and decided that we'd like to have another child. I have always liked the fact that I am close in age to my brother and sister, and I thought it would be good for Zac to have a brother or sister who wasn't too much younger than him. Oscar was born in October 2007. Another little miracle, although a slightly less boisterous little miracle than the first one.

I was always up front with Chloe about the fact that I didn't want to get married again. She wasn't absolutely comfortable with that, but she understood my reasons. I was reared a Catholic. I was a churchgoer when I was in Ireland, I used to go to mass every Sunday, and I believe in God and all that that entails. But I also believed that, when you got married it was for life. I always said, before I got married to Jane, that when I got married that would be it, no other women, no messing. When you stand up there in front of the altar, in front of God, and you say 'forsake all others' you have to mean it and you have to do it. Well I didn't, and I felt guilty about that. Then we got divorced and, on top of everything, it cost me a fortune, so I said never again. If I do meet someone else, no matter who she is or what she says, no matter how much I love her, I am not getting married again.

I bought Chloe an eternity ring that Christmas and I gave it to her just to let her know that I wanted to be with her, that she was my life partner, but I just didn't want to get married. I wanted her to know that, just because I didn't want to get married, it didn't mean that I didn't want to be with her for the rest of my life. She understood, that's the type of person she is.

Then I had my fall.

It's amazing how your perspective can change in an instant. One minute you are flying high, travelling well in the Grand National, all you are thinking about is your race plan, how you are going to ride your horse in order to maximise your chances of winning the race. Then in one bad step and the blink of an eye, you are wondering if you will ever be able to walk again.

National Hunt jockeys think they are invincible. How else would they be able to bring themselves to fire half a ton of horse at obstacles that are bigger than themselves six or seven days a week. It's like, you believe you can fly, then one day, you realise that you can't, you're not invincible, time for a rethink. My fall from L'Ami in the Grand National changed everything for me.

One of the things that shone like a beacon was how much love one person could have for another. It had always been there, Chloe's love for me, she wasn't behaving out of character, and I was aware of it, but I probably didn't take the time to take full cognisance of it with all the noise that went with being a jockey. Lying on the flat of my back in Liverpool Hospital, I could see it very clearly.

Chloe did everything for me then. She dropped everything. It didn't matter what else was going on in the world or in her life, all she was concerned with was me, my well-being and the boys. It was Chloe who moved heaven and earth to get me transferred from Liverpool to Oxford, and she was always there with me, by my side, on the phone, she never left me during all that time. One of the days that I was on the flat of my back in hospital, I was on the phone to her, and it just felt right. We weren't on a gondola in Venice, we weren't at the top of Mount Kilimanjaro, but I proposed to her right then, on the phone, from my hospital bed in Oxford.

We were married in August 2008 and we had a hell of a party.

# CHAPTER 25

## ON OUR HEADS BE IT

Cheltenham 2007 was frustrating as hell. It all started poorly and didn't get any better.

I thought that Amaretto Rose was a certainty in the opener, the Supreme Novices' Hurdle. She had won a bumper and two hurdle races earlier in the season, she was all class and I thought that she was my best chance of a winner for the week. I had her lined up in a good position, the starter called us in, come on then, but he didn't let us go. By the time he did let us go, I had lost my good position. To make matters worse, a horse checked in front of us and Amaretto Rose ran into the back of him, so that set us back further. We were behind the wicket even before we crossed the start line.

She travelled really well through the race, though, got into the firing line on the run to the second-last, but Granit Jack, Ruby's mount, tried to duck out to his left, then ducked back in and cannoned into my mare. She's only a little thing, and that blow just knocked the wind out of her sails. She still travelled well into the home straight, but she couldn't muster the energy to get past Granit Jack nor to withstand the later surge of Ebaziyan. We finished third. Disappointing start.

I was third on Jack The Giant in the next race, the Arkle, third on Afsoun in the next race, the Champion Hurdle, and then set out on Juveigneur in the William Hill. I did everything right on Juveigneur. I got him switched off out the back, got him jumping well, made nice ground down the hill, arrived there at the last just behind Distant Thunder, and settled down to drive him up the hill. We made a bit of a mistake at the last, which didn't help, but I always felt that we were getting to Distant Thunder. Slowly on the final climb to the line, we were clawing him back, a neck down, a head down, level 25 yards from the line, one last surge and he's up. Juveigneur sticks his willing neck out, claims Distant Thunder, another Cheltenham victory for sure, then from nowhere, this thing whizzes past me on the right. Davy Russell on Joes Edge, from nowhere. It's close between the three of us, I'm sure I've got Distant Thunder beaten, but I'm afraid that Joes Edge has just got us on the line. The photo revealed that he had.

That one just ripped my insides out. I was as close to being physically sick as I had ever felt on the back of a horse. I watched that replay a fair few times. The finish that Russell conjured from Joes Edge was quite incredible. It was as if he had just joined in at the second-last. A stride before the line he was a neck behind, a stride after the line he was a neck up, that's how fast his relative finishing speed was. Regrettably, on the line, he was a nostril in front of us.

I had a big argument with the handicapper after that race. Juveigneur had gone up 14lb without winning a race, discounting one novice hurdle. Joes Edge had won a Scottish National off a mark of 132 and he was racing in the William Hill off 130. I was baffled by it. I put it to Phil Smith, the handicapper, and he told me that if I had jumped the last better I probably would have won. That was a bit cheeky of him. Actually, the winner hardly jumped a jump at all the whole way round, so he was probably actually value for more than the winning margin.

Juveigneur was a ten-year-old. I don't agree with putting ten-year-olds or 11-year-olds up significantly in the handicap. It's not as if they are improving. Juveigneur was fully exposed, he had no secrets from anybody. He went up in the handicap after this run too.

So I came home after the first day at Cheltenham, not in very good form. Third on Amaretto Rose, third on Afsoun, beaten a whisker on Juveigneur. Tuesday was my big day at that Festival, I knew that Tuesday was my best chance of riding a winner. If I came home without a winner on Tuesday, there was a good chance I'd go through the week without one, so I was a little bit down in myself when I got home. Zac was seven months old at the time. I walked in the door and he said, 'Dada', and all my disappointment just evaporated. It was amazing, all of a sudden it didn't matter how many winners I had ridden. He didn't care, it didn't

Left: *Landing Light jumping in front of Baracouda and Thierry Doumen in the Ascot Hurdle in November 2002.*

Bottom left: *En route to winning the 2002 Charlie Hall Chase at Wetherby aboard Marlborough.*

Bottom right: *Battle-scarred after getting unseated off Azertyuiop at the first fence in the Haldon Gold Cup at Exeter in November 2003: "Travelling well, unseated first".*

*The smiles say it all. With Tony Martin and Xenophon after winning the 2003 Coral Cup.*

*Lining up a putt in a ProAm tournament at Forest of Arden in May 2004.*

*Kauto Star on the way to landing the Tingle Creek Chase at Sandown in December 2005. He was electric.*

*In the winner's enclosure at Newbury after Trabolgan had won the 2005 Hennessy Cognac Gold Cup, with Nicky and Corky Browne (right).*

*Jumping the last in the 2006 Racing Post Plate on Non So. I didn't know it at the time, but this was my 14th and last winner at the Cheltenham Festival. Note how Non So has his legs crossed in mid-air. Luckily he straightened them out again before they hit the ground.*

Above: *Winning the 2006 Ryanair Chase on Fondmort.*

*With Nicky Henderson, exchanging views.*

*Schooling Zebra Crossing at Seven Barrows.*

Above: *With Nicky and Punjabi after we had won the Champion Four-Year-Old Hurdle at Punchestown in April 2007.*

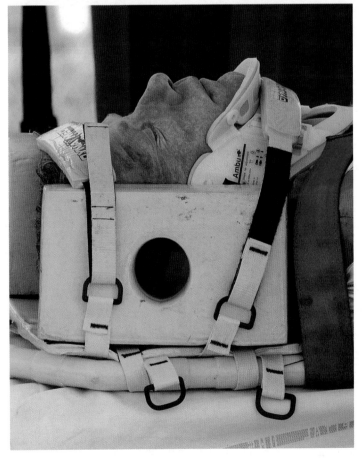

*Being carried off in a neck brace after L'Ami had fallen at the second fence in the 2008 Grand National, and wondering if I would ever walk again.*

*X-rays, from the side (right) and from the front (below), showing the extent of repair work the surgeon had to do to my neck after the fall on L'Ami.*

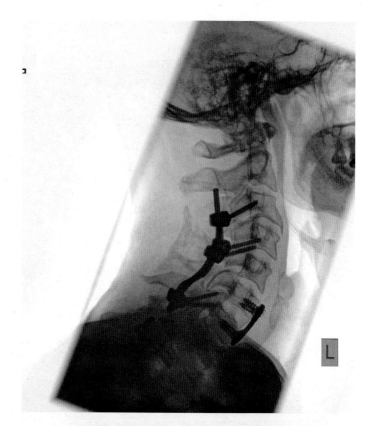

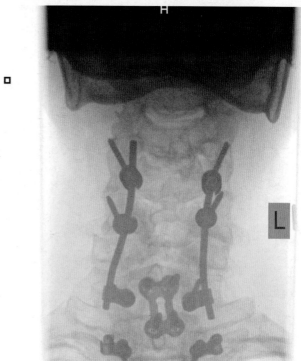

*With Chloe at Nicky's open day in 2008.*

*Throwing my son Zac around at home, although Zac seems to be more interested in the camera than in his dad.*

*Best man and best mate Shane Donohoe.*

*Chloe with Oscar on our wedding day.*

matter to him if I had ridden all six winners, I was just Dada. Chloe put her arms around me. 'Ah, bad luck.'

I was right about the rest of the meeting though. I finished seventh in the Gold Cup on L'Ami, fourth in the Triumph Hurdle on Punjabi, and Crozan fell with me at the top of the hill in the Ryanair Chase when he was travelling well in front, although he was a soft horse, he had no heart, and I really doubt he would have got up the hill. Lots of placed horses, but I never got to celebrate a winner.

I rode Snowy Morning for Willie Mullins to finish second to Denman in the Royal & SunAlliance Chase the following day. Ruby is obviously Willie's regular rider, but he is also Paul Nicholls' regular rider, and he, unsurprisingly, chose to ride Denman in the SunAlliance. Willie had called me six weeks before to ask me to ride him. As I was on the phone to him, I was texting Ruby:

'wots dis snoy mrnn'

Ruby texted back:

'hez ok gud hrs got a chnc'

Snowy Morning travelled well just behind Aces Four and Denman, who set the pace from early, but Cailin Alainn fell in front of us at the second-last fence on the first circuit, and Snowy Morning actually did well to stay on his feet. He totally lost his place, and did well to battle back to take second spot. It wouldn't have mattered though if Denman had done the splits at the back of the second-last and the last, we wouldn't have beaten him, he had that much in hand.

I didn't ride that often for Willie Mullins, but I was over at Leopardstown to ride Royal Paradise in a piece of work before the 2006 Cheltenham Festival. It was nine days before the start of the Cheltenham Festival, the day when a lot of the Irish Cheltenham hopefuls work after racing, it's almost a tradition at this stage.

There was another meeting on in Ireland that day at Clonmel, and some of Willie's jockeys were delayed getting to Leopardstown, so Willie asked me if I would mind riding Hedgehunter in a schooling session. I didn't mind at all, in fact I was very happy to school Hedgehunter, the previous year's Grand National winner. I gave him a smack down the shoulder when we got to the straight and he took off. He was seriously impressive. Willie was off looking after some other horse when I pulled up, but Jackie, Willie's wife, was there and she asked me what I thought.

'Jackie, he's flying,' I said. 'He'll run a big race in the Gold Cup.'

'Really?' she said, 'because we're not sure about running him in it.'

'If you run him in it,' I said, 'he'd have a big chance of being placed. And if your boy [Ruby] doesn't want to ride him, I'd be delighted to ride him for you.'

Ruby did ride Hedgehunter in the 2006 Gold Cup, when he finished a gallant second to War Of Attrition. I was talking to Willie at the drinks party that evening.

'I never thanked you for riding Hedgehunter,' he said. 'You did say he'd be placed in the Gold Cup and you were right. We'll get you to ride a winner for us some time.'

In April that year I was over in Ireland for the Punchestown Festival. I was riding on the Tuesday, had no rides on the Wednesday, then I was riding on the Thursday, so I went out on Tuesday night with Shane Donohoe and a few of the boys, gave it a bit of a lash. I was on the golf course the following morning, feeling a little the worse for wear, still pissed I'd say. I checked my phone on the ninth hole and there was a missed call from an unknown number and a text from Ruby asking me if I would ride Quatre Heures in the four-year-old hurdle that day. So I texted Ruby back, saying no problem, and when I finished my round I rang the number back. It was Willie.

'Ruby says you're ok to ride Quatre Heures today,' he said.

'Yeah, no problem.'

I'm feeling a little the worse for wear now still, but I get to the racecourse, have a good sweat, and I'm feeling a lot better. Ruby is riding Willie's other horse in the race, Mister Hight. I have never sat on Quatre Heures before, I've never seen him, I don't know very much about him, but he gives me a great spin, I go down the inside the whole way, take it up just before the last and win going away. Mister Hight falls at the last flight, but we have him well beaten at the time. So Willie was true to his word, he did get me on a winner, although I didn't expect that it would be a Grade 1 winner. I have a photo of Quatre Heures hanging up in my downstairs toilet, so I am reminded of him quite often.

Back at Punchestown in 2007, I won the champion four-year-old hurdle on Punjabi. It was important for Nicky to have a winner of a Grade 1 at Punchestown after having a Cheltenham of so many near-misses. And I rode Chief Dan George for Jimmy Moffatt to win the Sefton Hurdle at Aintree, getting up on the run-in to beat AP on Wichita Lineman after he and Richard Johnson on Massini's Maguire had gone toe to toe from too far out. They were never going to get home by putting the gun to their horses' heads from so far out. I think I told AP that as I went past him on the run-in.

In April I announced that I wasn't retiring at the end of the season after all. It barely made a couple of lines in the *Racing Post*. I had fooled nobody.

*

I had two rides for Nicky at Towcester one day in June 2007, so I got there early to walk the track. During the summer it was always imperative that Nicky or I walked it in order to determine if the ground was safe enough for the horses that we had running. I called Nicky.

'It's too firm,' I said.

'Grand,' he said, 'take them out.'

'Fine,' I said. 'Listen, I've been thinking, I'm thinking of taking a holiday for two or three weeks, this summer racing isn't suiting me, it's fast ground and we don't have many runners anyway, so I was thinking of taking a bit of a break.'

'Great idea,' he said. 'Take as long as you want.'

So I finished walking the track, went up to withdraw the horses, and the phone rang again. Nicky.

'Look, why don't you take longer?' he said. 'Take two months, come back at the end of August fresh and ready to go when the season gets going in earnest. I'm going to be turning a lot of these horses out now for the summer anyway.'

That was great, it was just what I needed and what I should have been doing every year. The falls are harder on the summer ground, and as I was getting older it was taking me just a little longer to recover from each one. I didn't go too far, we had Zac and Chloe was pregnant with Oscar, so I played a lot of golf and I was doing a fair bit for ISM, so I had a really good summer and came back in August, batteries recharged, dying to get going again.

We got off to a very bad start that season. October, November, December, the Henderson horses are usually flying, but it just wasn't happening. They just weren't firing, the horses were under a little bit of a cloud, and Paul Nicholls was cleaning up. So when I won a big handicap hurdle at Cheltenham in December on Jack The Giant, it was a big fillip for the yard. I thought he was a certainty, he was rated 30lb lower over hurdles than he was over fences, so he really ought to have been winning, but it was a huge relief when he did. Then he followed up a week later by winning the Ladbroke Hurdle at Ascot. That was a massive win for us at the time, it was really important for the yard.

A yard like Seven Barrows needs to be churning out winners, big winners. It's important for everything, for owners, for jockeys, for staff morale. When a yard is having winners, you can see it in the staff, everyone is happy, everyone goes about with a smile, but when a yard is going through a quiet spell lads are bickering, this is wrong and that's wrong and he can't ride, and it's all that fellow's fault.

I rode Binocular to win a juvenile hurdle at Ascot in January. I thought that he was a machine, bought by JP McManus out of Elie Lellouche's yard in France. AP is obviously JP's jockey, and Binocular was his ride even though he was trained by Nicky. AP called me after the race to ask me how he got on.

'I'm telling you Champ,' I said, 'this is a proper horse.'

I won the Adonis Hurdle on him as well at Kempton in February, but he wasn't that impressive there. I couldn't understand it. He didn't travel as easily as he had at Ascot and he kicked a couple of hurdles out of the ground. It was funny old ground that day and they said that they went no pace, but the time was good and I timed my run well, and he still only just got home from a Nicholls horse, Pierrot Lunaire.

JP was there that day, and Frank Berry, JP's racing manager, and Minty, David Minton, who heads up the Million in Mind Syndicate and who is a very good friend of Nicky's.

'I can't believe that's just as good as he is,' I said to them when I dismounted. 'I know he has won, and the second is ok, but I'm telling you, he's much better than that.'

'Sure he won,' said JP, ever the glass-half-full man.

JP had a clutch of top novice hurdlers that season, which was lovely for JP but presented a small problem for him in terms of Cheltenham targets, and an even bigger one for AP McCoy. Franchoek was his, trained by Alan King, winner of four of his five hurdle races and favourite for the Triumph Hurdle, so he was definitely running in that race. Binocular was also a juvenile, so he was eligible for the Triumph, but there was the option of running him in the Supreme Novices' Hurdle instead. But JP also owned Captain Cee Bee, who was trained by Eddie Harty in Ireland, and the talk was of him running in the Supreme Novices', and just to further complicate matters, there was also Jered, trained by Noel Meade in Ireland, who was apparently a machine, who was also eligible for the Supreme Novices' and the Triumph.

Looking at it from my point of view, AP was going to ride as many of them as he could, so I just hoped that he wouldn't ride Binocular in whichever race he ran. If they ran Binocular in the Supreme Novices', I wasn't sure whether AP would ride him or Captain Cee Bee or Jered. But if they ran him in the Triumph Hurdle, I was certain that AP would ride Franchoek. I desperately hoped they would run him in the Triumph. The way he was working before Cheltenham, to my mind he was back to his Ascot form. If Binocular was at the top of his game, I was certain that they wouldn't see which way he had gone.

I met Frank Berry at Warwick a couple of weeks before Cheltenham. They still hadn't decided on running plans for the Festival.

'How do you think Binocular would get on in the Supreme Novices' Hurdle?' Frank asked me.

'Run him in the Triumph, Frank!' I said. 'Because your man will ride Franchoek and I'll win it for you on Binocular.'

Frank laughed. He knew that I was half-joking, but he knew that I was half-serious too. Unfortunately, it didn't work out for me. They decided to run him in the Supreme Novices', as well as Captain Cee Bee. AP rang me beforehand to ask me what I thought. I couldn't lie. AP is one of my best mates and it's not my style anyway. AP chose to ride Binocular, Choc Thornton rode Captain Cee Bee and he beat Binocular by two lengths, the pair finishing first and second of the 22 runners.

It was a great result for JP. Of course I would have preferred it if they had finished the other way round, if Binocular had won it. Even though I didn't ride him, he was Nicky's horse, he was one of our team, and I would have loved for Nicky to have opened the meeting with a winner, especially a winner for JP McManus.

JP has only had horses with Nicky since the 2005-06 season, Tarlac was the first horse he sent to Seven Barrows, so Nicky is a relatively recent addition to JP's roster of trainers. JP is a good man. He puts so much into the game, both in terms of finance and in terms of energy and effort, that you really love to see him being successful, having winners at the big meetings, especially at Cheltenham.

*

The Queen didn't want Barbers Shop to run at Cheltenham. She thought that he was too inexperienced, and she was right to an extent. I was beaten a neck by Big Buck's on him on his chasing debut at Newbury in December, and I was annoyed with myself that we hadn't finished second or third in the Feltham Chase at Kempton on Boxing Day. Nicky wasn't sure about running him in the Feltham on just his second ever start over fences, but it looked like a fairly weak Feltham, so we said we would have a go.

He blundered his way around Kempton. He made a mistake at the third, another one at the fourth, he clobbered the second-last on the far side and then, just when he was finishing well, he made another mistake at the last. It was infuriating because I knew that he had loads of ability, he just needed to pay attention more, he just needed to put his head down and get on with it instead of fluffing about all over the place, which, I suppose comes with experience. So Her Majesty was right.

I suggested the Jewson to Nicky, you've got to run him in the Jewson, the two-and-a-half-mile handicap chase for novices at Cheltenham. It was the ideal race for him. I agreed that he didn't have the experience for the SunAlliance Chase, which is a real war of attrition, but two and a half miles would be perfect, and he was well handicapped, having only run twice and finished well behind Joe Lively in the Feltham.

Nicky was uncertain. Because the horse was owned by the Queen, he wanted to do the right thing, or he wanted to avoid doing the wrong thing and, on the face of it, he shouldn't have been going to Cheltenham on the back of such an ordinary run at Kempton. But we both knew that Barbers Shop was better than that. After we danced in in a beginners' chase back at Kempton in early February, we discussed it again.

'You know,' said Nicky, 'the Queen is actually fairly relaxed about it, but she would prefer him not to run, unless we have a good argument as to why he should run.'

'Ok,' I said, 'I'll tell you what. I'll school him tomorrow, and I promise you I will be able to tell after schooling him whether he should run or not.'

'All right,' said Nicky, 'but on our heads be it!'

So I schooled him the following day. When I came back in, Nicky was smiling.

'I know what your verdict is going to be.'

'Look, I don't know what they have in Ireland,' I said, 'but off his rating of 136, there is no novice in England who will beat him.'

He was just a little bit green in the Jewson, but he travelled well through the race and he jumped brilliantly. I was on the outside of Barry Geraghty on Finger Onthe Pulse going down to the last, and I kicked him into it. Go on! He nailed it, came up on the long stride and soared. The only problem was that he jumped it so well he spent ages in the air. He was like an aircraft coming into land on a windy day. So I feel like I'm up in the air, like in a hot air balloon watching Geraghty wing the fence on my inside and set on off up the run-in while I'm still in the air. He battled on well up the run-in, but he was never going to get to the leader. We went down by a neck in the end, but he had run a cracker. At least my head was safe.

I loved riding for the Queen and the Queen Mother before her. Being Irish, you don't really have much affinity with the Royal Family growing up, but you really appreciate the place that they occupy in the English psyche when you are living in England for as long as I have been. There was an aura about the Queen Mother, she was a fantastic lady. It might be difficult for an Irish person to understand this, but I felt very proud when I rode for her. I saw what she meant to racing people, everybody stopped and just watched her when she was at the races and it was amazing to be a part of that. She was so lucid, and she knew her racing inside out. She thought the world of her horses, and she loved coming down to see them school at Seven Barrows. She was a phenomenal woman.

After the Queen Mother died, the Queen took her horses over. It was always very special to ride for the Queen or the Queen Mother. Even though I am Irish, I still felt honoured to ride for both of them, to ride a winner in the Royal colours. Richard Hughes – son of Monksfield's jockey Dessie Hughes, who engaged in all those Ireland v England battles against Sea Pigeon and Night Nurse at Cheltenham and Aintree in the late 1970s and early 1980s and who couldn't be more Irish – was the same when he rode the Queen's Free Agent to win the Chesham Stakes at Royal Ascot in 2008.

The Queen didn't come down to Seven Barrows as often as the Queen Mother did, but she still came down a couple of times, and it was nice to school her horses for her. I felt privileged to ride for her, very privileged.

Cheltenham was hammered out of shape a little bit in 2008. High winds caused the cancellation of the second day, with the result they ran all the races that were due to be run on Wednesday on the Thursday and the Friday. Combined with the original Thursday and Friday cards, that meant a ten-race card on Thursday and a nine-race card on Friday. It didn't make it any easier to ride a winner.

I finished third on Chomba Womba in the new mares' race, the David Nicholson Hurdle, the first race on the Friday. I was really disappointed with her run, she just didn't travel like the same mare that I had won on at Doncaster. We only beat Alan King's mare Theatre Girl by three-quarters of a length at Doncaster and we finished about four lengths in front of her at Cheltenham, but still I didn't think that my filly had given her true running. Horses have off-days, they are not machines (although ask Lewis Hamilton and he will probably tell you that Formula One cars are not machines either), and I'm sure that, although we only finished two and a half lengths behind Whiteoak and Refinement, Chomba Womba had an off-day that day.

I was really disappointed for her owner, Richard Kelvin Hughes, and his wife Lizzie. I desperately wanted to have a winner for them at Cheltenham. That was probably the main reason why they began to have horses with Nicky in the first place, they knew that he knew how to train Cheltenham winners. They are such nice people, so thoughtful, I used to get a hamper from them every time I rode a winner for them.

They got even closer with My Petra in the Grand Annual. That was a race I really wanted to win for Nicky, the Johnny Henderson Grand Annual Chase, as well as for her owners, and it had been My Petra's aim from a long way out. She's a great filly, a plain old yoke to look at, but as hard as nails, riding her is like riding a gelding. If there is a mare to jump around Aintree, it's her, and she was only five years old going to Cheltenham.

We thought she was the ideal type for the Grand Annual and she had run really well to finish second to Noland, the Arkle favourite, at Sandown on her last run before Cheltenham. She was on her head for most of the way before staying on really well up the hill to take second spot, but she was never going to catch Tiger Cry, a ten-year-old who seemingly had no secrets from the handicapper, but trained by one of the wiliest Irish trainers in the business (and that's saying something) Arthur Moore, who apparently had.

The following morning, the morning after Cheltenham, I received a phone call from a number I didn't recognise.

'Hello?'

'Hi,' the voice on the other end said. 'This is Ben Tullough, racing manager for Mr and Mrs Hughes, who own My Petra.'

'Hi Ben,' I said. 'How are you?' I'm not exactly bouncing now, another Cheltenham where I hit the crossbar and the post, but didn't stick one in the onion bag.

'I'm fine,' said Ben. 'There's just one thing about My Petra. Do you think maybe if you had made more use of her she might have won?'

I couldn't believe it. There were so many things that were so very wrong with this phone call on so many different levels. Astounding. I bit my lip. There were lots of things that I wanted to say. Maybe in my younger days I would have said all of them, or at least some of them, but I bit my lip again, trying to see through the red mist that had descended.

'Ben,' I said carefully. 'How many horses in your lifetime have you seen lead the whole way in a handicap at the Cheltenham Festival?'

Ben was silent for a minute. I don't know if he was trying to think of one or if he was regretting making the call or if he was crawling back under the stone that had been his hiding place before he had extricated himself to make this really important phone call, the point of which I was, and still am, at a loss to figure out.

'I can't think of any just at the moment,' he said.

'There y'go,' I said. And hung up.

# CHAPTER 26

# NATIONAL NIGHTMARE

John Hales rang me ten days before the 2008 Cheltenham Gold Cup. As well as owning Golden Bear Toys and bringing the Teletubbies toys to the UK, and owning Azertyuiop and One Man, John also owns Neptune Collonges, who won the Guinness Gold Cup at Punchestown in 2007 and who was set to join fellow Paul Nicholls inmates Kauto Star and Denman in the line-up for the Cheltenham Gold Cup. I know John well. I have been on holiday with him a fair bit. Carl Llewellyn and AP and I used to go out to his villa in Portugal quite a bit a few years back.

'Do you have a ride in the Gold Cup?' he asked.

'I don't really at the moment, John,' I said. 'I have a couple of options, but nothing definite yet.'

'Will you ride Neptune Collonges?' he asks.

'I'd love to,' I said. 'But what will Paul say about that?'

'Don't worry about Paul,' said John. 'Lisa and I have discussed it and we want the best available, we think you would suit our horse and we want you to ride it. I'll sort it out with Paul.'

I hung up, delighted. According to the bookmakers, there were only two horses who had a chance of winning the Gold Cup, Kauto Star, the previous season's hero who had won his previous three races including the King George, and Denman, the latest steeplechasing sensation who had never been beaten in eight starts over fences and who had won the Hennessy under top weight, the Lexus Chase in Ireland and the Aon Chase at Newbury that season. But if there was one other horse in the line-up who was capable of getting into the mix, it was Neptune Collonges.

I had never ridden Neptune Collonges before, but I had ridden against him. I was really impressed with him in the Country Gentlemen's Association Chase that he won at Wincanton on his last run before

Cheltenham. I rode Butler's Cabin in the race, the horse that AP would choose to ride instead of L'Ami in the 2008 Grand National. I thought he could go a fair gallop. I watched the race again a couple of times on video and, take nothing away from Liam Heard, but I thought that the horse made a couple of mistakes that he probably shouldn't have made. I thought if he jumped slightly better he could be even better than he was that day.

The next morning, John phoned again.

'Paul's gone mad,' he said simply.

'Well, are you surprised John?' I asked.

'I told him that I didn't want Liam Heard,' said John. 'Liam's a nice lad and a nice rider, but he's got no experience. I want you to ride the horse, so don't worry, you're riding him.'

Paul rang me later that day.

'What the fuck is going on with Neptune Collonges?' he blurted.

'Look Paul, John has asked me to ride the horse,' I said, 'and I said I would.'

'But I want my jockey to ride him,' said Paul.

'Well what was I supposed to say to John?' I asked. 'Was I supposed to go, 'No John, I won't ride him, let Liam ride him'? I'm happy to ride the horse if the owner wants me to ride him.'

A couple of days go by and I'm still not fully sure that I am riding him. There's a bit of it in the papers, Fitzgerald rides Neptune Collonges but Nicholls isn't happy about it. John is on to me a couple of times to reassure me. He tells me that Paul still wants Liam to ride the horse, and that he has said a couple of things about me that aren't too nice, but that's grand. I know what Paul is like. He'll call you all the names under the sun, but ten minutes later he'll shake hands, he'll regret what he has said. I have been friends with Paul for a long time, and hope to be friends with him for a long time to come.

Friends with Paul or not, I still don't know for sure if I'm riding Neptune Collonges or not until the 48-hour declaration stage, when the declared runners and riders appear in the paper. My name is down beside Neptune Collonges. I breathe a sigh of relief.

Neptune Collonges reminded me a lot of See More Business, a typical Nicholls horse, a hard horse, hard-fit and a resolute galloper, rock-solid. John told me before the race that he wanted me to go a good even gallop. He said that he didn't want me to be a pacemaker, or to set the race up for any of the other horses, but just to go my own pace. Paul gave me my instructions, just pop him out, ride him handy, he jumps, he stays, he gallops. There's no talk of team tactics, nothing like that, Paul actually tells me that Denman might take me on if I try to lead.

Circling at the start, Ruby, who was riding Kauto Star, asked me what I was going to do. I told him that I was going to jump out handy and see how it goes. I was happy to make the running or happy to sit in second or third, I was just going to be going my own pace wherever that left me in the race. Sam Thomas on Denman said that he was going to be handy.

We jumped off in front, I went a good gallop from the start, and I loved him. I had never sat on him before that day, and he wasn't very big, but he was really neat, well put together, a lovely type, he just gave me a good honest feel through the race and over his fences. He hardly missed a beat on the first circuit. Then going past the stands, one circuit completed, one to go, Denman came up on my outside and went on. I just thought, away you go. I couldn't have gone the gallop he was going, so I left him off, kept going at my pace, about 15 seconds a furlong, my horse couldn't have done any more or I would have burst him.

Denman was six lengths in front of us down the back straight, the gap was down to four at the top of the hill, and I thought, right, we can catch this fellow, he went too fast too early. We winged the fourth-last, winged the third-last, but just when I was thinking we had a chance, Denman was gone, he just took off. I thought, 'Well fair enough, if you can keep on going at that gallop, you're every bit as good as they say you are'.

My fellow was in top gear, absolutely flat out and giving all he's got, when Ruby and Kauto Star came past on the outside and set off after Denman. We made a mistake at the second-last, our first mistake of the race, and it halted our momentum a bit, but then I got him going again. Going to the last, Denman had flown, away up the hill, but I thought that we had a chance of doing Kauto Star for second. We set off up the hill out after him, clawing him back with every stride, but the line just came three strides too soon for us. Even so, Neptune Collonges had run his heart out. Third place behind Denman and Kauto Star was no disgrace, and it was some achievement by Paul to train the 1-2-3 in the Gold Cup.

John and his daughter Lisa were delighted, I told them they should be very proud of their horse because he had run his lungs out to finish third. In a normal year, a year that didn't have two superstars of steeplechasing in it, his performance would have been good enough to win the Gold Cup.

There was a little bit in the papers afterwards about Neptune Collonges having been used as a pacemaker for Denman, but that was wrong. Harry Findlay, who owns Denman in partnership with Paul Barber, actually thanked John Hales for his help in the winner's enclosure after the race, which may have been the source of the press comment. But he wasn't a pacemaker, no way. I rode him at the pace that suited him, at the pace that maximised his chance of winning the race.

John asked me about that afterwards. He asked me what Paul had said to me before the race, and I told him exactly.

'He wasn't a pacemaker then?'

'He was nothing of the sort,' I said. 'He has run a stormer, and you should be proud of him.'

So it was another Cheltenham for me without a winner. Again I had come really close on a number of occasions. I hate walking out of Cheltenham with no winners, and here I was doing it for the second year running. At the drinks party afterwards, what are you celebrating? I suppose you are celebrating walking out of there in the full of your health, which is huge, but it doesn't seem huge at the time when you haven't had a winner. The irony is that, in 2008 more than any other year, I consoled myself with the thought that I would be coming back in 2009, that I was riding so well and had so many good horses to look forward to, that I would certainly be back with live chances in 2009. Regrettably, for the first time in 14 years, I won't.

\*

Aintree 2008, day one, and I'm at Taunton. It's the first time in 15 years that I'm not riding at Aintree on the first day of the Grand National meeting. Nicky was only intending having two runners at Aintree on the day, neither of whom had any great chance of winning, and he had two going to Taunton, both of whom had real chances. So I told Nicky that I thought I'd quite like to go to Taunton. He couldn't believe it, go to Taunton for one in a Class 4 novice chase and another in a Class 4 maiden hurdle, both worth four grand to the winner, instead of going and having a nice day at Aintree. I wasn't interested in going through the motions at Aintree on horses who had no chance. I had done all that. I much preferred the idea of riding a winner or two at Taunton. I rang Dave Roberts to tell him, he couldn't believe it either, but he got me a nice spare on a horse of Colin Tizzard's, Bring Me Sunshine, in the handicap chase.

So I went to Taunton. The ground was on the fast side for Nicky's horse, Turfshuffle, in the maiden hurdle, so that left me with just two rides on the day, but I won on both of them, Menchikov in the novice chase and Bring Me Sunshine in the handicap chase. Perfect. Now off I go to Aintree on Friday, a jockey in form instead of just another jockey who had gone through the motions on a couple of also-rans at Aintree. Of course I didn't know the significance of Bring Me Sunshine's win. I didn't know that it was the last time that I would ever be led into the winner's enclosure as a winning jockey.

Friday at Aintree didn't start well. I got fined for using my mobile phone on the racecourse before the first race. I was doing a tipping thing for the Tote, I couldn't find the box, so I was phoning the guy to see where he was, and some bloody security guy spotted me and reported me. It wasn't even near race time for me, I wasn't riding for ages, but obviously it was in the red zone, less than 30 minutes before the first race, and he reported me. So that was £200 down before the day even started.

It didn't get any better. Crozan buried me in the Topham Chase at Becher's Brook, he gave me a right good kicking as well, got me in the face. So I came back in, got changed, went out to ride Khyber Kim in the next, the Top Novices' Hurdle, whom I really fancied, and he ran well, finished fourth behind Pierrot Lunaire.

I came back in after the novice hurdle and felt like shit. I had been wasting a bit to get down to 10st 4lb for Oedipe in the next, the three-mile handicap chase, so that, together with the kicking that Crozan had given me and the painkillers that I had taken, combined to make me feel really crap. I told Nicky that I didn't feel up to it, that I wouldn't be able to do justice to my final two rides on the day. He said fine. He got Andrew Tinkler to ride Oedipe, who won the handicap chase, and Paddy Brennan rode mine in the last, the mares' bumper, Ravello Bay, who got into all sorts of trouble and could easily have won with a clear run. Andrew actually won that race as well on another mare of Nicky's, Carole's Legacy, at 25-1, who wasn't as talented as Ravello Bay. So that was a right kick in the bollocks, I had missed definitely one winner, probably two.

I got back to my hotel and had a soak in the bath. Chloe was supposed to be coming up to Liverpool and we were going to the Grand National party on Saturday night, but Oscar was only five months old so she wasn't overly keen on leaving him for too long, it was going to be her first night away from him. She phoned to see if she should still come up, if I was even going to be able to ride the following day and if I would be up for going to the party on Saturday night. I felt a lot better after a good soak, I thought I should be fine.

Whatever about missing the party, or any of my other rides, I certainly didn't want to give up the ride on L'Ami in the Grand National. Despite the fact that AP McCoy had chosen to ride Butler's Cabin instead, I actually thought that L'Ami had a better chance of winning the race. I was delighted when AP chose Butler's Cabin, in spite of my advice to him. L'Ami was a super jumper who stayed well, had a nice weight and had a touch of class, enough class to have run Kauto Star to a neck in the Aon Chase just over a year previously. I slept well on Friday night, got up early on Saturday, felt grand, phoned Nicky, fine, phone Francois Doumen, L'Ami's trainer, great, all set. Chloe arrived and we had breakfast together, couldn't be better.

I rode Ingratitude in the first, and he ran poorly, which was disappointing as I really fancied him to run a big race. Afsoun was disappointing behind Al Eile in the Aintree Hurdle as well. We tried him in blinkers for the first time, thought they might sharpen up his ideas after a lacklustre run in the Champion Hurdle, but they didn't. If anything he ran worse. That was it for me until the big one. I watched the three-mile handicap hurdle from the weigh room and got ready for the National.

I wasn't really nervous before the National, I was excited about it, I was intent on savouring every moment of it, but I wasn't nervous. I had my plan, I knew what I was going to do, I knew who I wanted to track and who I didn't want to track and I had a fair idea where most of those would be in the race. It's like anything, a round of golf, a presentation, a slot on At The Races, when you have your preparation done, you don't feel nervous, you just look forward to the event happening and you are confident that you will be able to do your best. I was confident in my horse, I was confident in myself, and I felt great.

The parade ring was full of people, as it always is before the National. JP had quite a few runners, lots of green and gold hoops with an assortment of cap colours, so I was looking for a familiar face who was connected with L'Ami. I spotted Francois first, then JP, wished JP luck with all his runners, as he did me, and went over final plans with Francois.

The rest, I remember vividly. Getting legged up by Francois, leaving the parade ring, cantering down to the start, thinking that L'Ami felt great, looking back up at the stands and savouring the atmosphere, the occasion, getting to the start and circling there, final checks, some nervous banter among the jockeys, gathering my thoughts, seeing the starter on his rostrum, final butterflies laced with adrenaline as he calls us in, whoosh, and off.

My National adventure very quickly got hammered into a National nightmare.

# CHAPTER 27

## TRIPPING

The injury didn't appear to be too bad at first. Fazakerley Hospital in Liverpool, just up the road from the racecourse, is where they bring all the injured jockeys from Aintree. They have a busy time of it on Grand National weekend.

So they got me out of the ambulance and into Fazakerley, and did an X-ray and MRI scan. They had a look at the X-ray and said that it didn't look too bad, that they'd have me off the spinal board soon and get me something to eat and drink. Perfect. I told them that the last time, the X-ray didn't pick up my fractured vertebrae, that I had been going around for 11 days with a broken neck and didn't know about it. The doctor said fine, now that they knew about that they'd pay particular attention when examining the MRI scan.

I was thinking, happy days, it wasn't so bad, I would probably be home soon. Then they came back after the MRI scan and said that they couldn't take me off the spinal board. Ah. The injury was unstable. There was no spinal unit at Fazakerley, so they were going to transfer me to the Royal Liverpool, where there was a spinal expert who could perform the surgery.

Chloe arrived before I left Fazakerley. I couldn't understand why she was so upset, but they were consulting with her, they were giving her details of the injury that they were withholding from me. They told her that it was touch and go, that it was very, very serious, that I had to have the operation done to restabilise my neck, otherwise it could have been catastrophic, I could be paralysed. She was with me almost all the time, she was fantastic. She was still breast-feeding Oscar, so she had to go back to her mother's house to pick him up. Oscar was spending his days in Royal Liverpool as well.

The first operation took nine hours. They had to remove two discs that had penetrated my spinal cord. They had gone in 25 per cent, which normally results in temporary or partial paralysis; 50 per cent and you're paralysed, 100 per cent and you're dead. So the first operation was to stabilise that, remove the discs and put this cage on my head, which stabilised the whole thing. I had had so many drugs that when I came to I was in La La Land. I didn't have a clue what was going on. I'm still on the flat of my back, I'm off the spinal board, no more marble floor, but I have this weight on my head, I still can't move. It feels like you're inside a guitar, like you have a big box on your head and you're looking out through the hole, and all you can see are these two wires, but you can't move your head to have a look, you're pinned to the bed with this thing that feels like it weighs a ton, six pounds of cage, on your head.

My throat is killing me from the ventilator that they stuck down it for the surgery. I'm struggling to talk, I can hardly breathe. My mouth feels like it has been in the Sahara for six weeks, I'm desperately trying to get a drink of water, but I can't, because my mouth is so dry, I can't suck my lips together.

I was in the recovery area for a day and a half, before they moved me to a private room on a ward, which was fine, but I'm still lying there looking up at the ceiling, I still can't move my head, me and my guitar. I was tripping badly as well on morphine, suffering hallucinations, paranoia, the works. That first night in my private room was one of the worst nights of my life. You're lying there, staring up at this ceiling. You can't use some of your senses so they begin to shut down while the others become sharper. My eyes were redundant, once I had decided that the ceiling was grubby and needed to be repainted, but my ears and nose went into overdrive, as well as my imagination.

I didn't sleep a wink that night. I heard everything, everybody, the staff coming in to look on me, chatting about ordinary things, what they did the previous night, their plans for the week, this doctor that they'd love to shag, and here am I, lying on the flat of my back, wondering if I will ever walk again.

My imagination ran riot. I thought that there were people in the room when there weren't, plotting, scheming. And I had this vision about where I was, what the outside looked like, I thought that it was by the sea. I'm not sure if it's because I had played golf at Royal Liverpool Golf Club, or some other reason, but I thought that the room was a prefab, like one that you would have as the builder's office on a building site. It's as vivid now as if this were yesterday. Outside my door was the outdoors, you walked straight out my door into the car park, and just outside was the nurses' station in another prefab. Beyond the car park was the sea. I can see it as clearly as if it were a photograph in front of me. The reality is that I was on the ninth or tenth floor of a hospital building in the middle of Liverpool, surrounded by other buildings in a fairly rundown area.

The nurses were talking about some gangster who had been in, and there was talk of 20 grand that had been stashed. The police were on their way in. There was no record of your man having been admitted, yet he was in the hospital. It was like a scene straight out of *The Bill*. To this day I'm not sure if this was reality or hallucination. So I was lying there, hearing all this, my imagination running riot, spurred on by the drugs and the morphine. What if your man comes into my room? What if there is a shoot-out in the hospital? I wouldn't be able to take cover, I wouldn't even be able to move my fucking head!

The staff were good and the operation was fantastic, absolutely amazing. It's incredible that my entire future, the rest of my life, was in the hands of the surgeon. You can walk again, you can't walk again. Toss a coin. But the rest of the hospital, the rest of the experience, fell a long way short. The staff were worked to the bone and they appeared to be unhappy, disillusioned. There was a terrible atmosphere about the whole place. Depressing, dismal, hopeless, and it made me feel very sad.

When I was going to get my scans done, when I was being wheeled down, all I could look at was the ceiling. It looked terrible, dirty, scummy even, bits of the ceiling missing, lightbulbs missing, really depressing. It just didn't feel right. It was cold, freezing, they were talking about snow. There was building work going on at the hospital and the journey on the trolley down to have my MRI scan involved going through what appeared to be a building site. Is this a hospital or a back-street clinic? And these people chatting away among themselves, 'All right lad?', just carrying on as if everything was normal. I don't know what I expected them to do, but everything wasn't normal. The rest of my life was hanging by a thread.

I felt helpless, I was down in myself anyway, at the lowest point that I have ever been in my life. They say it happens to people when they have a serious accident. They go through this stage of paranoia because they are afraid that it is going to happen to them again. It was the first time in my life that my destiny had been taken out of my own hands and put into someone else's. In an instant, you go from this confident sportsman in the prime of your health, invincible, to a complete wreck who needs help getting a sip of water past his lips, totally dependent on others, his future out of his hands.

I was tripping away, immersed in this paranoia, this fear of being paralysed for the rest of my life. I was dozing for a couple of minutes at a time, but I was always awake. I was tired but I couldn't sleep with the pain, the discomfort, my mind racing. The hallucinations turned into semi-dreams, dreams that felt like they went on forever. I was separated from my body, I was on the flat of my back unable to move, the kids were being taken away from me and I couldn't move to stop it, I was pushing myself around in a wheelchair, and more. And I'd wake myself up and think, Jesus that was a horrible dream, but at least I got some sleep, and I'd look at the clock, ten past four, five minutes after the last time I had looked at the clock.

This went on all night so that, by the time the morning came around, I was at my wits' end. I was physically and mentally wrecked, absolutely drained, sore, uncomfortable, probably hungry and thirsty. I couldn't wait to get out of that hospital. I was sending text messages to Chloe all night, 'please come and get me, get me out of this place', which was unfair on her, it was putting a lot of pressure on her, she with a young child and trying herself to cope with the fact that the father of her two children could be paralysed for the rest of his life.

She didn't see it like that, she was brilliant, she just wanted what was best for me. All I wanted was to get moved closer to home, ideally to Oxford. She worked on it the whole day. It felt like weeks to me. We're moving you now, we're not moving you now, you can move today, it won't be for a couple of days. It drove me mad. Chloe moved heaven and earth, and the Jockeys' Association was great as well. By the end of the day I got moved to Oxford.

Moving to Oxford was like moving home. I still had this cage on my head, I was still on the flat of my back, still uncomfortable, still in pain, but the atmosphere was totally different to what I experienced in Liverpool. The ceilings were clean.

I was moved to Oxford on the Thursday and they operated again on me on the Monday. That operation took six hours. They took the cage off, realigned the other vertebrae and inserted some metal into my neck to stabilise it. I lost two litres of blood, that's almost four pints, which is quite a lot when you consider that you only have eight pints of blood in your body. They gave me some tablets to swallow after the operation, but I couldn't swallow them. I went to swallow them and they flew out of my mouth like torpedoes right across the room. I felt like my throat didn't fit my neck, it was all swollen and I couldn't get anything down. I thought I was going to choke.

Jeremy Fairbank performed the operation, and he was really happy with how it went. He didn't think that it was going to take as long as it did, but he was happy. It was a huge relief to get the cage off my shoulders and have it replaced by a neck collar, and to be able to sit up. Goals are relative. When you are lying on the flat of your back with six pounds of weight holding your neck and shoulders together, all you want to do is sit up. Being able to go to the toilet by yourself, being able to wash yourself are so unattainable as to be completely unrealistic. When you are able-bodied and in the prime of your health, all you want to do is ride a Grand National winner.

I was allowed to go home the following Saturday. That was brilliant. I sat on my chair in the sitting room with my feet up. I had ruptured the cruciate in my knee as well and that was in bits. I remember realising that it had been five weeks since my fall, and I couldn't believe it. I had a brace on my knee and was struggling to walk. I'd walk up the garden and back and I'd have to sit down for 15 minutes to recover.

I followed racing a bit. I watched the Scottish National in hospital and was delighted when Seanie Curran won it with Iris De Balme. Seanie was a weigh-room colleague for a long time, and he is doing well with a small string of horses now as a trainer. I watched Punjabi winning the Grade 1 hurdle at Punchestown for Nicky, under Barry Geraghty. I was delighted for Nicky. He got a little emotional afterwards when he was talking about Punjabi and about how I should have been riding him and how he missed me around. That was really nice. I got a bit emotional myself.

Maybe Nicky sensed at that time that I wouldn't be back at all. That was the first time it hit me. Nicky had been talking about sending Punjabi to Aintree, but I thought that the race at Punchestown was the one for him. The Aintree race was going to be tougher, over two and a half miles. The Punchestown race was over two miles, might not have been that hot a race and was worth a hundred grand more. Punjabi had won at the Punchestown Festival in 2007. It was a no-brainer. Then I wasn't able to ride him. I wondered if I would ever ride him again.

Of course I was hoping that I would ride Punjabi again, that I would ride again, but I was going to be realistic about this. I didn't want my career to end that way, unexpectedly at the second fence at Aintree, but I wasn't going to do anything that was going to put me in danger.

In the end, there was no decision to be made. I went through lots of rehabilitation work on my knee and on my neck, but, August 6, 2008, I went to see Jeremy Fairbank, who told me that it was just not an option for me to ride again. He said that, if I had another fall on my neck, I could be paralysed or killed. I didn't want to hear it. I've always been an optimist, but I'm also a realist. If you're riding a 33-1 shot, you have a chance of winning. It's a small chance, but it's a chance. You're in the race, you have nothing to lose. But if you're told that, if you have a fall, it is an even-money shot that you will be paralysed, well that's not a risk that is worth taking. The decision is made for you.

There are two ways of looking at what happened to me, at my fall in the 2008 Grand National. You could think how desperately unlucky you were to sustain such a bad injury when nine times out of ten you would walk away unscathed, woe is me, or you could think how lucky you were to be able to walk again given how bad the injury was and how close you came to paralysis. I'm a glass-half-full man myself. I realise how lucky I was.

My dad would say that it was God telling me it was time to stop, time to get out while I was still able to walk away. I don't fully believe that, but I wouldn't dismiss it out of hand either. I believe in God, or I believe there is something up there governing what we do, but I also believe you make your own choices. I had the choice of several horses in the Grand National and I chose to ride L'Ami. That was my choice. L'Ami got the fence wrong, it was uncharacteristic, but he made the mistake. Was that a higher authority at work, trying to send me a message? Unlikely, but not out of the question.

I still have flashes, daymares if you like, of the fall, the impact, the crash of timber, the silence, the pungent smell of bone on bone, and it hits me hard. Jamie Osborne said to me recently that I would miss being a jockey.

'You'll miss riding at racing pace over fences,' he said. 'You'll miss the attention and the craic in the weigh room and coming back in after riding a winner.'

'That may be the case, Jamie,' I said. 'But I won't miss lying at the back of a fence trying to feel my legs.'

I have been doing some work for At The Races for a couple of years now, and I will step up my involvement with them. I'm very lucky to have that available to me, I really enjoy working with them. Also, I'm lucky to have Jon Holmes as my agent, working on my behalf.

My perspective on life changed somewhere between hitting the ground on the landing side of the second fence at Aintree, lying on my back there, looking at my body thinking that it didn't belong to my head, and lying in that hospital room in Royal Liverpool looking at the ceiling. Somewhere in all of that, something clicked.

All of a sudden, riding horses wasn't the most important thing to me any more. Riding another Grand National winner, another Cheltenham Festival winner, schooling a young horse at Seven Barrows, it all fell into line behind Chloe, Zac and Oscar. Kicking a ball in the park, showing Zac how to swing a golf club, throwing Oscar up on my shoulders, suddenly became infinitely more important. These are the things that life is all about, and I intend to live the rest of mine to the full.

# RACING RECORD

**JUMPS WINNERS**

**1988**

| | | |
|---|---|---|
| Dec 20 | Lover's Secret | Ludlow |
| Dec 30 | Corston Springs | Hereford |

**1990**

| | | |
|---|---|---|
| Apr 16 | Sunset Sam | Hereford |
| Dec 27 | Duncan Idaho | Taunton |

**1991**

| | | |
|---|---|---|
| Jan 21 | Duncan Idaho | Leicester |
| Feb 23 | Duncan Idaho | Stratford |
| Mar 9 | Rafiki | Sandown |
| Mar 13 | George Buckingham | Newton Abbot |
| Mar 16 | Duncan Idaho | Uttoxeter |
| Apr 1 | Relief Map | Newton Abbot |
| Apr 1 | Sherzine | Newton Abbot |
| Apr 5 | Ashfield Boy | Exeter |
| May 10 | Valtaki | Stratford |
| Jun 1 | Ashfield Boy | Stratford |
| Sep 5 | Penllyne's Pride | Newton Abbot |
| Sep 14 | Penllyne's Pride | Bangor-on-Dee |
| Sep 16 | Slippery Max | Plumpton |
| Nov 30 | Premier Princess | Nottingham |
| Dec 4 | Military Band | Ludlow |
| Dec 7 | Knight In Side | Lingfield |
| Dec 16 | Erme Express | Newton Abbot |
| Dec 20 | Shipwright | Uttoxeter |
| Dec 27 | Broughton Manor | Taunton |
| Dec 27 | Tiger Claw | Taunton |

**1992**

| | | |
|---|---|---|
| Jan 1 | Shipwright | Exeter |
| Jan 7 | Its Nearly Time | Chepstow |
| Jan 15 | Romola Nijinsky | Ludlow |
| Jan 16 | Broughton Manor | Taunton |
| Jan 16 | Knight In Side | Taunton |
| Jan 17 | Skinnhill | Kempton |
| Jan 23 | Miss Purbeck | Newton Abbot |
| Jan 31 | Mottram's Gold | Lingfield |
| Feb 6 | Greyfriars Bobby | Wincanton |
| Feb 8 | Whippers Delight | Uttoxeter |
| Feb 10 | Schweppes Tonic | Hereford |
| Mar 5 | Broughton Manor | Wincanton |
| Mar 5 | Mottram's Gold | Wincanton |
| Mar 9 | Celtic Diamond | Taunton |
| Mar 14 | Meat The Foulkes | Uttoxeter |
| Mar 21 | Kalogy | Newbury |

| | | |
|---|---|---|
| Mar 25 | Brief Encounter | Worcester |
| Mar 26 | Pere Bazille | Taunton |
| Mar 27 | Bumbles Folly | Wincanton |
| Apr 3 | Rafiki | Exeter |
| Apr 3 | Miss Purbeck | Exeter |
| Apr 8 | Kelling | Ascot |
| Apr 11 | Catch The Cross | Bangor-on-Dee |
| Apr 11 | Burnt Fingers | Bangor-on-Dee |
| Apr 28 | Sir Crusty | Ascot |
| May 1 | Truism I | Newton Abbot |
| May 4 | Molojec | Exeter |
| May 6 | Tresidder | Wetherby |
| Aug 1 | Ricmar | Newton Abbot |
| Aug 3 | Mandalay Prince I | Newton Abbot |
| Aug 11 | Mandalay Prince I | Fontwell |
| Aug 24 | Mandalay Prince I | Hexham |
| Aug 27 | Always Alex | Worcester |
| Aug 29 | Nuns Jewel | Southwell |
| Sep 2 | Celtic Diamond | Newton Abbot |
| Sep 23 | Height Of Fun | Southwell |
| Sep 28 | Celtic Diamond | Fontwell |
| Oct 10 | Master William I | Southwell |
| Oct 13 | Faux Pavillon | Exeter |
| Oct 17 | James The First | Stratford |
| Oct 22 | Forest Flame | Wincanton |
| Oct 23 | Faux Pavillon | Exeter |
| Oct 29 | Jimmy The Gillie | Kempton |
| Nov 3 | James The First | Hereford |
| Nov 14 | Eau D'Espoir | Nottingham |
| Nov 21 | Welknown Character | Ascot |
| Nov 25 | Schweppes Tonic | Hereford |
| Dec 10 | Boscean Chieftain | Taunton |
| Dec 12 | Sillars Stalker | Doncaster |
| Dec 26 | Boscean Chieftain | Wincanton |
| Dec 26 | Broughton Manor | Wincanton |

**1993**

| | | |
|---|---|---|
| Jan 6 | Brandon Grove | Southwell (A.W) |
| Jan 22 | Broughton Manor | Kempton |
| Jan 23 | Its Nearly Time | Warwick |
| Jan 23 | Rafiki | Warwick |
| Jan 29 | Broughton Manor | Wincanton |
| Jan 30 | Country Lad | Cheltenham |
| Feb 6 | Sabaki River | Chepstow |
| Feb 8 | James The First | Wolverhampton |
| Feb 15 | Fearless Fred | Hereford |
| Feb 20 | Boscean Chieftain | Chepstow |
| Feb 26 | Factor Ten | Kempton |

| | | |
|---|---|---|
| Mar 6 | Far Too Loud | Newbury |
| Mar 8 | Chip And Run | Wolverhampton |
| Mar 13 | Pats Minstrel | Sandown |
| Mar 15 | River Orchid | Taunton |
| Mar 19 | Thatcher Rock | Fakenham |
| Mar 20 | General Merchant | Lingfield |
| Mar 20 | Kisu Kali | Lingfield |
| Mar 31 | Thatcher Rock | Worcester |
| Apr 6 | The Green Fool | Sedgefield |
| Apr 16 | Rochester | Taunton |
| Apr 17 | Mickeen | Stratford |
| Apr 21 | Sabaki River | Cheltenham |
| May 1 | Height Of Fun | Hereford |
| May 3 | Boscean Chieftain | Haydock |
| May 14 | Derechef | Stratford |
| May 20 | Rafiki | Exeter |
| May 20 | Sabaki River | Exeter |
| May 26 | Old Mortality | Cartmel |
| May 29 | Whitewebb | Hexham |
| May 31 | Rafiki | Uttoxeter |
| Aug 4 | Trust Deed | Exeter |
| Aug 23 | Trumpet I | Hexham |
| Aug 25 | Trust Deed | Exeter |
| Aug 30 | Parbold Hill | Newton Abbot |
| Aug 30 | Trumpet I | Newton Abbot |
| Sep 8 | Trust Deed | Exeter |
| Sep 9 | Killula Chief | Newton Abbot |
| Sep 22 | Height Of Fun | Southwell |
| Sep 23 | Killula Chief | Taunton |
| Oct 4 | Kingfisher Bay | Plumpton |
| Oct 9 | Howaryafxd | Worcester |
| Oct 14 | Abu Muslab | Taunton |
| Oct 15 | Killula Chief | Ludlow |
| Oct 16 | Billy Bathgate | Kempton |
| Oct 22 | Amtrak Express | Newbury |
| Oct 26 | Croft Mill | Newton Abbot |
| Oct 28 | Abu Muslab | Stratford |
| Nov 3 | Time For A Flutter | Haydock |
| Nov 10 | Saint Ciel | Worcester |
| Nov 12 | Light Veneer | Cheltenham |
| Nov 13 | Under Offer | Windsor |
| Nov 13 | Easthorpe | Windsor |
| Nov 19 | Jopanini | Ascot |
| Nov 27 | Arabian Bold | Warwick |
| Nov 27 | Gotta Be Joking | Warwick |
| Nov 30 | Kanndabil | Leicester |
| Dec 2 | Emerald Storm | Windsor |
| Dec 9 | Smartie Express | Taunton |
| Dec 11 | Sparkling Sunset | Lingfield |
| Dec 11 | Admiral's Well | Lingfield |
| Dec 14 | Top Wave | Folkestone |
| Dec 18 | Billy Bathgate | Ascot |
| Dec 27 | Radical Request | Huntingdon |
| Dec 30 | Peacock Feather | Fontwell |
| Dec 31 | Big Matt | Newbury |
| **1994** | | |
| Jan 1 | Easthorpe | Nottingham |
| Jan 3 | Mister Nova | Windsor |
| Jan 12 | Elegant King | Southwell (A.W) |
| Jan 18 | Top Wave | Folkestone |
| Jan 22 | Current Express | Kempton |
| Jan 26 | Elegant King | Southwell (A.W) |
| Jan 31 | Nathir | Plumpton |
| Feb 2 | Jailbreaker | Leicester |
| Feb 9 | Squire York | Ludlow |
| Feb 9 | Deependable | Ludlow |
| Feb 9 | Johnny Will | Ludlow |
| Feb 17 | Jailbreaker | Sandown |
| Feb 25 | Bibendum | Kempton |
| Mar 10 | Sunbeam Talbot | Towcester |
| Mar 17 | Raymylette | Cheltenham |
| Mar 18 | Hermes Harvest | Lingfield |
| Mar 19 | Whitechapel | Chepstow |
| Mar 19 | Rafiki | Chepstow |
| Mar 23 | Broughton Manor | Exeter |
| Apr 4 | Bally Clover | Newton Abbot |
| Apr 6 | Barna Boy | Ascot |
| Apr 12 | Rafiki | Uttoxeter |
| Apr 30 | Philip's Woody | Plumpton |
| May 2 | Sartorius | Towcester |
| May 10 | Holy Joe | Chepstow |
| May 13 | Deviosity | Newton Abbot |
| May 19 | Zanyman | Exeter |
| May 21 | Erckule | Warwick |
| May 28 | Lodging | Hexham |
| May 30 | Lor Moss | Hereford |
| May 30 | Palace Wolf | Hereford |
| May 30 | Sydney Barry | Hereford |
| Jun 2 | Zanyman | Uttoxeter |
| Aug 13 | Northern Trial | Stratford |
| Aug 18 | Mr Bean | Uttoxeter |
| Oct 1 | Four Deep | Kelso |
| Oct 1 | Regan | Kelso |
| Oct 12 | Abu Muslab | Exeter |
| Oct 13 | Chickabiddy | Taunton |
| Oct 18 | Monksfort | Plumpton |
| Oct 27 | Hurricane Tommy | Sedgefield |
| Nov 2 | Arabian Bold | Kempton |
| Nov 17 | Mad Thyme | Wincanton |

| | | | | | | |
|---|---|---|---|---|---|---|
| Nov 17 | Amtrak Express | Wincanton | | May 12 | Braes Of Mar | Market Rasen |
| Nov 18 | Mr Entertainer | Leicester | | May 13 | Sparkling Sunset | Worcester |
| Nov 19 | Raymylette | Ascot | | May 17 | Lady Peta | Hereford |
| Dec 3 | Really A Rascal | Chepstow | | May 19 | Arfey | Newton Abbot |
| Dec 5 | Easthorpe | Ludlow | | May 19 | Hostile Witness | Newton Abbot |
| Dec 6 | Pats Minstrel | Plumpton | | May 25 | Its Unbelievable | Exeter |
| Dec 7 | On Air | Haydock | | May 26 | Sayh | Towcester |
| Dec 8 | Cheryl's Lad | Taunton | | May 27 | Gallardini | Cartmel |
| Dec 14 | Grouseman | Exeter | | May 29 | Staunch Rival | Uttoxeter |
| Dec 16 | Mad Thyme | Uttoxeter | | May 31 | Robins Pride | Cartmel |
| Dec 17 | Raymylette | Ascot | | Jun 3 | Castle Blue | Southwell |
| Dec 21 | Sublime Fellow | Ludlow | | Jun 10 | Sohail | Market Rasen |
| Dec 26 | Who Is Equiname | Kempton | | Jun 17 | Succotash | Market Rasen |
| Dec 27 | Amtrak Express | Kempton | | Jul 31 | Bodantree | Newton Abbot |
| Dec 29 | Emerald Storm | Fontwell | | Aug 19 | Castle Blue | Market Rasen |
| | | | | Aug 25 | Little Hooligan | Exeter |
| **1995** | | | | Aug 30 | Chickabiddy | Newton Abbot |
| Jan 10 | Barna Boy | Leicester | | Sep 8 | Red Valerian | Worcester |
| Jan 11 | Rather Sharp | Plumpton | | Sep 22 | Easthorpe | Newton Abbot |
| Jan 12 | Conquering Leader | Wincanton | | Sep 29 | Red Valerian | Hexham |
| Jan 14 | Blast Freeze | Ascot | | Sep 29 | Trumpet I | Hexham |
| Jan 16 | Keel Row | Fontwell | | Sep 29 | Scorched Air | Hexham |
| Jan 18 | Mr Invader | Windsor | | Oct 4 | Squire Jim | Towcester |
| Jan 21 | Thumbs Up I | Haydock | | Oct 7 | Go Ballistic | Worcester |
| Feb 10 | Big Matt | Newbury | | Oct 9 | Kinoko | Sedgefield |
| Feb 10 | Star Player | Newbury | | Oct 9 | Pats Minstrel | Sedgefield |
| Feb 17 | Cuddy Dale | Sandown | | Oct 12 | Staunch Rival | Taunton |
| Feb 22 | Dear Do | Folkestone | | Oct 12 | He's A King | Taunton |
| Feb 24 | Big Matt | Kempton | | Oct 28 | Drummond Warrior | Ascot |
| Feb 25 | Thumbs Up I | Kempton | | Oct 28 | Jackson Flint | Ascot |
| Mar 1 | Conquering Leader | Wetherby | | Oct 31 | Chickabiddy | Exeter |
| Mar 4 | Go Ballistic | Doncaster | | Nov 1 | Easthorpe | Haydock |
| Mar 4 | Easthorpe | Doncaster | | Nov 10 | Wonder Man | Cheltenham |
| Mar 13 | Frown | Taunton | | Nov 13 | Braes Of Mar | Leicester |
| Mar 13 | Grouseman | Taunton | | Nov 15 | Coonawara | Kempton |
| Mar 14 | Rough Quest | Cheltenham | | Nov 29 | Braes Of Mar | Hereford |
| Mar 21 | Dear Do | Fontwell | | Nov 30 | Dear Do | Windsor |
| Mar 22 | Magic Junction | Ludlow | | Dec 6 | Plunder Bay | Leicester |
| Mar 25 | Conquering Leader | Newbury | | Dec 8 | Cheryl's Lad | Cheltenham |
| Mar 27 | Mariner's Air | Nottingham | | Dec 8 | Our Kris | Cheltenham |
| Mar 31 | Elflaa | Huntingdon | | Dec 14 | Tudor Fable | Towcester |
| Apr 1 | Arabian Bold | Ascot | | Dec 15 | Ebullient Equiname | Hereford |
| Apr 8 | Thinking Twice | Aintree | | Dec 19 | Dear Do | Southwell |
| Apr 12 | Abu Muslab | Exeter | | | | |
| Apr 15 | Pats Minstrel | Plumpton | | **1996** | | |
| Apr 24 | Bo Knows Best | Chepstow | | Jan 13 | Big Matt | Ascot |
| Apr 27 | Rough Quest | Punchestown | | Jan 15 | Hag's Way | Fontwell |
| May 2 | Big Matt | Ascot | | Jan 15 | Silverfort Lad | Fontwell |
| May 5 | Speaker's House | Newton Abbot | | Feb 1 | Aly Daley | Sedgefield |
| May 5 | Hostile Witness | Newton Abbot | | Feb 1 | His Way | Sedgefield |

| | | | | | | |
|---|---|---|---|---|---|---|
| Feb 3 | Amtrak Express | Sandown | | Nov 23 | Olympian | Ascot |
| Feb 3 | Whattabob | Sandown | | Nov 27 | Lady Peta | Windsor |
| Feb 16 | Hooded Hawk | Fakenham | | Nov 29 | Golden Spinner | Newbury |
| Feb 17 | Thinking Twice | Chepstow | | Dec 2 | Mister Oddy | Worcester |
| Feb 17 | Pete The Parson | Chepstow | | Dec 4 | Sublime Fellow | Southwell |
| Feb 23 | Decide Yourself | Kempton | | Dec 5 | Lets Be Frank | Windsor |
| Feb 23 | Silverfort Lad | Kempton | | Dec 10 | Sharpical | Huntingdon |
| Feb 24 | Kimanicky | Kempton | | Dec 11 | Circus Line | Leicester |
| Feb 28 | Ebullient Equiname | Nottingham | | Dec 13 | Disallowed | Cheltenham |
| Mar 2 | Tudor Fable | Newbury | | Dec 13 | Elburg | Cheltenham |
| Mar 2 | Golden Spinner | Newbury | | Dec 17 | Rough Quest | Folkestone |
| Mar 9 | Amancio | Sandown | | Dec 19 | Whattabob | Towcester |
| Mar 11 | Jovial Man | Plumpton | | Dec 26 | Tim | Kempton |
| Mar 15 | Sorbiere | Folkestone | | | | |
| Mar 18 | Easby Joker | Lingfield | | **1997** | | |
| Mar 20 | Silverdale Fox | Towcester | | Jan 10 | Edge Ahead | Southwell |
| Mar 25 | Churchtown Port | Fontwell | | Jan 14 | Garnwin | Leicester |
| Mar 27 | Hag's Way | Chepstow | | Jan 14 | Amancio | Leicester |
| Mar 30 | Rough Quest | Aintree | | Jan 16 | Fastini Gold | Ludlow |
| Apr 1 | Pete The Parson | Exeter | | Jan 17 | Summer Spell | Kempton |
| Apr 2 | Sorbiere | Folkestone | | Jan 18 | Fine Thyne | Kempton |
| Apr 3 | Go Ballistic | Ascot | | Jan 22 | Splendid Thyne | Lingfield |
| Apr 6 | Dear Do | Plumpton | | Jan 24 | Salmon Breeze | Doncaster |
| Apr 9 | Merlin's Lad | Uttoxeter | | Jan 27 | Amancio | Plumpton |
| Apr 10 | Super Gossip | Worcester | | Jan 30 | Fiddling The Facts | Folkestone |
| Apr 10 | Litening Conductor | Worcester | | Feb 13 | Tristram's Image | Taunton |
| Apr 11 | Proud Sun | Cheltenham | | Feb 15 | Friendship | Windsor |
| Apr 17 | Tight Fist | Cheltenham | | Mar 8 | Sublime Fellow | Sandown |
| Apr 17 | Mister Oddy | Cheltenham | | Mar 14 | Sharpical | Folkestone |
| Apr 19 | Merlin's Lad | Ayr | | Mar 14 | Sunday Venture | Folkestone |
| Apr 19 | Dear Do | Ayr | | Mar 15 | Red Bean | Lingfield |
| Aug 10 | Yaakum | Market Rasen | | Mar 19 | Stormyfairweather | Towcester |
| Aug 26 | Sydmonton | Huntingdon | | Mar 26 | Garnwin | Ascot |
| Aug 29 | Brave Patriarch | Sedgefield | | Mar 29 | Kinnescash | Plumpton |
| Sep 7 | Fine Thyne | Stratford | | Mar 31 | James The First | Chepstow |
| Oct 14 | Ambassador Royale | Newton Abbot | | Apr 1 | Plunder Bay | Uttoxeter |
| Oct 18 | Sublime Fellow | Hereford | | Apr 2 | Melody Maid | Worcester |
| Oct 22 | Regal Pursuit | Plumpton | | Apr 5 | Bimsey | Aintree |
| Oct 25 | Plunder Bay | Newbury | | Apr 9 | Kinnescash | Chepstow |
| Nov 2 | Go Ballistic | Ascot | | Apr 16 | Stormyfairweather | Cheltenham |
| Nov 5 | Allow | Exeter | | Apr 17 | Fiddling The Facts | Ayr |
| Nov 6 | Fine Thyne | Kempton | | Apr 19 | Philip's Woody | Stratford |
| Nov 8 | Elburg | Uttoxeter | | Apr 19 | Barford Sovereign | Stratford |
| Nov 9 | Crack On | Sandown | | Apr 21 | Who Is Equiname | Towcester |
| Nov 12 | Lady Peta | Ludlow | | Apr 25 | Summer Spell | Ascot |
| Nov 15 | Hunting Lore | Cheltenham | | Apr 29 | Sea Patrol | Ascot |
| Nov 17 | Gloriana | Fontwell | | May 2 | Easter Ross | Newton Abbot |
| Nov 18 | Ritto | Plumpton | | May 3 | Fenian Court | Warwick |
| Nov 20 | Fine Thyne | Kempton | | May 5 | Embankment | Ludlow |
| Nov 21 | Wayfarers Way | Wincanton | | May 5 | Sigma Run | Ludlow |

| | | | | | |
|---|---|---|---|---|---|
| May 7 | Song Of The Sword | Chepstow | Dec 6 | Friendship | Sandown |
| May 7 | Blotoft | Uttoxeter | Dec 8 | Freeline Fontaine | Ludlow |
| May 9 | Philip's Woody | Stratford | Dec 9 | Camera Man | Huntingdon |
| May 10 | Kinnescash | Worcester | Dec 9 | Get Real | Huntingdon |
| May 10 | Embankment | Newton Abbot | Dec 9 | Serenus | Huntingdon |
| May 10 | Apachee Flower | Newton Abbot | Dec 10 | Who Is Equiname | Leicester |
| May 11 | Sublime Fellow | Wolverhampton | Dec 10 | Be Brave | Leicester |
| May 12 | Stormyfairweather | Towcester | Dec 11 | Wayfarers Way | Fakenham |
| May 14 | Song Of The Sword | Hereford | Dec 13 | Lord Jim | Cheltenham |
| May 23 | Salmon Breeze | Towcester | Dec 15 | Ideal Partner | Warwick |
| May 26 | Song Of The Sword | Hereford | Dec 15 | Even Flow | Warwick |
| May 26 | Kinnescash | Hereford | Dec 17 | Bassey | Bangor-on-Dee |
| May 31 | Diamond Fort | Stratford | Dec 18 | Pete The Parson | Towcester |
| May 31 | Cuillin Caper | Stratford | Dec 19 | Hooded Hawk | Uttoxeter |
| Jun 7 | Review Board | Worcester | Dec 20 | Celibate | Ascot |
| Jun 18 | Searchlight | Worcester | Dec 22 | Oh Donna | Ludlow |
| Jun 27 | Colossus Of Roads | Stratford | Dec 26 | Fiddling The Facts | Kempton |
| Jul 9 | Drummond Warrior | Worcester | Dec 26 | Serenus | Kempton |
| Jul 12 | Apachee Flower | Southwell | Dec 27 | Arfer Mole | Kempton |
| Jul 14 | Wilkins | Wolverhampton | Dec 30 | King Mole | Stratford |
| Jul 14 | Chocolate Ice | Wolverhampton | | | |
| Aug 2 | Shehab | Market Rasen | **1998** | | |
| Aug 8 | Irie Mon | Market Rasen | Jan 1 | Pete The Parson | Cheltenham |
| Aug 16 | Wilkins | Stratford | Jan 21 | Mountain Path | Windsor |
| Aug 16 | Coasting I | Stratford | Jan 22 | Sovereigns Parade | Ludlow |
| Aug 16 | Walter's Dream | Stratford | Jan 24 | Three Farthings | Kempton |
| Aug 23 | Irie Mon | Market Rasen | Jan 28 | Calm Down | Lingfield |
| Aug 25 | I Have Him | Huntingdon | Jan 28 | Kings Rhapsody | Lingfield |
| Aug 25 | Fraser Carey | Huntingdon | Jan 30 | Classy Lad | Doncaster |
| Aug 25 | Bigwheel Bill | Huntingdon | Feb 7 | Big Matt | Sandown |
| Aug 25 | Northern Fleet | Huntingdon | Feb 9 | Dear Do | Fontwell |
| Sep 1 | Irie Mon | Hexham | Feb 12 | Oh Donna | Wincanton |
| Oct 17 | Easy Listening | Hereford | Feb 12 | Melody Maid | Wincanton |
| Oct 29 | Canton Venture | Fontwell | Feb 14 | Sharpical | Newbury |
| Nov 9 | Philip's Woody | Sandown | Feb 14 | Golden Spinner | Newbury |
| Nov 14 | Yahmi | Cheltenham | Feb 20 | Mountain Storm | Sandown |
| Nov 15 | Better Offer | Huntingdon | Feb 20 | Philip's Woody | Sandown |
| Nov 19 | Friendship | Kempton | Mar 2 | Ile De Librate | Plumpton |
| Nov 20 | Sublime Fellow | Warwick | Mar 6 | Calon Lan | Newbury |
| Nov 21 | Pennybridge | Aintree | Mar 13 | Mountain Path | Sandown |
| Nov 24 | Get Real | Ludlow | Mar 16 | Just Nip | Plumpton |
| Nov 24 | Sunday Venture | Ludlow | Mar 20 | Veridian | Folkestone |
| Nov 26 | Ekeus | Windsor | Mar 25 | Ramallah | Towcester |
| Nov 26 | Easter Ross | Windsor | Mar 26 | Muhtadi | Plumpton |
| Nov 27 | Northern Nation | Uttoxeter | Mar 26 | Ballygriffin Lad | Plumpton |
| Nov 28 | Stormyfairweather | Newbury | Mar 27 | Tough Act | Newbury |
| Nov 29 | Sounds Fyne | Newbury | Apr 11 | Sounds Fyne | Carlisle |
| Dec 1 | Dream Leader | Folkestone | Apr 11 | Jack Robbo | Carlisle |
| Dec 4 | Shahrur | Windsor | Apr 14 | Supreme Genotin | Wetherby |
| Dec 5 | Tough Act | Sandown | Apr 16 | Hidebound | Cheltenham |

| | | | | | | |
|---|---|---|---|---|---|---|
| Apr 20 | Naughty Future | Hexham | | Nov 19 | Macgeorge | Warwick |
| Apr 24 | Woodstock Wanderer | Taunton | | Nov 23 | Garrison Friendly | Windsor |
| Apr 25 | The Land Agent | Sandown | | Nov 24 | Mountain Path | Worcester |
| Apr 28 | Big Matt | Punchestown | | Nov 26 | Country Beau | Taunton |
| May 2 | Classy Lad | Hereford | | Nov 26 | Jefferies | Taunton |
| May 6 | Philip's Woody | Wetherby | | Dec 1 | Royal Toast | Newton Abbot |
| May 6 | Auto Pilot | Wetherby | | Dec 3 | Grecian Dart | Windsor |
| May 8 | Mountain Storm | Wincanton | | Dec 3 | Copper Coin | Windsor |
| May 9 | Sir Dante | Worcester | | Dec 9 | Auto Pilot | Leicester |
| May 9 | Bitofamixup | Worcester | | Dec 9 | Tempestuous Lady | Leicester |
| May 15 | Song Of The Sword | Aintree | | Dec 10 | Perfect Venue | Taunton |
| May 15 | Just Bayard | Aintree | | Dec 11 | All Gong | Cheltenham |
| May 17 | Sun Alert | Fakenham | | Dec 12 | Philip's Woody | Doncaster |
| May 17 | All Gong | Fakenham | | Dec 15 | Salmon Breeze | Folkestone |
| May 20 | Mighty Phantom | Uttoxeter | | Dec 18 | Buckside | Lingfield |
| May 21 | Baranov | Exeter | | Dec 19 | Get Real | Ascot |
| May 25 | Song Of The Sword | Huntingdon | | Dec 19 | Hidebound | Ascot |
| May 28 | Prussia | Uttoxeter | | Dec 22 | Tempestuous Lady | Ludlow |
| May 30 | Hazaaf | Stratford | | Dec 26 | Grecian Dart | Kempton |
| Jun 1 | Mighty Phantom | Hereford | | Dec 26 | Serenus | Kempton |
| Jun 1 | Appearance Money | Hereford | | Dec 26 | Eagles Rest I | Kempton |
| Jun 10 | Majestic Affair | Uttoxeter | | Dec 26 | Melody Maid | Kempton |
| Jun 17 | Volunteer | Worcester | | Dec 28 | Lyreen Wonder | Chepstow |
| Jun 17 | Call My Guest | Worcester | | Dec 28 | Storm Damage | Chepstow |
| Jun 19 | Spartan Heartbeat | Hexham | | Dec 29 | Yokki Moppie | Taunton |
| Jul 25 | Call My Guest | Market Rasen | | Dec 29 | Top Skipper | Taunton |
| Aug 31 | Coh Sho No | Huntingdon | | Dec 30 | Deep C Diva | Stratford |
| Sep 1 | Toski | Uttoxeter | | Dec 31 | Premier Generation | Warwick |
| Sep 12 | Majesty | Worcester | | | | |
| Sep 14 | Infamous | Plumpton | | **1999** | | |
| Sep 22 | Tiger Lake | Fontwell | | Jan 6 | Park Royal | Lingfield |
| Sep 27 | Haunting Music | Huntingdon | | Jan 6 | Shoofk | Lingfield |
| Oct 3 | Toski | Chepstow | | Jan 8 | Majors Legacy | Towcester |
| Oct 7 | Treat Me Bold | Towcester | | Jan 14 | The Land Agent | Wincanton |
| Oct 8 | Woodstock Wanderer | Wincanton | | Jan 15 | Amoroso | Folkestone |
| Oct 9 | Tiger Lake | Huntingdon | | Jan 18 | Kings Boy | Doncaster |
| Oct 9 | Haunting Music | Huntingdon | | Jan 18 | Looks Like Trouble | Doncaster |
| Oct 9 | Long Lunch | Huntingdon | | Jan 18 | All Gong | Doncaster |
| Oct 15 | Ginzbourg | Taunton | | Jan 21 | Perfect Venue | Taunton |
| Nov 3 | Buckskin Cameo | Warwick | | Jan 23 | Kingsmark | Kempton |
| Nov 10 | Katarino | Newbury | | Jan 23 | Marlborough | Kempton |
| Nov 11 | Wreckless Man | Newbury | | Jan 23 | Tiutchev | Kempton |
| Nov 11 | Hidebound | Newbury | | Jan 26 | Centaur Express | Leicester |
| Nov 13 | Premier Generation | Cheltenham | | Jan 26 | Makounji | Leicester |
| Nov 14 | Katarino | Cheltenham | | Jan 29 | All Gong | Doncaster |
| Nov 14 | Stormyfairweather | Cheltenham | | Jan 29 | Goodtime George | Doncaster |
| Nov 17 | Collier Bay | Newton Abbot | | Feb 2 | Lizzys First | Taunton |
| Nov 18 | Mountain Storm | Kempton | | Feb 12 | Makounji | Newbury |
| Nov 18 | Tax Exempt | Kempton | | Feb 13 | Celibate | Newbury |
| Nov 19 | Country House | Warwick | | Feb 15 | Allez Wijins | Plumpton |

| | | | | | | |
|---|---|---|---|---|---|---|
| Feb 15 | Deep C Diva | Plumpton | | Aug 30 | Dun Coady | Fontwell |
| Feb 18 | Looks Like Trouble | Sandown | | Aug 31 | Destiny Calls | Uttoxeter |
| Feb 18 | Tempestuous Lady | Sandown | | Sep 4 | Bodfari Signet | Stratford |
| Feb 19 | Bacchanal | Sandown | | Sep 17 | Golden Hawk | Huntingdon |
| Feb 20 | Buckside | Ascot | | Oct 2 | Soldat | Uttoxeter |
| Feb 24 | Stormyfairweather | Doncaster | | Oct 5 | River Bay | Fontwell |
| Feb 26 | King's Banker | Kempton | | Oct 5 | Ritual | Fontwell |
| Feb 27 | Premier Generation | Kempton | | Oct 9 | Ma Barnicle | Worcester |
| Feb 27 | Makounji | Kempton | | Oct 16 | Calon Lan | Stratford |
| Feb 27 | Katarino | Kempton | | Oct 18 | Damus | Plumpton |
| Mar 2 | Catherine's Way | Leicester | | Oct 23 | Galapiat Du Mesnil | Worcester |
| Mar 2 | Eltigri | Leicester | | Oct 23 | Fard Du Moulin Mas | Worcester |
| Mar 2 | Centaur Express | Leicester | | Oct 23 | Highland | Worcester |
| Mar 8 | The Minder | Fontwell | | Oct 27 | Mr Collins | Cheltenham |
| Mar 10 | Kissair | Bangor-on-Dee | | Oct 28 | Wrangel | Stratford |
| Mar 10 | Mister Blake | Bangor-on-Dee | | Oct 30 | See More Business | Wetherby |
| Mar 11 | Tequila | Wincanton | | Oct 30 | Silver Wedge | Wetherby |
| Mar 11 | Basman | Wincanton | | Nov 3 | River Bay | Kempton |
| Mar 13 | Bacchanal | Chepstow | | Nov 6 | Rollcall | Wincanton |
| Mar 13 | Garolsa | Chepstow | | Nov 6 | Falmouth Bay | Wincanton |
| Mar 13 | Dusk Duel | Sandown | | Nov 9 | Serenus | Newbury |
| Mar 17 | Call Equiname | Cheltenham | | Nov 10 | Polish Pilot | Worcester |
| Mar 18 | Katarino | Cheltenham | | Nov 11 | Admiral Rose | Ludlow |
| Mar 18 | See More Business | Cheltenham | | Nov 13 | Silence Reigns | Cheltenham |
| Mar 18 | Stormyfairweather | Cheltenham | | Nov 17 | Artemis | Kempton |
| Mar 23 | Kerry's Oats | Fontwell | | Nov 18 | Captain Miller | Folkestone |
| Mar 24 | Royal Toast | Towcester | | Nov 19 | Galapiat Du Mesnil | Ascot |
| Mar 26 | Masamadas | Newbury | | Nov 19 | Pembroke Square | Ascot |
| Mar 27 | Majesty | Newbury | | Nov 19 | Get Real | Ascot |
| Apr 3 | Blue Royal | Towcester | | Nov 20 | Carole's Crusader | Ascot |
| Apr 7 | Kings Boy | Ascot | | Nov 21 | Solvang | Aintree |
| Apr 16 | Calon Lan | Ayr | | Nov 22 | River Bay | Ludlow |
| Apr 17 | Esprit De Cotte | Stratford | | Nov 23 | Matchless | Market Rasen |
| Apr 17 | Tissue Of Lies | Stratford | | Nov 25 | Lets Be Frank | Uttoxeter |
| Apr 22 | Yeoman Sailor | Fontwell | | Nov 26 | Clandestine | Newbury |
| Apr 26 | Amoroso | Plumpton | | Nov 26 | Highland | Newbury |
| Apr 26 | Otago Heights | Plumpton | | Nov 27 | Bacchanal | Newbury |
| Apr 29 | Katarino | Punchestown | | Nov 29 | Admiral Rose | Folkestone |
| Apr 30 | Blue Royal | Punchestown | | Nov 29 | Fast Fiddler | Folkestone |
| May 3 | Via Del Quatro | Fontwell | | Dec 2 | Captain Miller | Leicester |
| May 5 | Admiral Rose | Chepstow | | Dec 2 | Ad Hoc | Leicester |
| May 5 | Goodtime George | Uttoxeter | | Dec 3 | Tiutchev | Exeter |
| May 11 | Far Horizon | Hereford | | Dec 10 | Mister Banjo | Cheltenham |
| May 15 | Brandy Snap | Bangor-on-Dee | | Dec 13 | Hooded Hawk | Plumpton |
| Jul 11 | Hunting Lore | Stratford | | Dec 13 | Tiger Grass | Plumpton |
| Jul 30 | Hunting Lore | Bangor-on-Dee | | Dec 16 | Boro Sovereign | Towcester |
| Jul 30 | Gower-Slave | Bangor-on-Dee | | Dec 18 | Get Real | Ascot |
| Jul 31 | Captain Tancred | Market Rasen | | Dec 18 | Blue Royal | Ascot |
| Aug 7 | Sawlajan | Stratford | | Dec 21 | Silver Wedge | Folkestone |
| Aug 30 | Beauchamp Noble | Fontwell | | Dec 27 | See More Business | Kempton |

| Date | Horse | Course | | Date | Horse | Course |
|---|---|---|---|---|---|---|
| Dec 28 | Mister Banjo | Chepstow | | Apr 15 | Ad Hoc | Ayr |
| | | | | Apr 22 | Fanfaron | Plumpton |
| **2000** | | | | Apr 25 | Weet And See | Uttoxeter |
| Jan 3 | Regal Exit | Cheltenham | | May 1 | Salmon Breeze | Fontwell |
| Jan 5 | Cambrian Dawn | Catterick | | May 2 | Get Real | Punchestown |
| Jan 8 | Tiutchev | Sandown | | May 4 | Tiutchev | Punchestown |
| Jan 12 | Marlborough | Kempton | | May 16 | Obelisk | Hereford |
| Jan 13 | Wayward King | Wincanton | | May 20 | Cullen Bay | Bangor-on-Dee |
| Jan 14 | Eltigri | Folkestone | | May 24 | Sorrento | Worcester |
| Jan 15 | Dusk Duel | Ascot | | May 24 | Alexander Nevsky | Worcester |
| Jan 17 | Tenseesee | Doncaster | | May 29 | Damus | Hereford |
| Jan 17 | Silver Wedge | Doncaster | | Jun 6 | Native Recruit | Uttoxeter |
| Jan 19 | Mountain Path | Huntingdon | | Jun 7 | Coxwell Cossack | Market Rasen |
| Jan 22 | Inca | Kempton | | Jun 10 | Violet Express | Worcester |
| Jan 29 | Makounji | Cheltenham | | Jun 10 | Heliette | Worcester |
| Jan 29 | Mister Banjo | Cheltenham | | Jun 10 | Hot Plunge | Worcester |
| Jan 31 | Royal Toast | Plumpton | | Jul 2 | Native Recruit | Uttoxeter |
| Feb 1 | Easter Ross | Kempton | | Aug 2 | Hope Value | Newton Abbot |
| Feb 5 | Roi De La Chasse | Wetherby | | Aug 4 | Native Man | Bangor-on-Dee |
| Feb 5 | New Inn | Wetherby | | Aug 5 | Saif Majrour | Worcester |
| Feb 5 | Dusk Duel | Wetherby | | Aug 23 | Running Man | Perth |
| Feb 10 | Captain Miller | Huntingdon | | Sep 23 | Brandy Snap | Plumpton |
| Feb 11 | Wayward King | Newbury | | Sep 24 | Chief's Song | Huntingdon |
| Feb 12 | See More Business | Newbury | | Oct 1 | Kingsmark | Kelso |
| Feb 12 | Geos | Newbury | | Oct 4 | Brandy Snap | Towcester |
| Feb 17 | Steel Blade | Taunton | | Oct 6 | Masamadas | Huntingdon |
| Feb 18 | Silver Wedge | Fakenham | | Oct 13 | Montpelier | Hereford |
| Feb 18 | Kings Rhapsody | Fakenham | | Oct 14 | Kingsmark | Market Rasen |
| Feb 18 | Esperanza IV | Fakenham | | Oct 19 | Ghadames | Ludlow |
| Feb 18 | Bella Macrae | Fakenham | | Oct 20 | Donatus | Fakenham |
| Feb 24 | Landing Light | Wincanton | | Oct 22 | Fadalko | Wincanton |
| Feb 26 | Serenus | Kempton | | Oct 24 | Montpelier | Cheltenham |
| Mar 2 | Tempestuous Lady | Ludlow | | Oct 24 | Kadarann | Cheltenham |
| Mar 3 | Regal Exit | Newbury | | Oct 28 | See More Business | Wetherby |
| Mar 4 | Lakefield Leader | Newbury | | Nov 2 | Woodward Street | Haydock |
| Mar 4 | Zabari | Newbury | | Nov 3 | Soeur De Sentier | Uttoxeter |
| Mar 14 | Tiutchev | Cheltenham | | Nov 30 | Ceanannas Mor | Leicester |
| Mar 14 | Marlborough | Cheltenham | | Dec 4 | Specialize | Fakenham |
| Mar 16 | Bacchanal | Cheltenham | | Dec 5 | Ifni Du Luc | Fontwell |
| Mar 16 | Stormyfairweather | Cheltenham | | Dec 7 | Premier Generation | Ludlow |
| Mar 17 | Runaway Bishop | Folkestone | | Dec 7 | Deep Sunset | Ludlow |
| Mar 17 | Mystic Isle | Folkestone | | Dec 8 | Marlborough | Cheltenham |
| Mar 20 | Clandestine | Folkestone | | Dec 9 | Mister Banjo | Cheltenham |
| Mar 21 | Borotown Lord | Fontwell | | Dec 9 | Dusk Duel | Cheltenham |
| Mar 22 | Memsahib Ofesteem | Chepstow | | Dec 9 | Geos | Cheltenham |
| Mar 23 | Futona | Wincanton | | Dec 18 | Kadarann | Fakenham |
| Mar 24 | Lord York | Newbury | | Dec 18 | Hooded Hawk | Fakenham |
| Apr 6 | See More Business | Aintree | | Dec 26 | Fondmort | Kempton |
| Apr 14 | Lord York | Ayr | | Dec 26 | Bacchanal | Kempton |
| Apr 15 | Iris Royal | Ayr | | Dec 26 | Dusk Duel | Kempton |

| | | | | | |
|---|---|---|---|---|---|
| Dec 27 | Jocko Glasses | Kempton | Jun 3 | Red Hare | Fakenham |
| Dec 27 | Geos | Kempton | Jun 9 | Kahtan | Worcester |
| | | | Jun 10 | Classic Jazz | Worcester |
| **2001** | | | Jun 23 | Stratco | Newton Abbot |
| Jan 5 | Gastina | Ludlow | Jun 23 | Demasta | Newton Abbot |
| Jan 6 | Artic Jack | Haydock | Jun 23 | Lady Peta | Newton Abbot |
| Jan 8 | Bassey | Fakenham | Jul 1 | Genuine Article | Stratford |
| Jan 8 | Native Bid | Fakenham | Jul 8 | Demasta | Market Rasen |
| Jan 10 | Pedro Pete | Kempton | Jul 15 | Genuine Article | Stratford |
| Jan 11 | Iris Collonges | Wincanton | Jul 25 | Lady Peta | Worcester |
| Jan 15 | Captain Zinzan | Doncaster | Jul 25 | Moon Spinner | Worcester |
| Jan 16 | Dungarvans Choice | Chepstow | Aug 11 | Arabian Moon | Stratford |
| Jan 18 | Cupboard Lover | Taunton | Aug 24 | Arabian Moon | Uttoxeter |
| Jan 27 | Landing Light | Cheltenham | Aug 27 | J Dee | Southwell |
| Jan 27 | See More Business | Cheltenham | Aug 27 | Ozzie Jones | Southwell |
| Jan 30 | Carbury Cross | Musselburgh | Oct 2 | Rebel Son | Sedgefield |
| Feb 1 | First Love | Towcester | Oct 4 | Lord Youky | Hereford |
| Feb 10 | Landing Light | Newbury | Oct 10 | Miracle Kid | Exeter |
| Feb 17 | Bacchanal | Ascot | Oct 13 | Kahtan | Bangor-on-Dee |
| Feb 17 | Tiutchev | Ascot | Oct 13 | Barton Dante | Bangor-on-Dee |
| Feb 19 | Gastina | Fontwell | Oct 27 | Fondmort | Kempton |
| Feb 22 | Marlborough | Wincanton | Oct 27 | Ceanannas Mor | Kempton |
| Feb 24 | Chauvinist | Kempton | Oct 30 | Brother Joe | Cheltenham |
| Feb 27 | Lord O'All Seasons | Leicester | Oct 31 | Phar From A Fiddle | Cheltenham |
| Mar 10 | Irish Hussar | Sandown | Nov 1 | Martha Reilly | Stratford |
| Mar 14 | Dark Shell | Huntingdon | Nov 3 | Lord York | Ascot |
| Mar 15 | Calon Lan | Huntingdon | Nov 3 | Greenhope | Ascot |
| Mar 29 | Spring Margot | Exeter | Nov 7 | Surprising | Kempton |
| Apr 5 | Kingsmark | Aintree | Nov 7 | Native Society | Kempton |
| Apr 14 | Iambe De La See | Newton Abbot | Nov 10 | Jericho III | Wincanton |
| Apr 21 | Najjm | Ayr | Nov 14 | Got One Too | Newbury |
| Apr 21 | Carbury Cross | Ayr | Nov 17 | Greenhope | Cheltenham |
| Apr 27 | Ikrenel Royal | Sandown | Nov 18 | Frenchman's Creek | Cheltenham |
| Apr 27 | Marlborough | Sandown | Nov 19 | Lord North | Leicester |
| Apr 28 | Goguenard | Sandown | Nov 22 | Shayzara | Warwick |
| Apr 30 | Skye Blue | Plumpton | Nov 25 | Better Days | Aintree |
| Apr 30 | None Stirred | Plumpton | Nov 25 | Calling Brave | Aintree |
| May 4 | Westwinds | Folkestone | Dec 4 | Montpelier | Hereford |
| May 7 | Imperial Rocket | Fontwell | Dec 5 | Caballe | Plumpton |
| May 7 | Shuil's Star | Fontwell | Dec 5 | S'Assagir | Plumpton |
| May 7 | Karinga Prince | Fontwell | Dec 5 | First Day Cover | Plumpton |
| May 8 | Mister Benjamin | Taunton | Dec 7 | Bacchanal | Sandown |
| May 9 | Arabian Moon | Fakenham | Dec 7 | First Love | Sandown |
| May 14 | Polish Baron | Newton Abbot | Dec 8 | Fondmort | Sandown |
| May 15 | Got One Too | Hereford | Dec 10 | Clandestine | Folkestone |
| May 18 | King's Banker | Aintree | Dec 10 | Guru | Folkestone |
| May 19 | Najjm | Lingfield | Dec 10 | Artic Jack | Folkestone |
| May 24 | Tyrolean Dream | Wetherby | Dec 11 | Polish Baron | Fontwell |
| May 28 | Iambe De La See | Hereford | Dec 13 | Falmouth Bay | Huntingdon |
| May 29 | Ghadames | Hexham | Dec 13 | Deep Sunset | Huntingdon |

| | | | | | | |
|---|---|---|---|---|---|---|
| Dec 19 | Green Ideal | Newbury | | Jul 17 | Tarski | Worcester |
| Dec 19 | See You Sometime | Newbury | | Aug 4 | Scarletti | Perth |
| Dec 21 | Scots Grey | Ascot | | Aug 4 | Swift Pearl | Perth |
| Dec 21 | Cornish Gale | Ascot | | Aug 9 | Mumaris | Sedgefield |
| Dec 26 | Landing Light | Kempton | | Aug 26 | Ontos | Huntingdon |
| Dec 27 | Fondmort | Kempton | | Aug 26 | Joely Green | Huntingdon |
| Dec 27 | Greenhope | Kempton | | Sep 6 | Ontos | Sedgefield |
| | | | | Oct 1 | Little Tobias | Exeter |
| **2002** | | | | Oct 5 | La Landiere | Chepstow |
| Jan 11 | Jericho III | Huntingdon | | Oct 6 | Sungio | Fontwell |
| Jan 11 | Scottish Dance | Huntingdon | | Oct 6 | Arabian Moon | Fontwell |
| Jan 12 | Artic Jack | Ascot | | Oct 9 | Comex Flyer | Fakenham |
| Jan 15 | Non So | Folkestone | | Oct 10 | Noble Comic | Wincanton |
| Jan 15 | Castle Prince | Folkestone | | Oct 12 | Mighty Strong | Southwell |
| Jan 15 | Alice Reigns | Folkestone | | Oct 23 | Halexy | Chepstow |
| Jan 16 | Dungarvans Choice | Huntingdon | | Oct 25 | Existential | Fakenham |
| Jan 16 | Clandestine | Huntingdon | | Oct 26 | Comex Flyer | Kempton |
| Jan 19 | Ifni Du Luc | Haydock | | Oct 26 | Running Man | Kempton |
| Jan 22 | Non So | Fontwell | | Oct 27 | Thisthatandtother | Wincanton |
| Jan 22 | Cullen Bay | Fontwell | | Oct 27 | Iverain | Wincanton |
| Jan 24 | Pealings | Plumpton | | Oct 27 | Valley Henry | Wincanton |
| Jan 26 | Kates Charm | Cheltenham | | Oct 28 | Dorans Gold | Bangor-on-Dee |
| Feb 2 | Tiutchev | Sandown | | Oct 29 | Arabian Moon | Cheltenham |
| Feb 2 | Volano | Sandown | | Oct 30 | Simber Hill | Taunton |
| Feb 5 | Valerio | Market Rasen | | Oct 30 | Red Hare | Taunton |
| Feb 6 | Isio | Ludlow | | Nov 1 | Epervier D'Or | Wetherby |
| Feb 9 | Bacchanal | Newbury | | Nov 2 | Marlborough | Wetherby |
| Feb 14 | Dungarvans Choice | Sandown | | Nov 9 | Tysou | Sandown |
| Feb 15 | Lord Sam | Sandown | | Nov 9 | Nas Na Riogh | Sandown |
| Feb 20 | Rolling Tide | Ludlow | | Nov 12 | Scots Grey | Huntingdon |
| Feb 21 | The Bushkeeper | Huntingdon | | Nov 12 | Caballe | Huntingdon |
| Feb 23 | Cappadrummin | Kempton | | Nov 20 | Isio | Kempton |
| Mar 1 | Lord Joshua | Newbury | | Nov 20 | Calling Brave | Kempton |
| Mar 1 | Irish Hussar | Newbury | | Nov 26 | Tom Costalot | Warwick |
| Mar 2 | Stormhill Stag | Newbury | | Nov 29 | Chauvinist | Newbury |
| Mar 2 | Mel In Blue | Newbury | | Nov 30 | Bacchanal | Newbury |
| Mar 8 | First Love | Sandown | | Dec 4 | Ibal | Plumpton |
| Mar 9 | No Shenanigans | Sandown | | Dec 5 | Irish Hussar | Wincanton |
| Mar 19 | Just Murphy | Hereford | | Dec 6 | Lord Sam | Sandown |
| Mar 19 | Cybele Eria | Hereford | | Dec 7 | Hermes III | Sandown |
| Mar 19 | Tollbrae | Hereford | | Dec 12 | Regal Exit | Ludlow |
| Mar 20 | Old Bean | Ludlow | | Dec 14 | Fondmort | Cheltenham |
| Mar 23 | Isio | Newbury | | Dec 18 | Saintsaire | Newbury |
| Mar 30 | Phar Jeffen | Towcester | | Dec 18 | Iris Royal | Newbury |
| Apr 1 | Long Shot | Fakenham | | Dec 18 | Caracciola | Newbury |
| Apr 17 | Fadalko | Cheltenham | | Dec 18 | Calling Brave | Newbury |
| Jun 7 | Hermes III | Perth | | Dec 18 | Royal Rosa | Newbury |
| Jun 12 | Arctic Sky | Hereford | | Dec 20 | Far Horizon | Ascot |
| Jun 22 | Guid Willie Waught | Market Rasen | | Dec 27 | Non So | Kempton |
| Jul 10 | Native Approach | Worcester | | | | |

**2003**

| | | |
|---|---|---|
| Jan 6 | Placid Man | Fontwell |
| Jan 12 | Xenophon | Leopardstown |
| Jan 13 | Barito | Plumpton |
| Jan 13 | Dancing Bay | Plumpton |
| Feb 11 | First Love | Folkestone |
| Feb 22 | Avalanche | Kempton |
| Feb 24 | Dancing Bay | Plumpton |
| Feb 25 | Irish Hussar | Leicester |
| Feb 27 | Deep Sunset | Ludlow |
| Feb 28 | Handy Money | Doncaster |
| Feb 28 | Iris Royal | Doncaster |
| Mar 1 | Got One Too | Newbury |
| Mar 2 | Nas Na Riogh | Fontwell |
| Mar 2 | Major Shark | Fontwell |
| Mar 8 | Royal Rosa | Sandown |
| Mar 12 | Xenophon | Cheltenham |
| Mar 17 | Poppet | Hereford |
| Mar 19 | Forest Tune | Ludlow |
| Mar 20 | Tysou | Wincanton |
| Mar 23 | Cybele Eria | Warwick |
| Mar 23 | Benrajah | Warwick |
| Mar 23 | Benson | Warwick |
| Apr 4 | Irish Hussar | Aintree |
| Apr 11 | Tysou | Ayr |
| Apr 17 | Amorello | Cheltenham |
| Apr 19 | No Need For Alarm | Stratford |
| May 5 | River Pirate | Ludlow |
| May 14 | First Love | Perth |
| May 18 | Brereton | Fakenham |
| May 21 | Just Murphy | Kelso |
| May 22 | Le Passing | Bangor-on-Dee |
| May 24 | Handy Money | Market Rasen |
| May 26 | River Pirate | Hereford |
| Oct 4 | Bid For Fame | Uttoxeter |
| Oct 8 | Cush Jewel | Towcester |
| Oct 10 | Volano | Huntingdon |
| Oct 25 | Rigmarole | Kempton |
| Nov 4 | Ceanannas Mor | Exeter |
| Nov 5 | Arctic Sky | Kempton |
| Nov 8 | Orswell Crest | Sandown |
| Nov 8 | Caracciola | Sandown |
| Nov 8 | Iris Royal | Sandown |
| Nov 12 | Mighty Strong | Newbury |
| Nov 14 | Ceanannas Mor | Cheltenham |
| Nov 15 | Fondmort | Cheltenham |
| Nov 22 | Calling Brave | Aintree |
| Nov 25 | Kercabellec | Warwick |
| Nov 25 | Ambition Royal | Warwick |
| Nov 27 | Lilium De Cotte | Uttoxeter |
| Nov 30 | Mighty Strong | Newbury |
| Dec 4 | Optimaite | Leicester |
| Dec 6 | Hersov | Sandown |
| Dec 10 | Maharbal | Newbury |
| Dec 10 | Mighty Strong | Newbury |
| Dec 13 | Iris Royal | Cheltenham |
| Dec 15 | Non So | Plumpton |
| Dec 16 | Calling Brave | Folkestone |
| Dec 19 | Trabolgan | Ascot |
| Dec 19 | Perle De Puce | Ascot |
| Dec 27 | Caracciola | Kempton |
| Dec 27 | Diamant Noir | Kempton |
| Dec 27 | Scots Grey | Kempton |
| Dec 27 | Greenhope | Kempton |

**2004**

| | | |
|---|---|---|
| Jan 3 | Calling Brave | Sandown |
| Jan 4 | Old Bean | Plumpton |
| Jan 4 | Non So | Plumpton |
| Jan 7 | Tanikos | Hereford |
| Jan 8 | Grande Jete | Wincanton |
| Jan 10 | Isio | Ascot |
| Jan 14 | Trabolgan | Newbury |
| Jan 22 | Fleet Street | Taunton |
| Jan 22 | Lady Of Fortune | Taunton |
| Mar 21 | Billesey | Stratford |
| Apr 4 | Lisa Du Chenet | Lingfield |
| Apr 10 | Magic Mistress | Newton Abbot |
| Apr 12 | Tollbrae | Plumpton |
| Apr 14 | Copsale Lad | Cheltenham |
| May 6 | Sea Captain | Ludlow |
| May 8 | River Pirate | Warwick |
| May 11 | Shamdian | Hereford |
| May 30 | Waimea Bay | Uttoxeter |
| May 30 | Gallik Dawn | Uttoxeter |
| Jul 3 | Smoking Barrels | Limerick |
| Jul 7 | River City | Worcester |
| Jul 18 | River City | Stratford |
| Jul 21 | Everready | Worcester |
| Jul 27 | Talking Cents | Galway |
| Aug 24 | River Pirate | Worcester |
| Sep 21 | Deferlant | Fontwell |
| Sep 23 | Aimees Mark | Listowel |
| Oct 3 | Antony Ebeneezer | Uttoxeter |
| Oct 11 | Royal Paradise | Roscommon |
| Oct 12 | Deferlant | Fontwell |
| Oct 12 | Gallery God | Fontwell |
| Oct 17 | Renvyle | Market Rasen |

| Date | Horse | Course | | Date | Horse | Course |
|------|-------|--------|---|------|-------|--------|
| Oct 17 | My Will | Market Rasen | | Mar 4 | Tanikos | Newbury |
| Oct 17 | Music To My Ears | Market Rasen | | Mar 16 | Trabolgan | Cheltenham |
| Nov 3 | The Market Man | Kempton | | Mar 24 | Roi De L'Odet | Ludlow |
| Nov 5 | Gallery God | Fontwell | | Mar 27 | Capitana | Plumpton |
| Nov 6 | Lord Buckingham | Wincanton | | Apr 2 | Schapiro | Newbury |
| Nov 6 | Briery Fox | Wincanton | | Apr 21 | Reel Dancer | Fontwell |
| Nov 9 | Nuit Sombre | Huntingdon | | Apr 29 | Feel The Pride | Southwell |
| Nov 10 | Papini | Newbury | | May 4 | Lawaaheb | Fakenham |
| Nov 11 | Out The Black | Ludlow | | May 8 | Gallik Dawn | Uttoxeter |
| Nov 16 | Johann De Vonnas | Towcester | | May 8 | Master Marmalade | Uttoxeter |
| Nov 16 | The Bar Maid | Towcester | | Jun 5 | Tigers Lair | Stratford |
| Nov 18 | Nas Na Riogh | Wincanton | | Jun 5 | Boomshakalaka | Stratford |
| Nov 20 | Jones's Road | Windsor | | Jun 22 | Shakerattleandroll | Worcester |
| Nov 20 | Oscar Park | Windsor | | Jun 29 | Tihui Two | Worcester |
| Nov 24 | Trabolgan | Lingfield | | Nov 25 | The Market Man | Newbury |
| Nov 28 | Mighty Strong | Newbury | | Nov 26 | Trabolgan | Newbury |
| Dec 2 | Cunning Pursuit | Wincanton | | Dec 2 | Its A Dream | Sandown |
| Dec 4 | Fashions Monty | Wetherby | | Dec 3 | Green Iceni | Sandown |
| Dec 7 | Johann De Vonnas | Fontwell | | Dec 3 | Kauto Star | Sandown |
| Dec 8 | Afrad | Newbury | | Dec 4 | Royal Corrouge | Warwick |
| Dec 9 | Mesmeric | Taunton | | Dec 8 | Natal | Taunton |
| Dec 9 | Bill Owen | Taunton | | Dec 10 | Afsoun | Cheltenham |
| Dec 30 | All Star | Taunton | | Dec 10 | Tysou | Cheltenham |
| | | | | Dec 14 | Restless D'Artaix | Newbury |
| **2005** | | | | Dec 14 | Craven | Newbury |
| Jan 1 | Lord Of Illusion | Cheltenham | | Dec 16 | Silkwood Top | Windsor |
| Jan 3 | Too Forward | Folkestone | | Dec 16 | Saintsaire | Windsor |
| Jan 3 | Roofing Spirit | Folkestone | | Dec 27 | Lustral Du Seuil | Chepstow |
| Jan 6 | Bathwick Annie | Wincanton | | Dec 27 | Blue Shark | Chepstow |
| Jan 12 | Papini | Newbury | | Dec 31 | Copsale Lad | Lingfield |
| Jan 13 | Beanney | Catterick | | Dec 31 | Play The Melody | Lingfield |
| Jan 15 | L'Ami | Warwick | | | | |
| Jan 15 | Oscar Park | Warwick | | **2006** | | |
| Jan 22 | Candello | Haydock | | Jan 1 | Fondmort | Cheltenham |
| Jan 24 | Redi | Southwell | | Jan 1 | Burnt Oak | Cheltenham |
| Jan 28 | The Market Man | Doncaster | | Jan 2 | Nas Na Riogh | Exeter |
| Jan 30 | Justified | Punchestown | | Jan 11 | Wogan | Newbury |
| Feb 3 | Sunset Light | Towcester | | Jan 14 | Tanikos | Warwick |
| Feb 4 | Demarco | Fontwell | | Jan 16 | Temoin | Plumpton |
| Feb 6 | Royal Paradise | Leopardstown | | Jan 16 | Brankley Boy | Plumpton |
| Feb 11 | Etendard Indien | Kempton | | Jan 19 | Au Courant | Taunton |
| Feb 11 | Up At Midnight | Kempton | | Jan 26 | Mam Ratagan | Warwick |
| Feb 13 | Sleep Bal | Exeter | | Jan 30 | Tooting | Ludlow |
| Feb 14 | Greenhope | Plumpton | | Feb 4 | Tysou | Sandown |
| Feb 15 | Its A Dream | Folkestone | | Feb 4 | Temoin | Sandown |
| Feb 17 | Sea Captain | Sandown | | Feb 7 | Jack The Giant | Market Rasen |
| Feb 18 | Chauvinist | Sandown | | Feb 8 | Adventurist | Ludlow |
| Feb 19 | Thames | Haydock | | Feb 9 | Afsoun | Huntingdon |
| Mar 3 | Beau Supreme | Ludlow | | Feb 12 | Its A Dream | Exeter |

| | | | | | | | |
|---|---|---|---|---|---|---|---|
| Feb 16 | Herakles | Huntingdon | | Dec 26 | Maharbal | Kempton |
| Feb 19 | Paix Eternelle | Fontwell | | Dec 27 | Afrad | Chepstow |
| Feb 22 | Karello Bay | Southwell | | Dec 27 | Good Bye Simon | Chepstow |
| Feb 23 | Tessanoora | Huntingdon | | Dec 29 | Duc De Regniere | Newbury |
| Mar 3 | Temoin | Newbury | | Dec 31 | La Dame Brune | Warwick |
| Mar 9 | Barbers Shop | Wincanton | | | | |
| Mar 11 | Karello Bay | Sandown | | **2007** | | |
| Mar 16 | Fondmort | Cheltenham | | Jan 6 | Papini | Sandown |
| Mar 16 | Non So | Cheltenham | | Jan 8 | Trompette | Ludlow |
| Mar 18 | Brankley Boy | Uttoxeter | | Jan 11 | Classic Fiddle | Hereford |
| Mar 21 | Haloo Baloo | Exeter | | Jan 15 | Ship's Hill | Fakenham |
| Mar 26 | Tessanoora | Worcester | | Jan 17 | Procas De Thaix | Newbury |
| Mar 27 | Trompette | Plumpton | | Jan 20 | Afsoun | Haydock |
| Apr 5 | Briscoe Place | Hereford | | Jan 20 | Amaretto Rose | Haydock |
| Apr 5 | Capitana | Hereford | | Jan 24 | Monfils Monfils | Huntingdon |
| Apr 11 | Herakles | Fontwell | | Jan 29 | Punjabi | Ludlow |
| Apr 16 | The Newsman | Plumpton | | Feb 1 | Karello Bay | Wincanton |
| Apr 16 | Kyno | Plumpton | | Feb 9 | Duc De Regniere | Kempton |
| Apr 18 | Star Award | Chepstow | | Feb 16 | Dancing Bay | Fakenham |
| Apr 20 | Classic Fiddle | Cheltenham | | Feb 16 | Tarotino | Fakenham |
| Apr 22 | Royals Darling | Ayr | | Feb 16 | Be Telling | Fakenham |
| Apr 27 | Quatre Heures | Punchestown | | Feb 16 | Fiddling Again | Fakenham |
| May 28 | Aitch Doubleyou | Uttoxeter | | Feb 24 | Punjabi | Kempton |
| Jun 2 | Keswick | Towcester | | Feb 26 | Juveigneur | Plumpton |
| Jul 4 | Mandingo Chief | Southwell | | Mar 4 | Classic Fiddle | Bangor-on-Dee |
| Jul 6 | Duke Of Stradone | Perth | | Mar 11 | Fiddle | Warwick |
| Aug 26 | Granite Man | Market Rasen | | Mar 21 | Ballyaahbutt | Lingfield |
| Sep 6 | Montevideo | Uttoxeter | | Mar 23 | Fleet Street | Newbury |
| Sep 21 | Irish Whispers | Fontwell | | Mar 24 | Karello Bay | Newbury |
| Sep 24 | Astyanax | Huntingdon | | Mar 25 | French Opera | Taunton |
| Oct 30 | Amaretto Rose | Warwick | | Mar 26 | Lester Leaps In | Plumpton |
| Nov 2 | Papini | Haydock | | Mar 28 | Treasury Counsel | Kempton |
| Nov 4 | Jack The Giant | Sandown | | Mar 30 | Shouldhavehadthat | Ascot |
| Nov 15 | Jack The Giant | Warwick | | Apr 1 | Ingratitude | Newton Abbot |
| Nov 16 | Legally Fast | Market Rasen | | Apr 5 | Sovietica | Wincanton |
| Nov 17 | All Star | Ascot | | Apr 13 | Chief Dan George | Aintree |
| Nov 18 | Neysauteur | Ascot | | Apr 26 | Punjabi | Punchestown |
| Nov 25 | Afsoun | Newbury | | Apr 29 | Dariak | Ludlow |
| Nov 26 | Mountain Approach | Newbury | | May 5 | Dave's Dream | Uttoxeter |
| Nov 26 | Schiehallion | Newbury | | May 10 | Boomshakalaka | Newton Abbot |
| Nov 27 | Sir Jimmy Shand | Folkestone | | May 15 | Ingratitude | Huntingdon |
| Dec 3 | Mr Dow Jones | Warwick | | May 17 | The Polomoche | Ludlow |
| Dec 7 | La Dame Brune | Huntingdon | | May 19 | Working Title | Uttoxeter |
| Dec 13 | Sir Jimmy Shand | Newbury | | May 22 | No Regrets | Towcester |
| Dec 13 | Fiddling Again | Newbury | | Jun 3 | Barbers Shop | Southwell |
| Dec 15 | Barbers Shop | Ascot | | Oct 13 | Run For Moor | Chepstow |
| Dec 23 | Treasury Counsel | Hereford | | Oct 16 | Calusa Caldera | Huntingdon |
| Dec 26 | Ungaro | Kempton | | Oct 21 | Tinagoodnight | Kempton |

| | | | | | |
|---|---|---|---|---|---|
| Oct 21 | Alph | Kempton | Jan 14 | Gold Award | Fakenham |
| Oct 31 | Scots Dragoon | Huntingdon | Jan 19 | Binocular | Ascot |
| Nov 3 | Papini | Ascot | Jan 21 | Dave's Dream | Folkestone |
| Nov 5 | Shoreacres | Plumpton | Jan 23 | Princess Flame | Musselburgh |
| Nov 8 | Calusa Caldera | Huntingdon | Jan 24 | Classic Fiddle | Fontwell |
| Nov 13 | Zebra Crossing | Kempton | Jan 25 | Mad Max | Newbury |
| Nov 13 | Chomba Womba | Kempton | Jan 26 | Chomba Womba | Doncaster |
| Nov 20 | Sovietica | Folkestone | Jan 28 | Doubly Guest | Ludlow |
| Nov 23 | Psychomodo | Ascot | Jan 29 | Bay Hawk | Folkestone |
| Nov 24 | Seven Is My Number | Ascot | Feb 2 | Afsoun | Sandown |
| Nov 27 | Procas De Thaix | Kempton | Feb 3 | Bay Hawk | Fontwell |
| Nov 27 | Boomshakalaka | Kempton | Feb 6 | Menchikov | Ludlow |
| Dec 14 | Jack The Giant | Cheltenha | Feb 7 | Stellino | Taunton |
| Dec 19 | Petit Robin | Newbury | Feb 8 | Barbers Shop | Kempton |
| Dec 19 | Valdas Queen | Newbury | Feb 9 | Mad Max | Newbury |
| Dec 22 | Jack The Giant | Ascot | Feb 10 | Classic Fiddle | Exeter |
| Dec 26 | Boomshakalaka | Kempton | Feb 15 | Punchestowns | Sandown |
| Dec 29 | Khyber Kim | Newbury | Feb 19 | Chantaco | Taunton |
| Dec 31 | Maggie Mathias | Warwick | Feb 23 | Binocular | Kempton |
| | | | Feb 23 | Riverside Theatre | Kempton |
| **2008** | | | Feb 24 | Galient | Fontwell |
| Jan 2 | Jean Le Poisson | Folkestone | Mar 1 | Working Title | Kempton |
| Jan 3 | Isintshelovely | Fontwell | Mar 3 | Kingscape | Stratford |
| Jan 4 | Duc De Regniere | Lingfield | Mar 5 | Honour High | Fontwell |
| Jan 5 | Chomba Womba | Sandown | Mar 6 | Dr Hart | Lingfield |
| Jan 8 | Jack The Giant | Leicester | Mar 9 | Carole's Legacy | Warwick |
| Jan 8 | Fleet Street | Leicester | Mar 15 | Punchestowns | Uttoxeter |
| Jan 11 | The Polomoche | Huntingdon | Mar 20 | Galient | Ludlow |
| Jan 12 | Royals Darling | Kempton | Mar 30 | Chantaco | Wincanton |
| Jan 14 | Working Title | Fakenham | Apr 3 | Menchikov | Taunton |
| Jan 14 | Fondness | Fakenham | Apr 3 | Bring Me Sunshine | Taunton |

# INDEX